Ensoulment

By
Lorís Simón Salum

www.ChironPublicatons.com

Interior and cover design by Danijela Mijailovic
Illustrations created by Patrick Smith
Printed primarily in the United States of America.

ISBN 978-1-63051-389-4 paperback
ISBN 978-1-63051-390-0 hardcover
ISBN 978-1-63051-391-7 electronic

Library of Congress Cataloging-in-Publication Data

Names: Salum, Lorís Simón, 1988- author.
Title: Ensoulment : exploring the feminine principle in Western culture / Lorís Simón Salum.
Description: Asheville, NC : Chiron Publications, 2016. | Includes bibliographical references and index.
Identifiers: LCCN 2016025903| ISBN 9781630513894 (pbk. : alk. paper) | ISBN 9781630513900 (hardcover : alk. paper) | ISBN 9781630513917 (e-ISBN)
Subjects: LCSH: Feminism. | Women—Psychology. | Women—Interviews.
Classification: LCC HQ1154 .S165 2016 | DDC 305.42—dc23

LC record available at https://lccn.loc.gov/2016025903

Contents

Introduction,
A note from the writer and director of the film *Ensoulment*

The initial idea for *Ensoulment* came after a long afternoon conversation with my mother, Rose Mary, during my sophomore year in college. I had caught that notorious sickness among soon-to-be graduates that makes you fall under the delusion that you must find the meaning of life before graduation . . . or else. In addition, I was struggling to understand the after effects from my first encounter with BodySoul Rhythms, a women's retreat held by the Marion Woodman Foundation. I remember feeling awakened yet confused about who I was and where I was going in my life. "What do you feel passionate about?" my mother asked from across the café table where we were seated. I watched as a woman came into the café and walked to the front counter. "Women," I thought. "Women fascinate me." True to her tendency to underestimate the amount of work involved in just about any project, my mother answered without flinching, "Why don't you make a movie about women?" And I, struggling to find a project I could call my own, replied, "Okay."

During the remaining two long years of college that followed this conversation, the idea held fast at the heart of my deepest ambitions. It became the kind of dream that is so precious you may not want to face the reality of it in the light of day. I did not know if I was certain I would do justice to that moment's spontaneity, but the certainty that I would make a film about women became my personal light at the end of the tunnel. It became "the thing I would do after I finish this indefinite thing I'm doing now . . ." and my answer to everyone's question, "What will you do after college?" "A documentary about women," I would respond, with a knowing grin on my face. I pretended to know exactly what I was going to do and how I would go about it, and the illusion tripled its effect when I wore my eyeglasses: They have never failed me to make me look a little more intelligent than I am.

My confident image may not have been successful in convincing everyone of what I planned to do, but I did create an army of words against my own insecurities. The more I planned the film out loud, the closer I came to convincing myself. A couple of months before graduation, the army attacked. I will admit to having wanted to take the easy way out, to go to grad school or find a job, but those easy paths quickly got lost in a forest of pressing need. No longer did I want to swallow the empty books and essays I had been asked to read and write as a student. No longer could I contain the pressure between what was being requested of me and what I was living, breathing, and seeing every day. If you ask me, I would have said I had no option. Someone inside of me was in control now, and she wanted to make a documentary.

And so I began to do research. I sought out those hidden traits that women surely held deep in their bosoms, the womanly forces that must hold the key to inner liberation and world peace. I was adamant about finding the narrative that would break all glass ceilings: "If only women knew X, the world would be a better place." I began reading anything I could about women—from different cultures all over the world and here at home, from queen bees to CEOs to stay-at-home mothers. I wanted to find a common thread that brought us all together. I became convinced that if we women could grasp a deeper sense of who we are, we could strengthen our understanding of the freedom we truly hold in our hands. I was sure of it.

At one point I ceased trying to find the right book and focused on trying to find the right person. Maybe oral wisdom could have a deeper impact on my thesis than intellectual essays. When it came to asking verbal questions, however, it was a tricky matter to hold the theme of "women" present while trying to stretch into people's inner lives. I wasn't getting the answers I wanted, not because they were "wrong" answers, but because when it came to leading happy, fulfilled lives, there was no difference between what was true for women and what was true for men. We all want to be economically stable, pursue our passions and cultivate the time we have with our families. All of us want it all.

There is a saying in Spanish that I've found to speak a simple truth: *El que busca, encuentra*, "He who looks, will find." However, the saying does not necessarily specify that a person will find what she intended. In the end, my search to unlock the keys for women's inner liberation extended far beyond just women and led me to a new understanding of gender and how it interacts with personal fulfillment and happiness.

Slowly but surely my focus started shifting toward something beyond gender. At this point, I was holding monothematic conversations with my family and friends at the breakfast, lunch, and dinner tables, bless their hearts. I trusted that those who knew me best would risk honest answers as I questioned them across the table, allowing me new insights into the inner lives of others. My mother had been present since the beginning, opening up her life-long store of knowledge as my very own, immediate library. When we moved to production, this store of knowledge would become fully spirited as her role shifted into an active participant. My brother, José Antonio, was quickly absorbed by the topic, too. I still don't know if his interest came out of a need to defend the male gender or out of genuine curiosity. He was one of the finest elements in the project (and in my entire life, I should add). Together, our questions went from asking about women, to asking about femininity, to asking about the feminine.

It was that term, "the feminine," that made it all click. Hearing that word again threw me back across time to my sophomore year in college. I was about 20 years old when my mother invited me to a women's retreat in Tepoztlán, Mexico. It was a week-long intensive that worked with the Jungian principle of "the feminine." I don't think I really understood back then what they were talking about, but I remember feeling how much the work resonated with me. It was my first true encounter with depth psychology. I was so young at the time that I don't believe I ever really got to choose what lens I would later see the world through: I was baptized Jungian. It may be that I am biased now, but I came to adore this sort of upbringing.

The term "feminine" is derived from Carl Jung's concepts of *anima* and *animus*, a Latin parallel of the oriental *yin* and *yang* (1982, p. 77). Modern terms might define these forces as right and left-brain thinking. For the Jungian, where the masculine represents limits and form, the feminine is that which infuses the form with a spirit, an impalpable substance that begins where the masculine ends and ends where the masculine begins.

A more approachable metaphor that holds this dynamic is the idea of language. On the one hand, we have an immense vocabulary, each word being specific to an action or thing, a feeling or maybe an abstraction. All words are held by grammatical structure; this is how we make full sentences, paragraphs and books. With language, we dictate to others what we want them to think in a way that no other system allows us to do. On the other hand, it is the intention that these words carry that we essentially want to convey. We need language as a vessel to enclose the millions of experiences we want the other to know and understand about us. As a result, we build a conversation, a vivid interaction that interlaces the masculine margins with their feminine insides in an enriching interchange of eternal stimuli. Together, humans have the magical experience of relating with each other in the most complex ways, and this magic is made possible through the interaction of the masculine and the feminine.

For many of us, this constant intermingling of the feminine and the masculine is hard to grasp. The Cartesian principle that delimits the boundary between the mind and the body has influenced Western thought profoundly, and the associations of masculine-mind and feminine-body have created a sense of either-or that makes it hard for us to recognize what's really going on inside of us. We like to believe our lives are guided by rational decisions, when in fact the majority of our choices are also composed of our body's reactions and our gut feelings. These forces behind our choices become even more complicated when we consider our heart's passions, another expression of the complex intermingling of masculine and feminine principles at play. I like to imagine that our necks are one of the most misleading features of the human anatomy. They have made us believe that there is an obvious separation between our head and the rest of our body. In reality, at no moment does our framework make an actual split. For centuries we have attributed our heads to reason and the masculine, and the rest of our uncontrollable body and nature to the feminine. A good look in the mirror will show you that we are all one big medley of flesh, bones, and energy. Other than our skin, we have no true indication of where we begin and where we end—though this also could be disputed. I have come to believe that the same standard can be credited to the feminine and masculine principles.

As I returned to the initial purpose of my project, however, and worked through these ideas in my readings and conversations, I attempted as best I could to separate the two, to detach what could be detached, to dissect what could be dissected, and to label what could be labeled. In this way, I came to focus my search on the concept of the feminine.

In our interview for this collection, Dr. Paula Reeves, author of *Heart Sense*, defines the Jungian principle of the feminine in the following terms:

> The feminine is a great cosmic principle, and as such it manifests today as a metaphysical principle . . . But it is also being used today as a psychological principle that has to do with different qualities that inhabit all human beings, qualities that manifest and express in different ways. The feminine has also been honored and relied upon across time in multiple cultures, primarily in Asia and Africa, certainly in South America. It's a centering principle. However, the feminine absolutely must have the masculine to make itself whole.

It's this whole business of Cartesian theory that I believe has knocked us off—the separation of them; because originally, it was an anchoring principle that helped us understand how to make sense of the totally irrational question of why we are born if it's only to die. So for my purposes, the feminine is an energy principle within the human psyche and soma. It's also a process—an energy process—between human nature and all of nature . . . It brings many of the energy principles that we use all the time into play, along with the masculine, to create the world as we know it (Reeves' interview, 2013).

Armed with a growing sense of the feminine, I realized that the principle encompasses all those qualities that Western culture has come to relate to women. The way we think about women is incredibly entangled with the concept of the feminine. I asked myself: at what point in history had the qualities of nurturance or delicacy been assigned to women and those of strength and force been appointed to men? When was it decided that men cannot be vulnerable but women can? How did we come to accept that women can be emotional, but men cannot? These differences are highlighted in Western culture where profits or productivity, factors that are believed to be the direct result of only masculine qualities, are seen as good; and inefficiency or vagueness, consequences thought to come only from feminine qualities, are seen as bad. Clear, analytical expression is desirable, and ambiguous or uncertain suggestions are unwanted. In a climate like this, emotional, passion-driven women are pushed aside from positions where decisions matter, and unambitious men who do not share an equal hunger for economic success can take a seat on the bench. One understanding followed another, and I began to believe that Western culture had reduced the feminine part of its collective psyche dramatically and then projected this diminished element onto an entire gender, arriving at the erroneous conclusion that women are by default less valuable than men.

Everything started to make sense. I had fallen into that trap as well. What I was really after was not the female gender, but a matter of the soul, the impalpable. I was trying to point to the things that were being overlooked in our society, trampled over and dismissed as "unimportant" or "hobbies." I wasn't looking for women, but for the nameless, the category-less, and the purely emblematic notion of the womb: that capacity to recognize, nurture, and bring to life. I was looking for this symbolism of a life cycle taken into the psyche and applied to each and every quality residing in the mind and soul. This was what was being devalued. This was what I was fighting for.

It became clear that my story had been with me all along—a young woman in search of the long lost feminine in her life. I decided to use an animated protagonist to depersonalize the narrative as much as I could and to create a more universal character. But it was impossible to speak my truth while leaving my personal life out of it, and I found myself giving in to the biographical. I divided the journey into the six areas in which the loss of the feminine had been the most significant in my life: the media, the body, men, relationships, the workforce, and religion. All my interviews were channeled through these six areas, while often exploring the distinction of women from the feminine.

Rose Mary, José Antonio, and I are still amazed to have had the honor to bring together such a fascinating group of intellectuals from so many different backgrounds. We were privileged to sit down with experts in cognitive psychology, depth psychology, women and gender studies, theology, philanthropy, biology, art, television, print media, and business. It felt like a banquet of ideas, and some days were just too good to be true. We traveled from Mexico City to Austin, Texas; from Miami to Atlanta to Santa Barbara and Los Angeles; along the East coast through New York, New Jersey, Rhode Island and Boston; across the puddle to London and back again to Ontario. Through it all we were also lucky to meet a number of astonishing people at home in Houston, Texas. In addition to the experts, we traveled the generation gap to interview younger crowds. It was equally important for me to make a space for the voice of my generation, people in their late teens and twenties.

We settled into a comfortable routine: I would research the experts and write the questions, and my mother would contact them and schedule an interview. I packed the equipment, and she booked the flights. I organized the set, while she entertained the interviewee. She asked the questions, and I dealt with the camera. The conversations we had after each interview on our way back to the hotel were solid gold. We thought we were the perfect team, and when my brother, José Antonio, decided to accompany us midway through the project, he completed our duo beautifully. Not only did he carry the heaviest bags, but he also offered humor, a fresh perspective, and of course a male presence that was more than welcome. It felt odd to be relieved at the inclusion of a man in the crew. His presence added balance to the dialogue and made it impossible for us ever to exempt men from the conversation, which I thought was profoundly important. As if that weren't enough, he later composed the entire film score. Despite all the talk about separating "the feminine" from "woman," the importance of balancing masculine and feminine energies was reaffirmed for me through this experience of a gendered perspective.

We conducted our first interview with three women from the Marion Woodman Foundation: Patricia Llosa, educator at the Metropolitan Museum of Fine Art in New York; Sheila Langston, professor at the Vancouver Film School; and Martha de la Garza, founder and director of the Central State Library and the Initial Education Center in Monterrey, Mexico. We were fortunate to grab them right after a weekend retreat in Austin, Texas, so that their words carried the honesty and depth with which they led the workshops. To our immense misfortune, this interview had to be redone due to technical failures and we lost the possibility of reuniting the three wise women. However, we were lucky to find Llosa and Langston again for a second try.

The next two interviews followed fast on the heels of the excitement of this first conversation. The first was with Gustavo Beck, a Jungian analyst from Mexico City, who led us to his former teacher, Dr. Ginette Paris, an author and professor at Pacifica

Graduate Institute in Santa Barbara, California. Dr. Beck emphasized the importance on marking that separation between the feminine and females. Dr. Paris enlightened us as she spoke about myth, goddesses, and the media. Both of these interviews were important to us, as the interviewees full-heartedly expressed their dissatisfaction with terms such as "masculine" and "feminine."

We kept in mind the cultural and academic variations in the meaning and essence of the feminine during our fifth interview with Dr. Brian Riedel, assistant professor at Rice University in Houston Texas. Despite his being the first academic to bring a non-Jungian perspective to the documentary, his words still resonated with our previous interviewees. He referenced an entirely new collage of intellectuals and studies that we had not taken into account before.

Our next interview waited for us in Miami, FL. By the time we arrived to meet with Michelle Villalobos, a sales, marketing, and personal branding specialist, our questions had become more specific. Villalobos's insight was most helpful when it came to women in the workforce. Even though she is very knowledgeable about the data related to gender disparity in the economy, her focus is on helping women make the change from the inside out, a stance that brought many of the theories we had explored into the practical world. Though she used different terms, her message advocated balancing masculine and feminine energies among business people.

Next came Dr. Terry Fassihi, founder and program director of the Houston Eating Disorder Center. Her interview was a second reality check. And even though she knew the cold statistics about girls and boys with eating disorders and image distortions, her work was directed towards inner change and keeping a healthy relationship with one's body.

We interviewed seven more people during our time in Houston: Dr. James Hollis, author and Jungian analyst; Dr. Jerry Ruhl, director of the Jung Center; psychotherapist Estela Seale; Dr. Debra Andrist, chair of foreign languages at Sam Houston State University; Aurora Losada, editor of the *Houston Chronicle*'s *La Voz*; Patricia Gras, former

PBS show host for *Living Smart*; and Dr. Brandon Mack, assistant director of admissions at Rice University.

I would be lying if I denied the sense of homecoming that accompanied our return to interviewing Jungian analysts. With elevated eloquence, Dr. Hollis accentuated the position of men in a patriarchal society. Dr. Ruhl, too, discussed this idea, often using the word "feeling" instead of "feminine." This subtle difference made his discourse that much more accessible, especially when it came to speaking to and about men. Dr. Mack introduced us to the term "effemiphobia," the negative feeling towards effeminate gay men by other gay men. He opened yet another door and showed us a parallel devaluation of the feminine in the LGBT community. Our journey continued with a conversation with Dr. Debra Andrist, a strong feminist who contributed sociological views to the discussion. Her firm stance was inspiring and contagious. She took my entire project and held it against the array of social movements from the past, pointing at how it blended in. In less than an hour, she charged my motivation and shook away my feelings of solitude.

I have known Dr. Seale all my life, and I've always believed our auras must vibrate at the same frequency. Each time I heard her answer one of my questions, her ideas settled and hardened around my judgments, my philosophies and my assertions. I like telling her that our similarities come from the fact that we're both Scorpios. She usually says she doesn't believe in astrology, but that she will make an exception just for me. Aurora Losada and Patricia Gras proved to be two women who do not take their beliefs lightly. Because both of them are involved in the media, we interviewed them together. I was fascinated to see the conversation bounce back and forth between them as they spoke of their frustrations and achievements as professionals, as women, and as Latinas in the United States.

Traveling to New York somehow changed the documentary's field of energy. It was as if we had passed our homegrown plant from its nursery container and set it into the earth to let its roots go wild. Our first scheduled meeting was with Dr. Abigail Disney, filmmaker and philanthropist. I remember feeling very nervous as I waited for her in her office. Looking around at her awards, recognitions, and Nobel Prize ceremony passes, I felt the adrenaline rushing through my body, but once she came in, her laughter overwhelmed the space as she filled it up with personal experiences and wisdom.

The next day was exhaustingly splendid. We drove to Montclair State University in New Jersey to see author and Professor of Religion and Philosophy, Dr. Cynthia Eller. I have never met anyone like her. In less than an hour, she made me question just about every particle of knowledge I had gained in my short, twenty-three years of life in relation to God. While I listened to her, doubts filled my thoughts until I had almost lost all hope, and then one phrase would make me regain it all back. Before I knew it, I was bombarded by a series of mini-epiphanies revealing the connections between human nature, theology, and biology.

I was reluctant to leave New York. I felt an urge to stay near these women and looked forward to my remaining interview with the Rev. Dr. Serene Jones, author and president of the Union Theological Seminary. Dr. Jones's eyes transmitted a zeal that can be found in only a few. The way she conveyed her views on the feminine in religion, women in Christianity, and the future of Christianity stirred the soul. Had I known I would be back, I would not have left in such sadness.

There was no time to take a breath. Two of the most emotional trips were yet to come. We flew to Ontario, Canada, to see Mary Hamilton, author and co-founder of BodySoul Rhythms, a program from the Marion Woodman Foundation. Meanwhile, author and Jungian analyst, Dr. Paula Reeves awaited us in Atlanta, Georgia. I cannot speak of Mary and Paula separately, for they have both been immense influences in my life since I attended my first retreat with my mother. Their names have become metaphors for inner strength, growth, and destruction. They hold in every cell of their bodies the key to what so much of the world calls happiness. For me, Paula and Mary sit at the core of all that represents human kindness and understanding.

Our second to last interview came with the Mankind Project (MKP), a global organization with the mission to offer men a higher sense of fulfillment in their lives through their programs. Greg Gondron, MKP training and operations coordinator, and Tom Hopwood, president of Executive Advice and former MKP counselor, sat with us to speak more about the feminine in men. Surrounded by Tom and Greg and my brother Jay, it was the first time I had felt such a nurturing energy surrounding me while in a room with three other men. The sensation was different than what I had experienced in women's circles, and somewhat foreign to me, but I felt embraced all the same. I understood that my past experiences of fully male environments involved detached, humorous comments thrown across the room, or swings of surging competition. I felt especially content after this interview to have included men in the documentary. Gondron and Hopwood sat still in confidence and spoke about their emotional experiences in response to society's expectations of men.

The last trip took us to Providence, RI, in search of what laid behind the study of biology. Dr. Anne Fausto-Sterling, author and professor of Biology and Gender Studies at Brown University, met us at her door along with her two dogs. Though I was able to better target my questions, having already performed so many interviews, Dr. Fausto-Sterling succeeded in shaking all our assumptions about science and gender, paving a safe path back to more objective viewpoints.

Just before I thought it was all over, I found a post on my Facebook newsfeed from Meggan Watterson, founder of the event Reveal and author of *Reveal: A Sacred Manual for Getting Spiritually Naked*. I had read about Watterson before, and when I came across this reference, I sank into a sort of regretful longing for not having been able to include her perspective in the film. In the blink of an eye, I sent her a shy message, and before I became too insecure about the awkwardness of my words, she responded. Another door had opened, and New York smiled back at me once more. To this day, I still can't get over the sense that the way we met was simply meant to be.

Introduction

In a moment of distraction, I was surfing the web and came across an article by Dr. Gary Bobroff, author of *Crop Circles, Jung & The Reemergence of the Archetypal Feminine.* His article shared my thesis about our society devaluating the feminine. After this introduction to his fascinating way of portraying his ideas, I realized I could not rest until my project had included everyone I came across who spoke of the feminine. Thus, I quickly contacted him, read his book and invited him to write in mine.

The honeymoon phase ended when the time came to edit the film. My mother and I were overcome with mini panic attacks each time I had to edit out answers due to time restrictions or when I was forced to cut entire interviews because of technical problems. We were so emotionally invested that it was as if we were erasing our own newly discovered ideas. Our biggest challenge was to form a conversation that included all the dialogues we had with all the interviewees, a conversation that remained true to their beliefs as well as to the documentary's theme. Forty-five minute segments had to be cut down to five minute segments. At the same time, we had to make sure that everyone made an appearance at the correct moment. If the feminine is responsible for encompassing chaotic qualities, then this was by far the most feminine period of the process.

Another issue that continued to haunt us, even after the documentary was released, was the automatic connection that kept emerging between the "feminine" and "woman." I was overwhelmed to find myself stumbling over this same stone again and again. How was I to separate an entire gender from a set of qualities that has been historically connected to it? Stuck once more in the linguistic confusion generated by the term, I found it impossible to escape without including an introductory segment about my use of "the feminine,"— a particular meaning that goes against the word's etymological roots. Calling the feminine "anima," as Carl Jung did, would detach the word from all the associations we Westerners have to its alternative, "feminine." Yet calling it "feminine" meant drowning it in too many associations to gender, in turn, also detaching it from our intended meaning. By the time I grew acquainted with more contemporary terms like "diffuse awareness" or even the eastern "yin," the interviews had been completed, and "feminine," had been repeated over and over. That word continues to trouble me even now.

Despite my attempts to clarify my intentions, the majority of people who watch the documentary continue to categorize it as a women's studies film. I came to think that I should have elaborated more on what the feminine represents with more examples or more academic abstractions. I asked myself if the audience deserved a longer, richer description of the term. Maybe I should have waited longer to make this film while I gathered a greater pool of words, or maybe I should have written the book before making the movie, as other filmmakers often do. As most art usually goes, despite my own ruminations about what I did, what I could have done, and what I did not do, the final piece has taken on a spirit of its own and has received a vast amount of positive reactions and awards.

A couple of months after I finished the film something still felt unfinished. My friends and family diagnosed me with post-partum depression. I denied the sudden emptiness that overtook my days by claiming that I was relieved to be done and excited about enjoying my free time again. But something was still missing, and I couldn't put my finger on it. I might have been able to convince my friends and even myself that I was ready to move on, but there was one person who never failed to see right through me. Since the beginning of time people have been able to lie to their friends, to their lovers, and to themselves, but no one escapes their mother. One day, my mother teased the truth out of me: All these wonderful interviews had included so much more than the film was able to encompass, and the project was still calling me to finish it more fully. "Why don't you write a book?" Rose Mary suggested, true to her tendency to underestimate the amount of work involved in just about any project. And I, longing to resolve this project I had made my own, responded, "Okay."

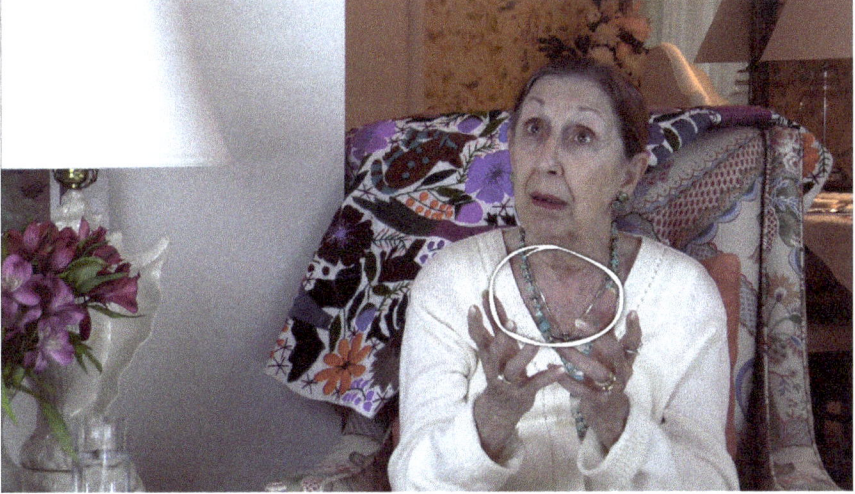

Paula Reeves

Dr. Paula Reeves, author of *Women's Intuition: Unlocking the Wisdom of the Body* and *Heart Sense: Unlocking Your Highest Purpose and Deepest Desires*, is a psychologist and workshop leader with a private practice in Atlanta, Georgia. As part of the Marion Woodman Foundation, she worked with Marion Woodman for over fifteen years leading women's retreats in the BodySoul Rhythms team. She also founded the Spontaneous Contemplative Movement and has held multiple retreats in Spain, Switzerland, Ireland, England, Canada, Mexico, and the US.

I was only nineteen years old when I first met Paula, and when I think of her, my mind is filled with the image of a long-standing tree: deep roots, solid trunk and abundant branches sprouting out and up, orna-menting the sky view. There are two pillars of truth that sit heavily in my consciousness, and she is one of them. I have given serious thought to kidnapping her and not allowing her to share her wisdom with the rest of the world except for me, but a better side of me has resisted. She is my one inspiration, my woman knight in shining armor, my utmost *wicca.*

Rose Mary. To you, Paula, what is the feminine?

For me, the feminine is a cosmic principle. I think of the feminine as a principle that has a number of qualities, and the qualities have been developed both metaphorically and sometimes energetically across time. I've done some thinking about where the whole notion of the "feminine" originated. I know that I am Jungian. I know that I am a mythographer. I love to use metaphors as teaching. But also I am basically a scientist. I came up through biology, and I lectured on how things are put together and on their origins. In reflecting on the origin of the feminine, I considered that it's one of the oldest cosmic principles. Like any of the origin myths in the Judeo-Christian tradition, for example, it speaks of the beginning in terms of the void, or it speaks of a vastness or a nothingness. That, we are told, is how the cosmos began, to the best of our knowledge.

We have forgotten over time that the concept of "void" doesn't mean without anything, just a bottomless emptiness; rather, it refers to what is full of all possibility though nothing has yet taken form. Thus, we are told that this great cosmos in which we all live came about when something penetrated that void of all possibility—just as sperm penetrates the egg—and form began to happen in the cosmos that we know. Before anything took shape, there was plasma, then stars and planets and galaxies formed.

Hence, the feminine is a great cosmic principle, and it manifests today as a metaphysical principle, as can be seen with the Sufis, but it is also being used today as a psychological principle that has to do with different qualities that inhabit all human beings who manifest and express it in different ways. The feminine has also taken form and been honored and relied upon across time in multiple cultures, primarily in Asia and Africa and certainly in South America. It is a centering principle. However, the feminine absolutely must have the masculine to make itself whole.

It's this whole business of Cartesian theory that I believe has knocked us off—the separation of the body and mind. For my purposes, the feminine is an energy principle within the human psyche and soma. It brings many of the energy principles that we use all the time into play, along with the masculine, to create the world as we know it.

Rose Mary. How did we come to define what is feminine and what is masculine? Is it purely a social construct? The majority of the population tends to pair femininity with women and masculinity with men. Should we pay attention to this?

We should pay attention to it. If you are asking if we should assign those qualities to gender, then that would be a mistake. In the distant past when culture was oral and humankind was doing everything possible to make sense of the challenges to their own survival and their observations of their environments and even beyond into the heavens, they were constantly having to deal with things greater than themselves: animals, earthquakes, plagues, etc. I believe that when human consciousness began to form words and to create tradition, they realized that females do in fact behave differently than males in the world, and that males do in fact have their own way of being in the world. They also saw that without both the male and female together, we would simply have no ongoing human race.

I have spent a lifetime nudging the folks whom I teach to recognize that the whole business of opposites does not exist anywhere in the world. Everything is complementary. What we think of as oppositional really is the extreme end of whatever we are using as an example. Jung had a saying that when you are working with change, if you can hold on tightly to the tension of what Jung calls the "opposites," and you give equal attention to the masculine and the feminine and hold on with your consciousness to each, they move closer and closer together until—Eureka!—they become complementary. When they become complementary, they form what Jung calls the transformational third, the new life, the new birth, the new idea.

This documentary is such an example of that, because here we stand, three generations in this room: the narrator, the wonderful woman behind the camera woman who just graduated from college; an older woman who happens to be the narrator's mother; and me, an older woman still—I am a great-grandmother these days! Without the documentarian's fresh new ideas, we would be stuck with our old ideas. Whereas, Lorís comes in and she asks the question, "Is there not something more to the whole notion of the feminine, from sociology, psychology, the literary perspective, and the arts?"

The Cartesian notion of separation has really set us on an awkward path. When we hold on to every principle without separation—especially to the feminine and masculine qualities in human nature—we recognize that there is a dance going on. The dance contains that exquisite piece of poetry, "So the darkness shall be the light, the stillness the dancing," which means that when we hold to both, the third will come through.

Rose Mary. When do you think the feminine became fractured, diminished, or weakened in history? Did it ever hold a high position in society?

I go to the oldest recorded tale of the feminine, recorded on clay tablets in Sumer, right there in that nexus between the Tigris and the Euphrates, now called Iraq. It is the tale of Inanna, a tale of the feminine, and I teach it as a mapping of the feminine as it presents itself in the psyche. Even in that culture in which the great deity that represented the feminine was so alive and so well, there were still the beginnings of rupture or separation.

I personally would hope that the principles of femininity never overwhelm any culture. Some cultures have been matrifocal, what we call matriarchal; but make no mistake, they had their own messes. Inherent in the principles of the feminine is a diffuse quality, a spiral, inward-pointing quality. What the feminine brings us that the masculine does not is a capacity for going inward and relating to everything. Relationship—intellectual, psychological, emotional, and ritualistic—is inherent in the feminine principle. It then happens to be carried by the female body, because the ability to conceive and incubate another human being, to wait without knowing, to give birth and then hold together the web of family, tribe, and clan is inherently the task of females across all cultures.

The center of the earth for the ancient Greeks used to be called "omphalos," the navel of the earth. The story tells how two eagles were sent out in opposite directions from Delphi. They flew and they flew and they encompassed the globe. When they completely circled the globe, they landed there at Delphi, and that was declared the center of the world, so an icon was erected there. The icon was a great ball of stone, wider at the base than it is as the top, so that it has a clear foundation. It is clearly delineated. That is the quality in the masculine. But it has the carving of a knotted net. That net depicts the feminine, and the two need one another. In any culture, feminine qualities exist to form a network. In our human body we have this exquisite, elegant loom. It's in our biochemistry, our immune system; it's even in the way our brains are filled with neural tracts and synapses that connect. All of those qualities are the feminine, but without definition through the masculine principles of uprightness and rigidness, it's a mess.

The net and the stone together create a metaphor that helps us see the dance of the masculine and the feminine. And we need only stand still and breathe in the state of the world today. We know what happens when we get an overly unconscious and ambitious masculine principle: it decimates humankind. Just decimates it. That's where we get our genocides and our wars for no reason, warriors who kill for the sake of killing. Women are joining those ranks now, just like men, because we had a period of time when we did our best to emulate all the masculine principles that really did not serve us well.

Rose Mary. Why do you think society rejects the feminine?

A misunderstanding. I believe that in societies like ours where there is a hierarchy, there has been not only a minimizing, but a degradation of the feminine in females and males—an absolute determination to teach our males to reject anything that appears "girlish" or "girl-like." A hierarchy has developed in which femininity is mistakenly thought of as female, and as weak, messy, unconscious, and incompetent. There's a long list.

In this culture, here in the United States, we had the witch hunts, whose absolute purpose was to eliminate both the intelligence and the capacity of females to know something about symbolic life, metaphoric life, and plant life; and to bring that into the culture. Consequently, as females have been devalued and males have had to maintain society and custom, females and feminism have been mixed together, and feminine qualities have been maligned. And males are not doing well at the top, not because they don't know how, but because culture itself shames them for the feminine. Shame on you if you weep in public; that is weak. Shame on you if you're watching a puppy or a kitten or a newborn, or even a flag that goes by or a meaningful song and tears roll down your eye because you are so deeply touched. That's silly. That's too girly or feminine.

Rose Mary. In your opinion, why do you think it's important for people to develop both the feminine and the masculine sides? Sometimes it might be difficult for people to translate this into their daily lives; could you give some examples?

This is why I wrote the book, *Women's Intuition*. Originally, the book was called *Embodied Intuition: The Sacred Witchcraft of the Soul*. I was referring in the most pristine manner to the ancient meaning of witch—Wicca, a woman of knowledge, of law, and authority. I wanted both male and female to have access to the book to understand that the nonverbal languages—the symbolic languages, the effectual language of our psyche and our soma—have much to teach us. They have ancient roots. In the book, I did all I could to point out that both male and female carried the nonverbal language of intuition inside. For males, we called it "hunches," for example. But we were always listening to and being taught by the intelligence of our body. Also, there's a great collective knowledge, always present, that we tap into in many ways—in our dreams, in a sudden slip of the tongue, in the impulse to do something in a certain way, or when you think of someone that you have not thought of in years, and then the phone rings and they are on the phone and it's happening almost simultaneously. Jung calls that a "synchronism," when two apparently unrelated events happen and they are reflective of one another.

My publisher decided that it wouldn't sell, reflecting the cultural bias that men would not be drawn to anything about the body and intuition, but women would; so it should be changed to *Women's Intuition.* In the first four programs that I had on PBS with the book, a good third of all the respondents were males. The first time I took my work to Australia and I talked about depression as the body's language of weeping and of sorrow, I had a room full of people who were weeping and saying, "In this culture, we have never been given permission to descend, to go inward." Therefore, I talked about how the great quality of the feminine is insight—self reflectiveness, not self-reference. It isn't "I," "me," "mine," but self-reflectiveness. How do I affect others? How does this connect to that? How can I bring disparate things together so they are related? The marvelous quality of the masculine is that it has the discernment for looking forward, "foresight," you see. When those two come together, it's an exquisite dance. The book still sells and has gone into a second printing, and I hear "thank you" so often, from male and female alike, because I give permission for females not to be messy with their intuition not to turn it into magic, or go to a dictionary with their dreams, but to listen to and move into the body. My second book was about how the heart knows before the brain knows. This is research-based, you see. With the heart, it's all about affect and response; it must have the mind to make sense.

For me to understand nature, human nature, and the nature of male and female, it takes a phenomenology. We can't speak about these things unless we are at least curious about how they have evolved across history, time, rituals, and cultures. I am concerned now, because the great god that stands at our altar today is Google. In some ways, it's absolutely divine; it's a miracle to me that I can go to a little computer that I hold in my hand and look something up that I used to have to go to the library for. But if we are to bring the feminine principle forward to help us heal and to honor the masculine and the feminine, there has to be human interaction. We must look deeply into the eyes of another human being and see our own relatedness, in compassion and understanding, and know that we are really not different. What we are is unique, and we must honor that uniqueness and always be willing to say, "You know, I disagree, but tell me more." My concern is that we will get more and more isolated with our rigidity or our restriction, because Google, the internet, cloud computing, none of that will ever take the place of the collective unconscious, the years and years of human experience that continues to inform us.

We have but to look at this vase of flowers next to me and know this is an old lady and she is just a regular hydrangea. You see her blue? Those are in a way the original hydrangeas. They just grow, and they have been growing since time began. Without the genetic knowing and history of this original lady and her seeds, these hydrangeas here could not have been born. They couldn't have come into being. We become clumsy in trying to separate ourselves from all that history and all of that energy that joins us, and in separating ourselves, we become alienated from the psychic and mythological dance that is going on in us. This dance that tells us that we need both principles: we need a physical DNA, and we also must have our psychic DNA. Together, it helps us relate to everything that seems different. It helps us understand our differences. And the masculine principle also helps us to say "no" as females; it is a complete sentence. The feminine brings us the "both/and," the masculine brings us the "yes" and the "no." They both need one another to form that great image of the rock upon which we stand, and the net which connects all of us.

Rose Mary. Even though women in Western societies pride themselves on being liberated from external oppression, would you agree that there are other internal obstacles that they have yet to overcome?

It's too easy to say, "Of course, I agree." I do know, and I would be foolish if I did not know it, that I am a secondary citizen in this culture in three ways. First of all, I am female. That's a given in this culture. Secondly, I happen to be an older woman, and elderhood is devalued in this "disposable society." The third way is that I have the misfortune of having educated myself. Some folks would say, "But you bought into a Ph.D." Well, I would answer, "I bought into nothing. I was starved for knowledge." Let me tell you what I have bought into. It's a good thing, but it will never provide me with the real depth that it provides my male counterparts with. I am self-employed, a self-sufficient woman who has been married for sixty years. I value marriage. My husband has supported me wholly and soulfully for decades. Now, as a self-motivated, educated and self-employed human being with licensure, etc., I will never be regarded with the same esteem as one of my male counterparts. Does that trouble me? Not in the least. Does it sadden me? Deeply. It saddens me deeply for what is being missed in our culture. In the course of working with human beings as a psychotherapist, I see hundreds of males and females alike who are so stressed with doing all they can. I see women who are trying to have it all. There is a tremendous pull at their core to have a timeout to relate, to cultivate that part of them that wishes just to be. The same is true in the case of the phenomena of the house-husband, the father who takes care of the children. They come in and say, "I'm just having such difficulty trying to manage it all."

This doesn't mean that we're not flexible, and it doesn't mean that females should be only one thing and males should be another. It means that we must ask ourselves, "What is the story I am telling myself when I acquire this or want this, and is that story true for me personally?" And if it is true, "How true is it?" That requires going to what I call "the altar of your being," and standing quietly and asking yourself, "In the end, is this what I want for me?" Sometimes, we don't even know. There is a mistaken notion in this culture that we can ever be like the other gender. We are wanting a kind of equity that society is not designed for yet.

Rose Mary. Do you think that our society's whole infrastructure is based on masculine principles? Do you think these principles are reflected in our attitudes toward the environment?

We have a metastructure and microstructure. Make no mistake, our microstructure is strong; but yes, our metastructure is based upon the principles of the masculine. I would say 75 percent of that is a blessing, because without those principles, technology would not be developed, organization would not be developed, and world commerce would not have developed. You would not have this exquisite camera, or this microphone, or the kind of medical care we all get. We can go on and on and on about what those masculine principles are and what a hierarchical system has brought us. Yet beneath all of that, there is a strong and pervasive system working, a system of networking and sisterhood.

One of the movies that so energized us a few years ago was *Divine Secrets of the Ya-Ya Sisterhood.* From time immemorial, females, in order to express their connection, their ideas, their folklore, their mother knowledge, etc., have met together in all sorts of ways. Currently, for example, we can see this in the eruption of the Middle East, where women will come together and educate one another when the outside world thinks they are meeting only to sew or to cook. Not at all! They're teaching women to read and write. There are two levels of culture, but primarily in this culture, we have become increasingly more industrialized, more technological, and more given to those hierarchal qualities that continually override our sense of collaboration and communication with the feminine and, therefore, with females.

I think if we had the scope to see it, we would find that, though the degradation of our environment is certainly a result of the wanton use of its resources for our own human purposes, it has also occurred because human beings have lost the capacity to relate to human nature, and to recognize that we are much lower on the food chain. Human beings are not in charge of this world. Nature is. I dare say, the day must come when we stand still and say, "Hooray! We have been born. Now, since we are here for such a brief moment in time, and then we will die, and then we will become ashes and dust, and we will feed these plants, and we will feed this planet; let us learn how to live by nurturing this womb into which we will return." So yes, when we lose sight of how deeply reliant we are upon the ecology of this planet, we have a tendency to disregard the necessity of being good stewards instead of consumers.

Rose Mary. When much of the world's population is made up of women, it's surprising to think that we have not acted together to fight for equity. What are some factors that you believe are keeping women from coming together? What can we do to change this?

To my ears those are two different questions. Women do not want equity. What we want is relationship and respect. I do not know of any woman who wants everything that she imagines men have. What she wants is respect for who she is, what she does, how she contributes, and the way in which she moves in the world. I don't know if it will even serve us to have equity, but it would certainly serve us to have something called "equality," and even that is a rather elusive word.

In addition to that, we think of the gender "woman" as being some sort of generic thing; it's not. Among womankind, we are different in what we want, how we want to be seen, how we relate across cultures, and even in social class. Women themselves have not extended equity to other women. Many women who went into industry and business denigrated their sisters who stayed home and reared children. The women who chose not to have children were denigrated by the women who chose to have children. We're not pack animals, and the consequence is that in our basic nature we are all unique. But we are relational. In being relational, I believe what we all want is respect.

Rose Mary. How can we change the fact that as women, we are sometimes separated?

I hear that we do not come together, but—my word—just look at the micro-businesses that are springing up! Those women are bringing their cultural voices and skills into play and at the same time establishing themselves economically and relationally. Look at all the many ways in which women are speaking out for their children. Take a look at the many ways in which women are finding small communities in which to join hands and make changes in small ways. My sense is that the reason why you don't see great projects mounted by women—corporations formed, and laws organized and legislated—is that this is not the woman's way. Our way is to care, to relate, to speak to one another, and to make changes woman to woman. If you doubt that women can bring about change, just go into any community where a woman has had a voice about the treatment of children, or about ecology that is affecting many of the people.

I'm just concerned about a time when we as females will have educated ourselves so well that we feel that we have a cachet and authority in the world, and so we hand ourselves over to book knowledge. We forget that the world is out there, alive and begging for us to roll up our sleeves and get out there and listen to every woman's story and every man's story. Because it's only when human beings feel seen, heard, and respected that we join hands and make a change.

Rose Mary. In your opinion, why is there such an obsession with the female body? Does religion play a role in it, or is our society hyper-sexualized?

These are important questions. I smile because we could do documentary after documentary about this. The pathos, the pain, suffering, and losses that have been suffered because of the idealizing of the female body, on the one hand, and the degradation of the female body, on the other hand; this pain is endless. All I can say is that any culture that represses its feeling side, and will not acknowledge the natural richness, the creativity, and the power in its own sensuousness and sexuality; this culture is then at risk for projecting all of that onto a gender. I don't believe it's any secret in the world that North America is terribly stunted in our expression of feelings and our ability to allow our sensuality to be part of us. When was the last time that you ate at a restaurant or were in someone's home when they ate something absolutely delicious and licked each finger while they were talking to you, and you stopped and observed that? You see, that is being present. When I touch my flowers, I have a tendency to caress them. These are examples of what I call a deep, deep, divine sensuousness. To be able to look at another person, even if they are someone you find reprehensible, you have to be able to think that, originally, that person came into this world with a fragment of the mystery of divinity, and when you make them nothing more than a carrier of your projections, then things that are sensuous become sexualized. Things that are forbidden become mocked. That may be a part of it.

Our folks have been taught that if you are fully developed as a male, you have an endless flow of testosterone, and as a female you are always receptive and delighted to be penetrated by any male because there is such delight in being seen as a sexual object. That's so bogus, and so false. It skews what it is to be masculine, feminine, sensuous, sexual; but also creative and relational. That is just the tip of a discussion we might have if we went into the pain and the awfulness that comes about when a culture is so repressed that it sexualizes an object, then negates the object of their sexualization.

Rose Mary. How are you having to work against this? Can you share the work you do and the results you have obtained?

Well, from an early, early age I learned to be a listener. I learned to listen carefully to what people were telling me. Whether it was the stories I heard from my large, Southern family, or what I learned as I began to travel—because by age seven I was traveling about the world. I was immediately attracted to indigenous practices of healing and of relating. What I began to recognize is that while we have cultural standards and laws, I was always more deeply interested in the human story and how the human being was affected by the mores, the folkways, the tradition—particularly the oral tradition—of their culture; and how that all came into conflict with the written law. I came of age before the sixties. I was born in 1933 you see, so I came of age before that great swelling of feminism, not to be confused with the feminine. The pushing back of feminism included the excellent work great warriors like Riane Eisler, who wrote the splendid book, *The Chalice and The Blade*, which spells out how the feminine was literally expunged from the literature, and why we have to bring back a sense of parity and equality. That happened after my coming of age.

For the first eighteen years of my marriage, I was a homemaker who was dedicated to rearing my children, teaching my children the kinds of foundational values that I hoped would sustain them. In many ways I was Christian, but I was also Buddhist, and I was also constantly seeking a broader view. As I grew towards the time for me when my children were grown and I could move into a professional life for myself, I moved quite naturally into two things. My love of story led me to become a mythographer. Using story, I described to other human beings how we were connected to the world, male and female alike. Therefore, I became not only a mythographer but also a psychotherapist. I have spent a lifetime helping people understand that they come into this world with an essential self that will never be replicated; I have listened to their stories and asked them: "Tell me, what is the story beneath your story? What is the story you are telling yourself about this law or this conditional society?" Every human being carries a fragment into this world that will never again come into a meaningful part of the whole web that is humankind if they do not manifest it; if they do not become conscious of it and live it.

I may not have legislated or protested or been active out in the world, but I have taught male and female communities alike to understand who they believe they are, who they believe they are capable of becoming, and then how to be absolutely practical about it. I have taught human beings how to be their essential self, to get in touch with their ensoulment. I have used "soul" as you have used "soul." It is your total personality. It is your ego in connection with divinity. It is your ego in connection with the rest of the world. I have taught people to understand their soulfulness and to take how they are affected by the laws of the world or of their culture very seriously. And if that gives them grief, they will learn to find a way to speak out without doing any harm.

I have also lived long enough to recognize that change comes about cell by cell, word by word and fragment by fragment, and every single bit of it counts as part of the whole. So, have I done my task for females? Yes, I believe so, just as I have for the males of the world. I have as much compassion and receptivity to the damage that the masculine way and the patriarchy has done to the men I know, as I have for what it has done to the women I know. Too much of the masculine principle leads to a hierarchical and patriarchal society that is much too full of itself and not enough encompassing of others.

Rose Mary. You have developed Spontaneous Contemplative Movement and Embodied Intuition. Can you describe this model?

I have been dedicated for many decades now to teaching human beings what they know—but do not know that they know—that their bodies tell them. A symptom is really a metaphor that has much to tell us about what is mattering in us, to us. A metaphor, you know, is the choice of a word or description that, when it is right for the listener, simultaneously attracts the mind, energizes the body, and deeply innovates our soulfulness. When I say, "symptom is metaphor," I am teaching human beings that there is so much more to us than our cognitive selves. There is always a dance going on within us between our psyches and our somas that gets expressed through our exquisitely elegant minds.

I have combined contemplative movement with the use of a mirror and metaphor. When people come to me with an ache in their heart or a hip that is literally locked down, I would say, "Let us listen to what your body knows that you don't even know that you know." I ask them to tell me the story of their symptom, but I ask them first to tell me the story while looking at me; and then to tell me the story while looking into their own eyes in the mirror. The reason I do this is that educated folks—by that I mean folks who no longer refer from the inside out but rather describe themselves by syntax and by language—oftentimes do not relate to the concept of "myself" as telling the story. When you look deeply into your own eyes and repeat the story, you begin to realize that you are speaking to yourself about yourself. Eventually the use of that mirror helps you be self-reflective in a very deep way.

Then, I ask them if they are willing to take their attention to their symptom and move spontaneously and contemplatively. I say, "Stand still and do nothing until you feel a spontaneous movement. I know you are reflecting on your aching heart or your arthritic hip, but the first movement might be an impulse to just move your finger. Move it, and let the energy continue until it comes to its own resting place, and then quietly just confer with yourself. You don't have to have an image or a story. Just wait for the next spontaneous movement." Sometimes, folks just do this for just two or three minutes, and they are finished. Other times, it will go on for forty-five minutes or more. Then, I ask them to come back and tell me the story again, looking into the mirror, and then reflect upon the movement and the contemplation. What happens is, across time, the relationship between "my symptom," "my story," and "me" begins to develop in the most unique way.

In *Women's Intuition*, I wrote many excerpts of the stories that, using this method, people began to move through and expand until they got to the understory that was nothing about the symptom as they knew it. It was not about healing the arthritis or taking some kind of medication for the heart; it was about, "What is mattering to me?" The mattering is just showing as heartspeak and hipspeak. When we do not know what matters most to us, then that will become the "matter" with us, and—blessed be—a symptom will develop. Do we give ourselves these symptoms? No. Is there such a thing as arthritis? Of course. But our psyches use the vulnerability of the body to let us know where we are vulnerable in our divinity, in our essential human being-ness.

I wrote the book, *Heart Sense*, based on the science of organ transplants and the mysterious relationship between the heart and the recipient of a donor organ, to help us understand that quite literally on a biochemical level, our hearts respond to everything we think before our mind can wrap itself around it. The heart and the brain are entrained with each other, as is our entire system. As human beings, when our hearts begin instantaneously to absorb what is going on in us at a really deep and intimate level, there is a chemical electricity that flies between the heart and the brain, and there are showers of neuronal activity—actually biochemical, hormonal activity—that go throughout the body and invigorate the whole body and our organ systems. We are being danced, and our hearts simply know it. In the literature on organ transplants you read about cases like that of a recipient of the heart of a donor who was in a motorcycle accident, who is very careful with their diet and keeps certain dietary restrictions, yet suddenly discovers an absolute hunger for McDonalds' French fries. The donor recipient must have them, adores them. Then this person learns that those French fries were one of the donor's favorite foods. Or a recipient suddenly thinks, "I just love to cha-cha." And then, "What am I thinking about? I never cha-cha'd in my life." But they go and take lessons. The donor loved to cha-cha, you see. Now, these are very rudimentary kinds of thumbnail sketches, but I wrote *Heart Sense* because what I wanted to convey, again, is that even when we don't know what matters most to us, it still matters deeply within the core of our being. Our hearts carry it, even when they are beating in the breast of another being. Once that donor heart is entrained with the brain of the recipient, things begin to change, you see. But in the transition, that essential-ness is carried even into the breast of another.

I suppose if I have asked anything of others or if I have carried any particular message in all the years that I have taught all over the world with my writings, and CDs and DVDs and what have you, is that all of us as human beings, male or female, are far more than our gender. We are far more than our cultural restrictions. We are much more than the legislation of our being-ness. We have a depth in us that is unplumbed and can speak to us about our essentialness. It can help us understand, whether we are an Australian living in aboriginal Australia or an

African that is still in the deepest part of Africa or a Ph.D. sitting right here in this chair next to you, that, essentially, we are connected. We are connected in a way that begs us to get to know our human nature and our own sense of relationship, and then not to be messy about it or make assumptions, but instead to bring in other fine masculine qualities of containment, of focus, and of interaction. Together, the penetrating logical quality and the receptive incubating quality come together, and we have what we have had this morning—a conversation.

Rose Mary. How do you envision a world that fully embodies the feminine as an equal to the masculine? What would this world look like?

I believe that has been described as Eden, and I personally would want none of it. I prefer the snake; I prefer consciousness and differences. Do I want to see things disintegrate as that old story of Eden did? No, but I believe that what you are describing to me, at least in my knowing of human nature, would require a level of unconsciousness that I would not welcome. If I were to give you an answer that had no meaning at all—and yet I am not in any way being flippant—I would say to you that we would all have to wait for death and return to that place from whence we came where surely the DNA of the Cosmos needed both the feminine incubation and the masculine penetration to be. We came from that place, and we will return to it.

I do live by principles of the feminine. I was born Judeo-Christian, and I spent many years apologizing to the Old Testament God. After much soul searching and trepidation, I'm over that now! I guess what I am saying, in conclusion, is that it's taken me seventy-nine years to get to this place, and I'm no template for how to do it. I just feel such a sense of gratitude and humility to have this time with you and to know that a female much younger than I has the courage to create this documentary, and to collaborate with her mother—no small thing—in these important questions and generational differences. So, blessed be.

Patricia Llosa

Patricia Llosa is originally from Peru but has lived in Israel and currently lives in New York, where she has worked at the Metropolitan Museum of Art for the past sixteen years as an administrator and educator. Patricia has studied archeology, art history, and visual arts, and she holds a master's in fine arts. A Jungian analyst by training, she completed the Marion Woodman Foundation BodySoul Rhythms Leadership Training Program in 2003.

Patricia was present at the very same retreat where I met Paula. Given the role of interpreting dreams, she had a tenderness in her voice that made you want to go hug her and fall asleep on her shoulder. At first I thought she was bringing out that side of her for the sake of the retreat, perhaps to welcome the women to open up without feeling judged. But when I met

Patricia at the MET for her interview, I sensed the
same tender energy, though with a brighter spark, and
I understood it to be her constant nature. Never having
met anyone like her, I wondered at her gentle spirit. If
I were to have met her when I was a child, I would
have immediately classified her as an angel. Now, I see
her as a sort of mythological princess, the feminine
incarnate.

*Rose Mary. What are other more approachable ways of looking at the
feminine? There seem to be so many associations with the word feminine.*

The feminine is such a big word as I understand it now. I grew up
in Peru, where I experienced several images of the feminine as gender.
It differed amongst the Indian population, *mestizo* women, and
Spanish women. They all had different ways of expressing and living
the cultural role of what it means to be a woman. This is what I
understood the feminine to be. Then, when I moved to Israel to study
archeology and Art History, I found very different images of the
feminine there among the young women my age who were toting
guns and considered the aspects of the feminine I had grown up with
to be wimpy and subservient. So, at a certain level, the image of
femininity is a cultural phenomenon and gender specific.

But your question reminds me of why I was attracted to the work
of C.G. Jung and Marion Woodman, precisely because it is about
seeking an essence below this surface. It was through them that I
learned about the feminine as essence. What resonated with me was
the dynamics which they put in the terms of the eastern idea of *yin*
and *yang*—with *yin* representing the cyclical, and flowing, the dark
and the deep. To think of the feminine as that *yin* quality, whether it
is in a man or a woman, made more sense to me. Through working
with Marion Woodman on images like the Black Madonna and images
of nature and the earth, I became more aware of the territory of the
body and the territory of matter. I am also interested in the Spanish

dynamic that we have talked about, *duende.*[1] So now I understand the feminine as what comes from below, from the earth, and what has that earthy, material quality rather than an angelic airy spirit.

Rose Mary. All these feminine images that you grew up with, could you also tell us about other images of the feminine you have studied in the past?

I remember my fascination at encountering the earliest images of the feminine found in Europe. The densely potent but portable images that can be held in the palm of your hand: the Venus of Willendorf[2] and the Venus of Lespugue.[3] These sculptures are carved out of stone, with very small heads and large breasts, bellies and hips, and very narrow feet. They are 20,000 or 30,000 years old. You get the sense from them not of a personal but of an archetypal feminine since they are of voluptuous shape and have no particularizing features. This sculpture next to me is a copy of a Cycladic figure owned by the Metropolitan Museum of Art. The Cycladic figures are also feature-less though perhaps they were painted, but they also keep well the secret of who they are and what they represented. They are about 5,000 years old, and many of them show the female figures with their hands squared on their bellies and with squared off heads.

I love tracking the images of the feminine through time; I see this every day at the Metropolitan Museum where I work. There are two images of the feminine in the 19th century galleries that are placed together in a wonderful juxtaposition. On one side is a painting of Salome[4]. Many Met visitors come to see her, sitting full bodied and carnal with her toes sinking into a fur rug. She reigns there as the sensual feminine, the seducer, one in her body and delighting in her

---

[1] A Spanish term referring to something newly created, a dynamic or a change of air. A direct translation of *duende* points to a little being, a dwarf or elf.
[2] An Austrian statue of a female figure from about 28,000 and 25,000 BCE.
[3] A French statue of a female figure from about 26,000 and 24,000 BCE.
[4] Queen of Chalcis and Armenia Minor in 34 AD. She is identified with the seductive dancing woman in the New Testament.

earthy abundance, her warm skin, her sparkling eyes—with a come-hither look and with her curls rolling down her shoulders. At a certain point she was removed by a curator but was returned due to public clamor. Right next to her is a totally different world in a painting of Joan of Arc[5]. You are knocked out by her piercing visionary blue eyes that seem to look into you and beyond you. Here is a woman who is so contained you see that she is engaged with another dimension, not the physical dimension—as she is depicted so separate from the nature that surrounds her—but the spiritual one. So the seductive and the spiritual are two very different aspects and images of "woman" that I especially appreciate.

Rose Mary. Do you believe there is space for the feminine in the workforce?

I think there is space for the feminine everywhere, there has to be! Yet it does come at a cost, and that is what your question brings forth. There is a tremendous cost because when you are connected to your feminine values, you would be listening to the rhythms of your body, to relatedness, to other people. It brings in more of a sense of the possibility of diffusion and relatedness and relating to one's own nature and other people's nature. Those are not necessarily the values in work environments. However, though it comes at a cost; it is what we have to stand up for!

Rose Mary. In the past times you were speaking of, was there space for the feminine qualities?

In those times, there was a shift in the relationship to nature. If you watch the sunrise or the sunset every day, you have a different relationship to cycles. If you are accustomed to walk out in nature, you notice the pace of nature. The problem is that we become disconnected from the cyclical life of nature, and its vitality, and live in a one-sided way in an ego-driven world. That world is brilliant,

---

[5] A French heroine and Catholic saint (1412 – May 30, 1431).

especially when manifested in New York City, for example. It is always amazing to me to see the city from far away when you drive in from the airport at Newark, you see it as a miniature cluster of buildings. Then you come closer, and closer, and closer, and once you are in it, it has such a force and rhythm of its own that it has its own laws, it becomes a gargantuan monster. You are brought down by the rhythm and the pace of the city. It is very hard to keep your own inner rhythm, whatever it may be, in the face of that rhythm or to struggle to integrate those two rhythms together. I think it is tremendously important to bring the feminine values into the daily life of those who live in a city, or work in an environment where they feel they cannot really listen to their body because they are seated in a chair all day. It is awful to not listen to the body's needs for emotional expression.

Rose Mary. In a way you feel a threat from patriarchal values.

It all comes down to what you value. It's important to ask, "What do you value?" Also, have you had an opportunity to develop a taste for this value? For example, there is a value to what Jung calls intuitive thinking, a value to daydreaming, to imagination, to resting and just dropping into your own internal rhythms, or the rhythms of the soul. But in order to give them space, you have to value them. It is a different set of values. Jung talks about the difference between directed thinking and intuitive thinking. Directed thinking is so linear. We mostly live in a linear world. The feminine brings in the curves. That is probably so politically incorrect! The feminine is the rhythmic, the circular and the intuitive—a different path. If you can develop a taste for that rhythm, you realize how it feeds the other. It is not about being one-sided, but about connecting with both the feminine and the masculine. If you only have that feminine energy, you can get heavy and dense. The matriarchy can be just as heavy and one-sided as the patriarchy. I would differentiate the feminine from the matriarchal. The matriarchal is the frozen or rigidified feminine, as the patriarchal is the frozen masculine—they both lack movement upwards, towards growth but are about clamping down and contracting.

I remember working with Marion Woodman in Brazil when she spoke about working with a group of women who were very much brought up as fathers' daughters. They were doing the seminar exercises, and they were mothering to such an extent that she called it "smother mother." It manifested as a dense, sentimental over-protection, which when discussed by the group was seen as a cultural expectation. If there is too much of that, there is not enough creative spark, that directive force that will create something. It really is about finding the balance between the two, but as your question brings out, there is a lack of balance in the world right now—and the appreciation of the feminine dynamic is what needs to be brought in before it turns against us with its rage of abandonment through climate change, etc. That is why it is so important that you make this film and bring in the question of what is the value of the feminine—not in terms of gender but as a dynamic—and for younger people to understand it as a dynamic and reparative need to balance.

It is such a hard question, what is the feminine? There are so many images out in the world that people identify with the feminine. Is it the little pink dresses, lace, curling your hair, makeup, is it swinging your hips, is it being flirtatious, is it being seductive, is it being motherly? How to get to the essence of what that means for you, for me? It really comes back to the sense of "being one in herself," as Marion Woodman says. The connection to that rhythmic, cyclical interior nature.

Rose Mary. In a way it is what is happening with this Cycladic sculpture as well as that piece that Marion Woodman always speaks about, right?

Yes. Marion Woodman loves this drawing of St. Anne by Leonardo da Vinci, and she describes the experience of coming upon it in the National Gallery of London and making it her own in her book, *Addiction to Perfection*. She references it when she teaches but most often to point to the importance of each person finding the image of the feminine that brings alive or renews the meaning of the feminine to them. This image was hers. At the same time she speaks of the collective upsurge of images of the black Madonna she witnessed in the dreams of the women she worked with.

Rose Mary. There is always that sign in Da Vinci's hands, the pointing.

Marion speaks about this pointing as "uniting earth and sky." It is symbolic of this encounter and the creative moment. As for the Cycladic sculptures[6], they are very mysterious. As there is no written history, no one knows what these figures mean. However, it is true that the way she has her arms around her center gives that sense of call to your full being or being one onto herself.

Lorís. One last question Patricia. What is something a person could do on a daily basis to ground this whole concept of being more in touch with yourself?

Taking the time to listen to yourself. What does that mean? Taking the time to investigate your inner life. Something wants to be heard but is usually drowned out.

So first you need to take the time to turn down the volume on the myriad impressions that are bombarding you from without and become aware of an inner space, and that you can actually take up residence there. Begin to relate to that space in which an authentic impulse can be discerned.

Nowadays, there is a hunger for more bodywork. How many people do yoga now compared to fifty years ago? However, when you do the yoga poses, and you work out and you connect to your bodies, you have to be careful not to do it with a patriarchal approach: as in pushing your body towards a goal; having an agenda for it; wanting it to be good, to be healthy, to be beautiful, to be thin!

What I recommend is to take a moment to drop all the agendas. Then, once you drop them, ask, "What does my body have to say? What are the agendas that live in my body?" Then begin to dialogue

---

[6] A Greek figurine belonging to early cultures from the Cyclades (ca. 3200 – 2300 BCE).

with them. One of the things that has been most helpful to me in the work with Marion Woodman and BodySoul Rhythms is how she talks about the creature self. Listening in that way has allowed me to reclaim the creaturely part of my body, letting it emerge and dialogue with me, so that I begin to get a sense of this particular body, my home that takes me around everywhere and does so much for me. How can I treat it with affection and say, "thank you," and relate to it without my ego agenda? Even if that just takes a few minutes a day, a dialogue opens up. Once you have a dialogue, you are no longer stuck in one side of yourself. Hopefully then the masculine and feminine values are dancing together.

Lorís. I think I have never looked at it that way, as a dialogue, but I guess that is what it is!

Marion taught that the dialogue is always underway even though you may not feel it directly. She often enacted the image of the healing staff of Asclepius[7], the dance of two snakes rising up, entwining and meeting each other which is a medical symbol to this day. You work and you work and you work and you come to a place where the feminine is rising up and you reach an understanding. That touches off another process. Basically, it is the dance of opposites that is essential to Jungian theory and symbolizes the path of individuation. In order to individuate, it is the balance of both yin and yang, masculine and feminine. What we are feeling much more right now in the world is the imbalance of the feminine values. We are trying to bring these values in as many ways as we can. What I am interested in right now is the leap of the irrational, as the breaking through of a radical new set of values. Robert Bly inspired me with his book called *Leaping Poetry*, and the whole idea of the risk in the form of a leap. It is about letting go of that structure of the goal and allowing there to be this little breath in between space for creativity and a new relationship and the irrational. It is a way of envisioning Jung's

---

[7] The god of medicine and healing in ancient Greek religion.

transcendent function. I think that is why I like the *duende* of Spain and Federico Garcia Lorca so much. In his autobiography, *Memories, Dreams, Reflections* (1989), it made me think about leaping into the *pupila*. The *pupila* is the center of the eye, but it also means a doll, or a little image of oneself, like a homunculus. That image has sparked my imagination, that the turn towards the inner life is a leap within, implying an inner drop towards inner reflection. The reflection in the body.

Rose Mary. In that sense, would the duende *be a feminine aspect? Or from the yin qualities?*

Well, where the *duende* is considered I can only throw out a guess it emerges from the earth, yet it has fire. I think the *duende* has both. It is a paradox—which Marion Woodman likes to say is the way of the feminine—an earthy spark. It is mercurial—you can't really pin it down even though I just tried to. Oops! Again, it comes from below; it comes from the earth and the darkness. Lorca talks about how in flamenco, it rises up from the soles of the feet. It is both. It comes from the world of matter as well as the spark of creativity. Thus, it is like dark matter, or dark spark. I think it is both. You know why? Because it is embodied. When it is embodied, it is both. Therefore, the *duende* is the spark. Yet when you dance it, when it manifests in the arts, that is when it is connecting to the feminine because the feminine is the body, is the way that it manifests in matter. I guess I would say that, for me right now, I understand the *duende* as what Jung called in the Nietzsche seminars the impulse in the blood (1997). An embodied, authentic impulse.

Rose Mary. Do you think Lorca was conscious about it? Or maybe he just felt it, and it came through.

I would think so. Lorca felt it deeply, or he would not have brought it through. As happens so often, the artist is the harbinger of the collective nature of the time. He paid for it with his life. All the structures of Spain are breaking down, all of the structures in

Europe! It is feeling the impending war coming on. It is very prescient, very intuitive. You know how poets and artists are the intuitive representative of our time, of our culture. He also felt that importance of being connected to an essence that was related to nature because he started to collect the aspects of what he understood as *duende*, the dancing halls in Southern Spain, listening to people sing who maybe were not educated, but were educated in life, in experience, even though they were not academic. When he talks about *duende*, he talks about breaking through this façade of academia. In a way, for example when I think of Latin American women, as I try to understand my past, I think of how we have this structure of behaving in a certain way with men, being very family-oriented, being very adaptive in many ways, and there being a lot of both positive and negative values to that. However how do you find your own voice? Your own voice when you have such a powerful structure? I think that is what *duende* is about, breaking through the structures and finding a voice that comes from within, that is yours, but is also from the ground of your own being and your experience. I want to write about this, especially for Latin American women, because it is a Spanish dynamic. It is part of our heritage!

Rose Mary. Yes, you need to! There is not much out there about this topic.

This is my passion. It comes out of the work with Marion [Woodman]. It reminds me of the stories of the creation of the earth and the great myths. The great mother Gaia is giving birth and she is in so much pain, she has to put her hands down into the earth while screaming with the birth pangs. Finally, she gives birth. From under her finger nails there are all these little pieces of earth that get stuck under there. These little gods emerge from there. They become grounded creativity, like the Kabeiroi[8], which I see as precursors to *duende*. It is very interesting.

---

[8] Mystic gods or daimones that appear in various fragments of the ancient world.

I think you are also asking, how to be feminine and have a force in the world, and be forceful. How to be one in yourself, related to your feminine values, but also connected to the masculine values and the values of the yang where you have an impact in the world. We want to have an impact. For me, the study of *duende* is how I am trying to understand how to both be creative in my pursuits and have an impact, yet at the same time value the cyclical nature of the feminine and be able to hold the opposites of the agenda and no agenda at the same time, which is really hard! Both have an aim but also allow it to have its own rhythm. It is really living on a creative edge. I think if we can live that way, it is true creativity! It really is.

I was talking about—with your question—what is the feminine? It is a question that stops you short. I feel some hubris trying to answer it. What I love about what you are doing is that you are circumambulating the question, as Jung would say. You are traveling, talking to people from all walks of life, all ages, and circumambulating: "What is the feminine, what is the feminine, what is the feminine?" All these different answers are creating a field that hopefully will bring another level of understanding as people watch your film and think about what it means to them. What are the images of the feminine and where are they stuck in their concepts about, "This is the feminine"? How do we bring movement into the question of what is the feminine? I think that is what you are doing! It is a great project! Circumambulating the feminine.

Sheila Langston

Sheila Langston works as a team leader for national and international Marion Woodman Foundation workshops. An experienced voice instructor, Langston has taught for over twenty-five years in Canada, the US, Mexico, and Europe. While her work focuses on the voice and the body, she also fuses her studies in myth, metaphor, images, and dreams into her coaching. Langston is presently in training as a Jungian analyst at the Centre for Research and Training in Depth Psychology in Switzerland.

I met Sheila at my very first BodySoul Rhythms retreat in Mexico. I may have been too young to understand many of the things that were covered in that intensive week, but somehow the lessons took hold and resurged later when I was able to recognize them. In particular, once I understood her insights into the power and place of the voice, the lesson struck me with a force I couldn't shake off. Every time I jump into a significant conversation with someone, I observe the movement in our words and in our faces. I may stop speaking when the other person talks, but my emotions and thoughts keep running, so that I'm not sure at what point conversations actually end. "Voice" has gained a new meaning for me that goes way beyond the vocal chords.

Lorís. To you, what is the feminine?

Receptivity, taking in, having the courage to stay in the moment and stay present and allow myself to be affected. I think for me, at this point in time, femininity is the ground of my body, the earth that my body represents. So it has a quality of earth and of containing, of the container of the body and the body as a holding structure, as a holding being.

Lorís. Do you believe that society agrees with that idea of femininity?

In my experience, when I do engage with somebody on this level and talk about these kinds of things, there is an agreement. People in my life do come to a deeper understanding of the feminine, or an appreciation, as if they're hearing something that they already knew but didn't know that they already knew. So, I think there is a possibility for this kind of consciousness or understanding of the feminine. It's somewhere there in a layer, but if you mean on the surface, no. Also, the behavior that may be considered to be feminine is rather light and girlish and non-threatening.

Lorís. Why do you think that, before, we had these goddesses that we praised, like Demeter, and now they've become so insignificant?

I think that the discussion about why it happened is a huge topic, and we don't really know how that transformation occurred from the veneration of goddesses and the great mother. What's important to me is that the feminine power has gone into the underground, into the shadow. We're talking about a bigger subject here, too. It's not even so much about the feminine and masculine; we're talking about the patriarchy, which is a whole other structure within which there is no room for either the masculine or the feminine to be in their fullness. There is a set of rules that disallows each of those aspects to be fully lived.

For me, in terms of the feminine, the depth and the breadth and the power of the feminine can be overpowering. You brought in the Kali figure in our previous conversations. There is a huge destructive aspect to the true feminine, as well as an incredible creative aspect. But if you speak in those terms, then where in our world do we have the opportunity to really be fully in our female bodies and stand in our place and speak with our full voice and our full hearts; how do we not then be considered to be a ball breaker, or an Amazon, or whatever all those different labels are that associate a strong feminine with too muchness?

Loris. This is a country that runs on illusions. You have to look like a girl, but then not act like one. Everyone rushes to look like the fourteen-year-old that they see on the cover of a magazine.

There is something in that for me in response to "supposed to be," so that, as women in this culture we are defining ourselves through an imaginary outside eye, which is completely disconnected from the feminine. The feminine is internal and in the body and in the flesh.

Loris. Does Western society lack femininity, or a place for femininity?

I'm just caught up by the use of the word "femininity"; it doesn't resonate with me the same way "feminine" does. I find that I'm curious about that and wonder whether femininity in my imagination and my experience is associated with the other that we were talking about— the light and the girlish. So, I'm just noticing this now, and I want to speak it in this moment. Because if I ask, "Well, is femininity honored or seen in our culture?" I think, "Yes, in that fluffy pink, girly way." But the true feminine, no. Although, maybe it's a "maybe." Maybe it could be, maybe it is starting to be. For me, I have to believe that the work that we're doing is rippling out in some way, which must mean that somewhere, on some level, the feminine is finding a place again. That's what I hope. That's what I'd like to believe.

Lorís. This patriarchal society, whether it does or does not give a place for the feminine, how do you think it affects relationships?

We spoke before about being inside one's own being, one's own body, and how that begins to allow a kind of connection or relationship. I know it's different in different places, from having been here working with Latina women, and from stories I have been told; but what I know about Canada is that the risk of being in one's body is enormous because there is emotion there. There is pain. There is memory. There is vulnerability. There is the immediacy of being present, which can be overwhelming. So, unless there is the opportunity to begin to trust that, people just don't live in their bodies, or they live in their bodies in a superficial way. They go to the gym and run on the beach, do their stretching and their yoga, but it's not a deep connection. And so there is a basic lack of trust in being together. Does that make sense?

I'm struck by the word "feeling," and it takes me in my imagination back to this idea of relationships and connections between men and women. I think that feeling belongs so much in the world of the feminine, and because the feminine has been pushed underground for so long, the risk then of being in true relationship is that there is going to be feeling there. In Canada, we have moved so far in terms of straight and gay relationships and bi relationships and transgender, and all of that causes a great deal of awareness and acceptance. But on some level there is still that lack of embodied trust than there is in a same-sex relationship. You know you can only get so close, and you cannot get any closer because then too much feeling comes up that we can't control. It gets subverted or diverted into a sexual kind of representation. So, bringing that flood of feeling back into this notion of body and feeling and connection, it's the same thing! It's as if we say, "If I get too close, there's going to be a flood of feeling and—oh!—who knows what's going to happen!"

Lorís. How does the feminine manifest in the voice?

The voice is an experience of the body. I believe that because our voice most often comes out in words, and words are like the last step of the process of the voice; they're the result of thought, of breath, and of body. So for me, the feminine aspect of the voice is—oh, that's such a big question! It's so many things! It's the sensation of the vibration in my body of my own sound. It's the pleasure of the movement of my own breath in each sound of my body. The feminine in the voice is—the word "surrender" came out earlier—it's surrendering to the movement of the breath. It's surrendering to receiving the question, and already the receiving of the question is the beginning of the voicing of my response. So there is no separation for me between the silence, the posing of a question, the expression of a thought, my response, and my expression in return. It's all part of the whole thing, which is the body.

And another thing there that I've been more curious about recently is in the sound of the voice. Because, what is the masculine nature of sound? What is the feminine? Right away I go, "Well, the feminine sound of the voice is somewhere up here" [high pitch voice], and I think there is some truth in that. I think there's a playful and light young sound in a woman's voice that somehow we don't respect. Particularly more recently, women have been expected to have these strong powerful present voices; whereas only thirty or forty years ago, a woman's voice was placed much more up here in this range. So there is a whole question for me surrounding power and presence in the voice. What's the masculine of that? What's the feminine of that? What's the body, and what's the sound? It's a book.

There's something else that's coming in that I would like to add, that I feel is important. Logos, which is associated with the masculine, is also associated with verbal expression. And Eros, more associated with the feminine, is more related to silence and secret, in the best possible sense of the word. So what I'm coming to believe is that voicing—i.e., being able to voice who we really are—requires a confidence, a trust in, and a reliance upon the feminine, the body of the voice; and also the Logos that is thought, and the masculine, the belief that my thoughts are clear enough. I'm making sense. So for me it's a real get-together of the two that result in this kind of conversation, or any conversation with substance.

Lorís. So, in relation to what you said, why do you think the feminine voice has not been heard in society?

Well, if I play around with what I just said, there is something about science and time, and the fact that there's not really ever enough time to be in the silence from which the feminine emerges. The floods of information that are constantly coming at us and our inability to process and receive all of it—that, too, is really keeping us up in our cerebral cortex, processing, thinking, understanding, remembering. There's no time in the space between these spades of information to really digest and feel, to ask, "How to I feel about this?" Not, "What do I think about it?" or, "What do I remember?" or, "What can I repeat?" But, "How do I feel about this? Do I feel anything, or is it just a bunch of stuff?" And I think we're constantly dealing with that.

Gustavo Beck

Gustavo Beck is a psychologist and graduate of the Pacifica Graduate Institute in Santa Barbara, California. He also received training in depth/archetypal psychology at the Institute for Depth Psychology in Mexico, where he currently teaches and serves as a clinical supervisor. His studies focus on archetypal theory and its impact on contemporary social, cultural, and political issues. In addition to a private practice in Mexico City, Beck is also a professor at Universidad Iberoamericana in Mexico City as well as a translator for psychology and humanities publications.

My mother was the first to tell me about Dr. Gustavo Beck. I'm not sure I had met a male Jungian analyst in person before. All this talk about the feminine that I had been exploring came from women, so I was extremely curious to see what a man had to say. In retrospect, my interview with Dr. Beck feels like a newly-opened bottle of wine; it seems like the more time passes, the better it tastes. His insistence on grounding the feminine and staying away from theoretical analysis has never been so relevant as now, three years later, when I have exhausted all hypothetical thinking and am desperate to bring all the words down to reality.

Rose Mary. To you, what is the feminine?

I feel extremely uncomfortable with the term feminine, as with the term masculine, precisely because it's a term. It can very easily become void, meaningless, or ideological. I can think about things that feel feminine or that feel masculine, yet I find it very hard to define it out of context, outside of a specific situation. Otherwise, we fall into categorizations, which would feel very unfeminine.

Rose Mary. If we wanted to put that in context, how do you think we came to relate femininity with women and masculinity with men?

That's a good question. On the one hand, I think it was very organic. Things that seemed to pertain to women became feminine, and those that pertained to men became masculine. However, throughout history and across geographies, those things that pertain to women or to men are not necessarily the same. There is a Jungian scholar named David Tacey[9] who emphasizes the importance on differentiating the "feminine" from the "female," and the "masculine" from the "male." That distinction is extremely important because otherwise the categories become rigid either way you approach them—"Because I'm a man, then I can't be feminine," or "because I'm a man I have to connect with the feminine." It becomes very stale, and

---

[9] Australian interdisciplinary scholar and author best known for his books *The Spirituality Revolution: The Emergence of Contemporary Spirituality* and *Edge of the Sacred: Jung, Psyche, Earth.*

everything becomes gendered: everything is either male or female. Thus our relationship to whatever the feminine is becomes very artificial, forced. Men have to cry because that is feminine. Who says that? It's a total construct!

At the end of the day all these terms are constructs that have historical context, which have social origins, which have theoretical backgrounds. There's nothing wrong with that. What is dangerous is forgetting that they're constructs and that they move. I think that's the key also, to understand that there is no such thing as "the feminine" or "the masculine." Femininity moves. Masculinity moves. There are types of femininity, types of masculinity; there are levels, depths. Narrowing maleness to masculinity and femaleness to femininity pins everything down narrowly so that everybody loses— men, women, the feminine; because everything has to fit somewhere. The terms lose their natural dynamism and become this or that: "This is the feminine," or, "This is the masculine," or, "Men are masculine," or, "Men have to be feminine." So, I don't think there is such a thing as "the feminine," per se.

Rose Mary. Do you think the feminine attributes in the psyche are fractured in our society?

I think that's a dangerous assessment. Again, it's much more useful to say that women are being oppressed, as opposed to saying that the feminine is. Why? For example, saying that women earn statistically 30 percent less salary than men is a problem you can deal with very quickly. Saying that the feminine is at jeopardy becomes extremely abstract. Paradoxically, this abstraction of the feminine is very masculine. It becomes an instrument of dominance in which, in defending the feminine, I actually don't honor the feminine.

For me the feminine is always there. Certainly, social structures are built from stances that are more masculine-oriented, but to me, the problem lies more in the definition, and the need to defend. If you want to defend something, defend people; defend women; defend men.

The abstractions become unnatural, ideological. That's why I have become very suspicious of it, because defending the men's movement or a feminist movement can very easily become ideological. It's very clear when a feminist is in contact with the true spirit of the movement; she, or he, doesn't care that much about the feminine. She cares about women; she cares about specifics; she cares about justice. It's very practical. It's very felt, in a sense. For me, I should not say that women and men should be equal because the feminine principle deserves a space, no. I should say that women and men deserve the same space because it's obvious! Why should I explain it? It should be self-evident for men and women.

Rose Mary. One of the things that moved us to undertake this documentary was Lorís's reflection that women are not fully liberated or fully themselves within the psyche, because what is considered the feminine is not fully accepted in society. The other day, Christina Aguilera gave a concert and she made a mistake in one of the notes. Patriarchal society, always in search of a perfect world, criticized her. What struck me is that instead of apologizing and saying it wouldn't happen again, she said, "I don't know why this happened. I'm going to give you free concerts, from this day to this day." Being human, making mistakes, all these things that could be feminine, are banned from society. How can a person, or a woman, liberate herself if from the inside she has so many constraints?

That's where my discomfort is. What bothers me is the obsession with perfection, and the guilt with not being perfect, this apologetic attitude that looks to compensate for not fitting into other's expectations. If we define the feminine, even with good intentions, women end up feeling guilty either for being too womanly or feminine, or for not being womanly or feminine enough. If they're not mothers, they're failures. If they are mothers; they're failures. We're living for categories and it becomes extremely unnatural. It's not that mothering is feminine. Mothering is an aspect of being feminine. Why not just approach it from the actual person? This woman wants to be a mother. This is her way of expressing her femininity.

Wonderful! This woman wants to be a dancer. That's her way of expressing. This woman wants to be a CEO. Why is that unwomanly? The problem is that we live a lot through categories.

Just yesterday I was teaching a class, and the topic of inter-sexuality came up. A younger man than me, probably twenty years old, said, "Maybe having the categories of just man and woman isn't enough. Who says that people are divided into men and women? What does that mean?" This is a psychology student, not someone with a clinical practice. He just intuitively says, "You know, maybe these categories are a little narrow." The establishment of categories situates people, both men and women, in this very apologetic situation in which they always have to be "in touch with the feminine." You don't have to be! If you enjoy doing it, do it! You don't have to be anything. It's a question of incorporating these concepts—the feminine, the masculine, perfection, imperfection, the mistake, etc.—in a more natural, organic, spontaneous mode in which, if I mess up, I mess up. If I cry, I cry. If I get angry, I get angry. It's just human!

Lorís. Language has a stronger impact on us than what we might imagine. Maybe we need to pay more attention to the labels we put on things.

Language is as necessary as it is dangerous. Yes, we need language; we need categories; we need to speak about male, female, feminine, masculine, etc.; but we always need to take it with a grain of salt, because it really doesn't mean anything by itself! What does it mean to be a man? Who knows? What does it mean to be a woman? That's where it's very important to be aware that maleness, masculinity, femininity are all a work in progress. More importantly, it's a work in progress that is built through relating. There's no such thing as an abstract femininity. Femininity moves through time, it moves through relationships. When I think of femininity, I might remember books. I could pull out three or four books and think, "Oh yeah, femininity— this is femininity." But for me, it's much more real, and it gives me a much more solid referent of what is feminine to remember a girlfriend, or my mother, or my sister, or my brother, or whomever. I can remember experiences that felt feminine, which may or may not accommodate to theory.

What is important is to situate femininity or masculinity in context and in situations of felt experience. Take the transgender issue, for example. In certain countries—I believe Argentina is one; I know Australia is one—they have a third gender. They're creating new possibilities of identity. That's the point. This all has to do with identity, with who we think we are. It's problematic to think of identity as something static. It becomes a burden! What does it mean to say, "You should become yourself"? What does it mean to be yourself? No one knows the answer to that. Whoever tells you they know is either lying or living in a fairy tale because being oneself is an action. It's a movement.

There is another Venezuelan, a Jungian analyst named Lopez-Pedraza[10]. He said that English-speaking people are screwed because of their use of the verb "to be." In Spanish, the verb "to be" has two forms: "ser" and "estar." "Ser" means "being" as an essence; it is ontological. "Estar" means "being" like being here, in this space. I think that part of the problem with talking about the feminine and the masculine is that we have dealt too much with "being" in the ontological sense—what is it to be feminine—and not enough with what it feels like to be feminine, what it feels like to feel masculine. How is the masculine presence different from a feminine presence? It's not abstract; it's "ser" and "estar." It's not "¿qué es lo femenino?"—what is the feminine essentially, ontologically? It's "¿cómo es estar en lo femenino?"—what is it like to be in the state of the feminine? The difference is that one has body and one does not. If I were to be technical, "estar" is more feminine than "ser." It's as though the verb "to be" in English only had the masculine connotation and not the feminine one; if I were technical, that is.

---

[10] Rafael López Pedraza was a Jungian analyst from Venezuela best known for his books *Anslem Kiefer: The Psychology of "After the Catastrophe"* and *Dionysus in Exile.*

That's the point for me. Who cares what the feminine is? Let's ask people, how they feel the feminine in their body. I'm trying to say we should not bring this down to concept, but down to earth—to "here," me relating to you. How does it feel different with a man than with a woman? Or how does it feel different to speak with this man, rather than to speak with that one? I think that's where you can find hints of what the feminine is—only hints, and then it goes away. Then you have another come and have another hint, and then that recedes. It's always a relationship and there is always an action. This tendency to abstract is again, very masculine.

Rose Mary. Yes. In a way the tendency to abstraction is very pervasive in society. It's what makes us do things. It's framing us in a situation in which we are victims of labels and categories. How do you think these labels and categories are affecting relationships between men and women?

I think it distances you from relationship. It would be naïve to think we can't live outside of language, but you have to be wary of living through labels. At the least, you need to be aware of the fact that, when we are saying something about which we have this very strong conviction, we are speaking through language, and therefore through categories, and therefore through labels, and therefore through constructs, and therefore through things that don't exist. What really grounds words is people, relationships, my girlfriend. I can give you a two-hour lecture on femininity, but you'll only really know how I experience femininity when you see me relating to my partner or interacting with the woman in the shop. That's when you're really going to see how I experience femininity, even though it doesn't tell you as much as a two-hour lecture where I quote twenty authors. This tendency to begin with a concept is very troublesome for me.

Rose Mary. I agree with what you're saying, but how do you get rid of those concepts that are imposed on you? Can you give us examples?

For me, it begins with humility. It's a question of being okay with not knowing, of being able to have conviction of desire without having certainty. How do you do that? The tendency to conceptualize is much more natural. This kind of acceptable uncertainty takes more energy; it's much more difficult. If you just follow what you have in front of you, I think that is the antidote. Have the issue of the feminine present, but anchor it in your relationship to your daughter, or to your mother, or to your brother, or to your dog! Anchor it with actual presence; that's the real. Instead of having these deep discussions, just relate. Have a picnic. Focus on the picnic.

The answer is not so much to do something differently, but to stop doing a lot of what we do. There is a time to be conceptual, to give lectures. I love it. I'm a teacher—I write. But this topic in particular must be anchored in reality because it's useless to be an expert on femininity and masculinity, and on men and women, if you can't handle a conversation with an equal, if you can't handle the actual execution, the experience. That's when you put yourself out there. Whatever femininity and masculinity are, they come out and their relationship is put in play in those interactions. If your starting point is experience and not concept, then you are open to surprises, "Oh, I didn't know this!" And you will know. You won't be sure, but you'll know. Anyone who has had a girlfriend or brother or friend knows that. That is what the real is.

Rose Mary. But another paradox comes in here because people know, and yet they still behave differently.

They're trying to fit these expectations and this image of what it means to be a man, a woman, a person. Jung made it very clear when he spoke about individuation, and about being authentic, becoming more you. Why did he make it clear? Because he was speaking about himself. He wasn't talking about a concept. He conceptualized it, but he was starting from his own experience, from his own demons, his own pain and relationships. As humans in the twenty-first century Western world, we have a natural tendency to conceptualize. That's just how it is. I think it's more a matter of unlearning than learning. Don't try too hard, it's not that difficult! My six-year-old niece can do it. She's very clear on what it means to be a woman. Why? Because she's not bothering with what it means to be a woman; she just is!

Rose Mary. Right, but when she gets older—

Yet that is part of living. Part of living is distancing yourself from yourself, then to return to yourself. That's a process that happens naturally. That's part of the experience of any man and any woman, starting to relate to the masculine and the feminine by unlearning everything he or she learned of what it is to be a man or a woman. I think in my case, as I unlearn what it means to be a man, I become more of a man. Why? Because I become my version of a man. What that means, I don't know. If I contextualize it, maybe I'm a woman for all I know. This is my version of a man. I certainly relate to the outer, to the conceptual, to the social, to the historical; and there is a tension between who I am as a man and how I build myself or understand myself as a man, or as a feminine being. I will always be in the process of becoming a man, or a woman, or becoming more feminine or more masculine. That is living.

Lorís. Is there anything else that you think is important to add to the conversation?

I'd point to a couple of things. On the one hand, I have spoken right now on an immediate level, but I do think it's important to consider that there are very concrete and dramatic social and political implications to this. The important thing for me is to attack those political and social issues in their concreteness, or to be more precise, in their specificity. The problems faced by women in the US—or even on the East Coast versus the Mid-West, South America, as opposed to Nairobi—are entirely different. Before being women or men, we are people. So, let's approach this person first as a person. Then, before entering the categories, let's just describe what they are experiencing. This person is experiencing oppression. This person is experiencing the hyper-conceptualizations. This person is experiencing the guilt of making mistakes, the pressure of having this or that body. What

I'm trying to say is that we are all subject to these situations, but each of us is subject to them in a very specific way. That would be for me a feminine approach, treating each phenomenon in its specificity. Instead of treating this woman as a victim of patriarchy, treat her as a woman in pain. What is this pain? Is it that she is oppressed by her husband? Let's deal with that. Implicitly, you will deal with the feminine or the masculine. If there's something to be done about the feminine, it will be done through that specific context.

Start with specifics. Start with women, with men, with everyone. Don't aim at a huge agenda; just know that if you work with women, you will be working with the zeitgeist of your time. You will implicitly be affecting our constructs of masculine and feminine, but through people, by relating and in action.

If you approach an injustice through the concept, it becomes an obligation, a heavy sense of duty. You say to yourself, "I have to be tolerant." The effect is to become detached from the phenomenon. You say, "We should not discriminate against Mexicans or black people." What do you mean you "should not"? Why isn't it just a matter of fact? Why doesn't it just outrage you to see anyone beat another, regardless of whether he is Mexican, or African-American? In the concept, you lose the person, and tolerance becomes a concept and not a matter of fact. It's wonderful to be tolerant, why? Because it just is! It's very animalistic and instinctual.

That's where I'll close; it's a matter of instinct. People are not instinctually discriminatory. I think that if we truly connect with this "estar," with this aspect of being that is more embodied, more animal, more instinctual, then, organically, it will lead to a different world—not a harmonic, peaceful, pinkish, Disneyland-ish world; but to one in which everything is always moving all the time and everything has its place.

I've been recalling this image all through the interview. Last night I had a patient here, and a mouse just ran through the office. It was a wonderful instance of the presence of the animal. Instead of thinking, "Oh, it's an office; it shouldn't have a mouse," it should just be about letting things be. Whatever pops out! I think that's why the image of the mouse popped up. We didn't interpret it or make anything of it. It was just a moment when the person and I connected. "What does a mouse mean? What does it symbolize?" Who cares! What's important is that we were both startled, and it was an experience of relating. Constructions, and conceptualizations, and interpretations, they have to come afterward. There are about ten steps before doing that, ten steps before building an agenda. The reference should always be the experience. How does it feel in the body? How does it feel here, in your chest? What is the idea or feeling that naturally pops out? Respect for this level of experience can help us penetrate the masculine and the feminine naturally, without being so deliberate. Specificity and instinct. Immediateness.

Ginette Paris

Dr. Ginette Paris is the author of many books, including *Heartbreak: Recovery from Lost Love and Mourning* and *Wisdom of the Psyche: Depth Psychology after Neuroscience.* Previously Professor of Communication at the University of Quebec in Montreal, Paris became a permanent resident of the US in 1985 and is now a psychologist, therapist, and core faculty member at the Pacifica Graduate Institute in California. Her research interests include mythology and somatics.

As I was booking my flight to the Pacifica Graduate Institute, I asked my father if he wanted to come along. Since my mother and brother were already part of the crew, we could make a family trip out of it. I remember my dad sitting in Dr. Paris's seat so I could prepare the equipment and use him as my subject before she was ready to get in front of the camera. My father had always been the symbol of responsibility for me, and the image of him in that chair would later resonate with Dr. Paris's emphasis on the important role of responsibility that a person takes on when speaking of the inner world.

Rose Mary: What is the feminine?

It's a quality. Femininity is a quality. In our field, we call it an archetype. This university for example, Pacifica Graduate Institute, if you look at the grounds, the gardens, it's a very feminine place. There's always food and beauty around. People take extremely good care of each other. That's the ancient idea of *yin* and *yang*. The feminine doesn't belong to women; it's an archetypal quality.

Rose Mary: Archetypes are often confused with gender, more so in sexist cultures. How does that affect society and culture?

I think this young generation is in a period in which they're degenderizing everything. The idea that masculine and feminine qualities don't belong to one gender or the other, but are human qualities; this is very important. It's important to recognize that when you look at a person you don't know what's in there. It might be femininity and it might be masculinity. For example, if a young father has to take care of a newborn, he does it with the archetypal qualities that used to be associated with motherhood. Does it harm his masculinity? Absolutely not. It was a huge mistake of French psychiatry and Freudian psychiatry to maintain that mothers had motherly qualities and fathers had fatherly qualities. That's why the concept of the archetype is interesting, because maybe in the family you were brought up in your dad was the compassionate one. The basic quality that defines femininity is supposed to be compassion, but in some families it's the dad who has all these feminine qualities and the mother who is ambitious and represents culture. Psychiatrists like Jacques Lacan used to say the world of the father is the world of the word and of culture, because culturally, fathers didn't touch their babies. Instead, they talked with them when they were capable of logical thinking. The truth is, today, we know that the baby will be attached to whomever takes care of it physically. Babies are little animals. They attach to smells and sounds. Whoever takes care of the young infant will have, what used to be called, motherly attachment and infant attachment. It was thought to be something that happens between mother and child. Not so. It happens between the child and the caretaker. Whoever this person happens to be.

It's something I very much like about young generations today. They don't care so much about gender. You develop whatever qualities you have. Often these days, very ambitious young women will develop the yang—the capacity to fight, to show her expertise, to win, to get out there in the world and accomplish something. They're very heroic. Sometimes young guys don't want to fall too soon into the clichéd stereotype of the ambitious male, so they float for a bit; they can be artistically inclined and intuitive.

It's the project of a whole generation. It started, of course, with feminism many, many years ago, many generations ago, and it's now being realized. I think it's one of the gifts of the younger generation, to be able to see if a person is mathematically gifted and tends toward a rational, scientific mind, regardless if they are a boy or a girl. It's the mind, not the biological sex. The same thing is true of intuition and the capacity for compassion. A Buddhist monk has a huge capacity for compassion. Is he less virile? No.

Rose Mary. In your book, Wisdom of the Psyche, *you suggest that the more sexist the society becomes, the more the mother has a power complex. Would you say this is one of the reasons we all grow up with diminished feminine qualities?*

I think so. Depending on how much sexism there was in our culture, we grow up with a sense of inferiority that diminishes the value of femininity. Let me give you an example. I once had a patient who was raised in a Muslim culture, and he told me how his father began teaching him how to order women around when he was six or seven years old. Here is this little boy, seven years old, telling his mother, "Do this! Do that! Get me a glass of water! Clean my shoes! Cook me this! I want that!" This was something that was supposedly necessary for him to learn in order to become a man.

Thus, here we have a child giving orders to his mother, his grandmother, his aunt. As he grew up, he realized that he was seeing through this sexist kind of division. The tragedy is that he took after his mother very much. He had her mind. Therefore, he felt he had received only half of his inheritance. He could not be like his mother because women are, in his culture, inferior and should obey the man. The first thing little boys learn is to thank God every day not to have been born a woman. You see, this is extreme genderization. That means he never learned to receive this maternal inheritance of a very good mind. The other problem is that a child is given power over an adult, and as a result, never gets over the Oedipus complex. He never learns how to deal with frustration because he has a slave at his service.

My patient said that once he lived in this country, in the US, his relationships with women were horrible because he had never learned to understand that the other has needs, too. It's like being given a slave in a way. The major transition between childhood and adulthood is that you learn that your needs are not to be met instantly. You learn to cope with frustration. Yet, how can you learn to relate to another who is not an object, if you have always had an object?

Rose Mary. Speaking about diminished femininity, how does this affect romantic relationships?

Romantic relationships are always filled with projections. No relationship starts off with the reality. It only begins when you retract your projection. The theory that Jung had about falling in love is that you always fall in love with the person who has the very quality that your own soul would need to develop. That means if you are this, you will be attracted to its opposite, or to somebody who has the quality that you have but do not know exactly how to use. Of course, you idealize this. At the beginning of a relationship, there is this huge, "My boyfriend is my hero. He knows so much. He's so great." You idealize that relationship. The same is true when a man falls in love with a woman. She becomes the goddess, not a human being. She is *the* woman, femininity incarnate. Then comes the disappointment. The other is not divine; it's love that is divine, not the other. The disappointment is what usually destroys relationships. "How dare you not be the god or goddess I thought you were! You disappoint me!" Since we carry a great wounding from our childhood—every child is wounded in one way or another—we expect the other one to repair all that and to be capable of giving, giving, giving. We don't tolerate the disappointment when the illusion is lost. However, in normal relationships that are based on both partners having a capacity to love, each slowly discovers their own projections onto the other and tries to develop these qualities in themselves. Then, they become more accepting of their partner's limitations.

Rose Mary. According to some spiritual leaders, including you, there is a child living in our psyche. The theory suggests that what differentiates the child psyche from the adult psyche is the fact that we all need compassion, but the latter is ready to take responsibility. Is responsibility part of why the feminine is so diminished? If so, why?

It is true; we all have a primitive child in us. Neuroscience has discovered that all of the fears and hurt of childhood are still in our brain. It is as if we remember that we are these fragile, vulnerable, incompetent little beings who need to be protected, need attention, need to be taken care of, because we don't have the ability to do it ourselves. We all have an inner, vulnerable little being, even when we are old and getting sick and getting vulnerable again. It's literally there, in the limbic level of the brain.

The big mistake that psychology made with the inner child fad, was to tell everybody, "Oh! You have this vulnerable little child in you. Identify with it and ask the child what it wants." The problem is, identifying with the inner child makes you a victim, because the child is incompetent, incapable, and needy. That whole period of psychology almost insisted on that vulnerability, that brokenness. Today we realize this was the wrong approach to take. The solution is not to deny the inner child nor to identify with it, but to educate the inner child. Show him and reassure him that there is an adult in the psyche that will take care of those needs. If you identify with the inner child, you ask everybody around—and most of all, your partner—to take care of that inner child. It breaks every relationship. "Why should I take care of you rather than you take care of me, or us taking care of each other?"

There is a whole period of psychology that has convinced people that they have all these needs that come from the inner child but were never taught how to take care of it. Instead of identifying with the inner child, we need to separate from the inner child. Here is his voice: "I'm here! I'm here! I'm vulnerable and I want you to pay attention to me!" We must tell this voice, "Take care of it yourself!" Don't ask the rest of the world to take care of that inner child. Grow up. Adopt the child and separate from it. Psychology's made a big mistake in victimizing a whole generation of believers in this theory.

Rose Mary. Would you say that mothers perpetuating patriarchy hurt the inner child?

The problem with women in patriarchal societies is that they feel they have to be in service to the child. If you look especially at American motherhood—I don't know how it is in other cultures—but in American culture, the task of a mother is of a servile character, subject to the needs of the child. This relationship is true, but only for very short periods. Soon enough, the role of the mother should be to teach the child to take care of his or her own needs. But the cultural messages here say, "You have to be the maid who keeps the house and the bedroom of the child, who cleans and cooks and acts as the chauffer." The role of the mother is that of a servant to the needs of the child.

Let me give you an example. The other day I was watching a woman in a restaurant with her child. He had a pacifier, and he was throwing it on the floor and the mother was picking it up. He threw it again and again, and the mother kept picking it up. The child was having fun. It was a game! Why did this woman not see what she was teaching the child? Her lesson said, "You can turn me into a slave anytime you want. You just throw it, and I'll pick it up." The same is true of children crying and saying "Mommy, mommy, mommy, as if mommy were a household appliance that did your tasks at the push of a button. It's very detrimental and it's because women think so little of themselves that they turn themselves into servants. It's not like that in other cultures. It certainly wasn't like that among eighteenth and nineteenth century nobility and peasantry. The mother had a lot to do. If she was poor, she was working in the fields. If she was noble, she had other tasks to do. We have turned the mother into a servant, and it is dangerous. It comes from the patriarchal attitude that says, "You take care of the kids."

Rose Mary. That may also be the reason why kids are raised with a diminished femininity, because the mother is not a role model.

Right, this is not a role model. Who wants to be a servant? Who wants to be a slave? How would you identify with your mother? How would you want to identify with your mother, especially if you are a young man? I read a biography of generals once, European and American army generals, and the point of the book was that all these men had had very strong mothers. Lady Churchill was a very noble woman. Do you think that she ever thought of her role as a servant? Never. My son, who is forty, doesn't feel it is a problem to say, "This talent I take from my mother, and this from my dad." Again, it's something I believe the younger generation is capable of understanding because many mothers today don't want to define themselves as servants, or as secondary, less than men. They have changed the culture enough that today a young man can say, "Well, my mother was a concert pianist," and this is what he wants to do, too. "My mother was a surgeon." "My mother was a scientist." I know a young man who wants to become a mathematician following the model of his mother. Really, if you define yourself as a servant, it perpetuates the harm done by patriarchy.

Lorís. You say that if you do not have that role model, you have no steps to follow. Do you think that, in a romantic relationship, you start seeking what is familiar to you? Do you seek the slave mother?

In romantic relationships, there are aspects that attract us for their sameness and there are aspects that attract us for their difference. Usually we are attracted to something in us that is unconscious, an ability that needs development. The other seems to have it, so you want that for your soul. You project it, saying, "You have it, and I do not." A good definition of projection is the example of the person who says, "Take off your sweater; I'm hot." Projections are not all negative, but if you've had a mother who felt inferior, who let herself be dominated, whose femininity was cheapened because of a cultural definition of womanhood based on the servants' role and intellectual inferiority; then you become attracted to somebody who, on a deep, deep level, you think and you feel is inferior. How can you relate in an egalitarian way and create a strong couple? The man who feels that the partner thinks, "I am inferior; I am the servant and he is the king," will not stay in that relationship. And she will try every trick in the book to manipulate and get her way, or become dependent, like saying, "Okay, I'm inferior, so you take care of everything!" There are all these unconscious dynamics when a culture is sexist. It doesn't teach people how to relate in a way that is sustainable. This is unsustainable. It is ecologically impossible when you don't develop your own self to always be clung on the other.

I love your questions; you keep asking questions about romantic relationships!

Lorís. That was a good answer! When we were writing these questions, there was something in me that wanted to bring this subject up and I couldn't seem to find the way to do so. After hearing you speak, it suddenly came to me.

Let me give you an example. Today, I'm sorry to see that very young girls have role models teaching them how to dress and what kind of makeup to wear. I am not against little girls, they are so cute and so beautiful, and it's fine to dress whatever original way. Yet it feels as if the culture is saying, "This is what it means to be a woman!" It's very reductive. What if you have a different talent in you, and it's not about makeup and hair? This is very dangerous because it's way too limited! Young boys today learn that a woman should be absolutely cute, thin, tall, whatever the culture dictates. If you're not; well, you're not in the game. This is very limiting.

Think of FDR when he met Eleanor. Here is the woman whose mother thought that she was ugly and used to tell her, "You look like a horse." Eleanor Roosevelt's mother was a very beautiful, feminine-looking, gracious woman; she had wonderful manners. She believed her daughter had to be just like her to succeed. This was a big wounding. Turns out she came to be one of the most loved persons in the history of America. However, she was still hurt by her mother's cruel words. When she was an old woman she said, "I wish I had been prettier." On the other hand, because she lived within a society and with a man who appreciated her for her intellectual qualities, she became a wonderful, loving and loved person. You see her milieu was rich enough to say, "Forget about this face, and become who you are."

If a culture limits the definition of either masculinity or femininity, it has an impact on romantic relationships and destroys them. You see plenty of actresses who fall into that cliché and seem to teach girls the wrong lesson.

Lorís. Not too long ago I had a dream about Beyoncé and Brad Pitt. I went to my therapist and told him about the dream. He analyzed it a little, and then he said to me, "It's curious how, before, femininity was represented by goddesses. Now, those goddesses have been replaced by…"

Actual people. Let's talk about that. If I understand well, your question has to do with goddesses being replaced by stars. The problem is, this represents a significant degradation. For example, the goddess of beauty used to be Aphrodite. Well, Aphrodite was not the most beautiful goddess. She was the goddess of beauty. This is a big, big difference. She was the goddess who allowed you to see beauty. In fact, for the Greeks, she represented the deep, deep mystery by which we begin to see the beauty in the other when we fall in love. This is quite mysterious. Why is it that I am attracted to this man? He's bald and fat, but the way he smiles just melts me. If you were to meet him, you would not find him attractive. I do. That's the mystery. When you fall in love, and especially when you make love, you look at the other and you see the beauty of the goddess. That was their point. You are not the goddess; you are her servant. Therefore, if you make love with respect, you serve the goddess because she is the goddess of beauty. Love is beautiful. Desire is beautiful. Through the act of lovemaking, you connect with this deep mystery by which loving somebody means you find someone beautiful, even physically. You begin to see little mannerisms and you get attached. That was the deep mystery of Aphrodite: the capacity to see beauty and to give beauty. That's why you make a bouquet. You serve the goddess by bringing beauty into the house. You serve the goddess.

The degradation can be seen when a person looks at the reflection in the mirror and finds that they are beautiful, instead of serving the principle of beauty for everyone around them. Aphrodite was the smile personified. If you look at models today, they all look enraged. They all look as if they want to spit on you! They have this face of anger that says, "Don't dare touch me! I'm expensive." They have no curves. They're basically the results of an ideal of woman seen as a boy of twelve. That's what the fashion designers desire. They don't want models with breasts and hips. So, there is a loss. We have lost our goddess of beauty. It's why we replace her with those figures that are completely degraded if you compare them with what used to be the real goddess of beauty. It's the same for all the other goddesses, part of our cultural loss.

Rose Mary. These role models also reflect nature. Do you think our problems with the environment are a reflection of not having cultivated the feminine?

I think patriarchy is just like a religion. It will take more than one generation to change it. We have been indoctrinated into thinking in patriarchal ways. That being said, it's not patriarchy in and of itself that is the problem, because there was a time when patriarchy was not corrupt. Patriarchy used to mean that the *pater familias* was responsible for the whole family. Women could not work because they were always pregnant, so men had to care for them and bring home the bacon, as we say. Patriarchy was a kind of structural society that made sense in a time were women were made physically much more vulnerable because they were always carrying babies. It made sense that the woman would take care of the house and babies, and the man would bring home the bacon. That was a deal.

The distortion of the deal worked the same as it does with the mafia. It starts with some *mafioso* coming to you and saying, "You pay me, and I'll protect you from all these little dogs and delinquents who'll break your window and steal the stuff from your store." That's a good deal: one hundred dollars a month for protection. It's hiring protection, just like the woman that needs a husband to protect her because she has a million kids. The twist that is the evil of patriarchy is the same as the twist with the protection racket. First you ask for one hundred dollars for protection against the enemy; then, you ask for more money to be protected against your own violence. "If you don't give me two hundred now, I'll beat you." That's the racket. And it's the first corruption of patriarchy. Now you need to do what I say or else I will beat you.

The second phase, which is even worse, is a historical dissociation of the idea of the patriarch and his responsibility. Therefore, the reason feminists became truly angry at patriarchy was because there had been a dissociation. "I want all the power, all the money, but none of the responsibility." Fathers abandon their kids, because they don't want to pay for them. Instead, they leave it to their mother who has a much lower salary because of the sexism in the culture; and who now has to take care of all those kids with nobody helping because the dad is just a grown up baby who wants to spend his money on a Maserati. "You do your thing," he says, "I'm out of here." You see the dissociation. Men wanted to keep the power and the advantage and the promotions and the big salaries, and—though some are very respectable patriarchs—many wanted the power but not the responsibility.

This is true of our politicians, who come from the Father arche-type. The politicians are supposed to be the fathers of the country, yet they want the goodies but not the responsibility. It's always somebody else's fault. They belong to the same archetype of the father—father of the family, father of the country—but it is dissociated from responsibility. That is what the feminists are still so angry about. It's the corruption of the system. You can't judge patriarchy as evil; it's the corruption that is so dangerous.

Lorís. If our goal were to embrace femininity, for males as well as females, what would be the best path to accomplish that, either as a society or as an individual?

Firstly, I would stop calling it "femininity" and "masculinity," because it genderizes the concepts and we need to move toward a degenderized society. Let's say you are a scientist. Well, you're somebody with an extremely rational capacity and that's why you're at the lab all day. You develop your rational mind; you control your emotions; you do your science, which is a very rational process, the best you can. You develop that to the maximum, and then you come home to a little baby, a newborn. Your wife is exhausted and you take the baby with all the compassion in the world and you become competent in that task. A newborn doesn't need a daddy who tells you what the laws of the outside world are and how it works. You need that when you grow up, when you need to learn how to manage the real world. Well, a dad would tell you, "You need to become competent in something. You need to follow the law, or establish the law, or break the law," if it is a revolution. This is the culture. Traditionally, the archetype of father means the outside world, and the archetype of the mother means the protection of the little vulnerable thing that is incapable of taking care of itself. If we didn't have those two polarities, humans would disappear. We are all born needy and fragile, and we all need a society that has laws and customs and traditions. This is what used to be called the domain of the mother and the domain of the father. If you degenderize it, it's clear that we all need to be capable of demonstrating one archetypal quality or the other archetypal quality as well. That, to me, would be the first step.

Everybody should receive education and become autonomous. Women should fight for their economic independence—this is crucial, absolutely crucial—and ask the rest of the world to do the same. I was very, very pleased when, in France, they decided that wearing the full burka veil would be illegal. In the US, the legal decision was framed around safety; if you can't see a person's face, it could be a burglar carrying out a crime. In addition, in court, you can't testify with the full veil. Therefore, they made it a safety issue. In France, they made it an issue of principle. I thought this was brave. A woman who does not have the right to show her face is losing the capacity to relate in the world. It is sexist; it is oppressive, and we will not have it. Of course, part of the Muslim community took it as religious oppression. However, the response was, "No. There is a value that is more important, and that is gender equality." I applaud it.

It's true; your face is the way you connect. If you weren't supposed to talk and smile and have facial expressions, what would that mean? Why is it that a culture would want that? Why do they ask for it? If you consider, you see it's because women are objects; they are property. They are the property of their husbands. They don't want to share any rights. That damages the sons as much as it damages the women, which is one thing we don't take into account when we criticize sexism. It damages the sons.

Last fall I was in Montreal where there was the tragic case of an honor killing. A father asked his son to kill the three daughters. It's called the Shafia case; the son and the father are in prison for life. In the system of honor killing, the father, the patriarch, can order the son to kill his sister. In this case he had to kill three sisters because they were educated in Canada and they wanted to wear short skirts and talk with the boys in their class. They had put a few pictures of themselves in a bathing suit on Facebook, and that was enough for the father to order the son to kill his sisters. This is called an honor killing. So you see, patriarchy is usually criticized from the point of view of the women, and we fail to see that it also destroys the son. They have to obey the patriarch as if he were the ultimate law in the family. In this example, it is not honor but dishonor that was in play; and the son, as well as the father, will spend their lives in prison.

Many are saying that equality of gender is the biggest revolution ever in the history of mankind. It has only been possible with contraception and control of our bodies, and with economic equality and freedom. Psychologically, it will take time. It's similar to what you see when you do therapy, you see how sexism—and exactly the same is true of racism—is a great myth. "If you are that color, you are inferior. If you are that gender, you are inferior." They are myths that need to be deconstructed and revealed as lies. A myth always portrays both a lie and a fundamental truth. Nevertheless, we always have to see that part of the myth is destructive, so we are going to have a new myth. "Black is beautiful" is the new myth. "Strong is female" is the new myth. Yet it is always a task that is never finished. However, in my lifetime I have seen so much. Although I feel sometimes that young women think it's all finished and all done and don't see the necessity of becoming conscious of how it was. Young women seem to think, "Oh, you've done the work! Thanks!" Sometimes it's quite difficult, because their own femininity may not be as developed as they want.

Brian Riedel

Dr. Brian Riedel is a social scientist and professor of the practice in humanities at Rice University. His work uses ethnographic and qualitative research to explore issues related to LGBT equality. His professional experience includes education and academic, government, and non-profit management.

I believe Dr. Riedel was one of the first witnesses of the birthing of *Ensoulment*'s ideas. In fact, I would say he was part of the reason of why they initiated in the first place. I remember meeting Dr. Riedel in a seminar and practicum program in Rice University's Center for the Study of Women, Gender, and Sexuality. It was one of those classes that nudges something inside of you, and something tiny changes position. A bit of time passes, and suddenly you're overwhelmed by the massive butterfly effect it has created. I think part of "it" was the idea of putting into practice what you believe in. I could never sit still in his class, there was too much energy waking up. I don't think that energy has gone back to sleep since then.

Rose Mary: In your opinion, how did we come to connect femininity with women and masculinity with men? Is it purely a social construct or are there biological roots that bring us to this understanding? Do you think people should pay attention to this?

I think we should pay attention to these connections regardless of whether we should make them or not, because they are categories through which we like to make the world meaningful. The idea of gender mapping neatly onto two different types of bodies, such that the feminine applies to bodies that look like this, and the masculine applies to bodies that look like that, is a clean, easy starting place. However, as we move through the world and get to see more of what the world is, we realize there is a lot of fluidity, not just between the two categories of feminine and masculine, but also among the types of bodies that exist.

Then there are the things that we do to stylize that body, whether it's the clothes, the mannerisms, the voice, the social arrangements, or how we comport ourselves at a party. Do we walk up assertively to somebody and introduce ourselves, or do we wait for someone else to introduce us? This, too, is a gendered activity in a way that has nothing to do with the body, per se, nothing to do with the genes, yet we are constantly explaining one register of these stylizations by reference to another. So, someone might be seen as more authentic to their gender if there is an imagined concordance between the body, the genes, the behavior, and the expression.

It's not stable across cultures and time, and that's the most interesting thing about it. We want somehow to be able to ground all of our behavior in some fundamental essence of who we are, when in fact that might change, even in the course of our own lives. So to tie femininity to women and masculinity to men is a social exercise that has to be done over and over again, partially because it isn't actually fixed.

Rose Mary. Is it common for people to misunderstand the word "feminine"? Many times people tend to associate it only with women.

The problem is that terms actually do describe things that we do. Regardless of what terms we use, there is still this real world out there that we like to try to sort as if it easily sorted into a binary. We know that there are bodies that escape the male/female gender binary, both on the level of the genes as well as on the levels of the body and behavior. There are XXY chromosomes and expressions of our chromosomes by which a body may come out appearing to be female but over time develop to be more male in its physiology. We could have any number of people whose behavioral landscape goes away from what we would expect to be this clean binary.

The terms themselves are still used because they describe things. However, it's not as if the terms themselves are real. There is a difference in description between the language that we use and that real world that we want to pin those words to. I think the presumption is that it's easy to talk in terms of a binary but better to think of a Venn diagram with two sets that overlap. There is set A and set B, and the intersection. However, a lot of people stop there and forget that there is stuff that is excluded from that whole binary, outside of those two groups. One of our challenges might be to re-conceptualize gender outside of that two-symbol binary. Maybe that's a better exercise than to change all the terms completely, because there is still something real to be described.

Rose Mary. And that's why we keep using them.

Absolutely. Our world is patterned in ways that make it very tempting for us to presume to describe the whole, because *most* things seem to fit into this box or that. We might like to assume simply that there are only two boxes, and that is rarely the case.

Rose Mary. In our interview with Dr. Gustavo Beck, he proposed eliminating the terms altogether. I wondered afterwards: How would we address those things that originally had those names? As humans, we categorize our world instinctively and then we move around those categories.

I recognize the ideal in the suggestion that we eliminate the terms; but it really indicates a category mistake in confusing the name that we give things for whatever reality they represent. This is even more true when we sense that the reality of our lived experience is somehow not described by the words that society might allow us to use to refer to it. For example, if someone grows up feeling themselves authentically a woman, and their attractions are to other women, does that undermine their belonging to the category of "real women?" That's a question that many theorists pose. Judith Butler, for example, or bell hooks, might go there. There are many theorists who have been thinking about gender and sexuality in these ways. At the philosophical level, it is a category error that's at the heart of this urge to try to ditch the terms, that mistakes the terms for the thing they represent. This is like pointing at the moon and mistaking the finger that is pointing for the moon itself. Many people question that level of mistake in this context.

The question that you really want to open up deals with understanding the claim that we need to let go of the categories. The idea represents a good social goal, because we know that the named categories don't actually describe the reality that we live. The motive behind getting rid of the categories is well-intentioned, yet in practice people are probably still going to want to describe the world in ways that seem easy enough to do it. The categories that become socially available always somehow fail to describe completely the real world that we actually live in.

Rose Mary. Men and women both have a side to them that's feminine. Do you think it could be detrimental to the development of men to deny their femininity? Should people seek to develop their femininity alongside their masculinity?

If you go about your life editing out a part of who you feel yourself to be, you are not a whole person, regardless of what we call that part—the feminine, the masculine—because even though we are thinking about femininity, we are also thinking about the ways that we police ourselves willingly into certain kinds of behavior, either because of social acceptance or the sense that we will be punished in some way if we fail to do it. This would be true for men who delete the feminine from their lives, or women who cut out what might be called "the masculine" from their lives.

Think about the kinds of things that have been said about powerful women like Hillary Clinton or Oprah or Madonna, describing them not just as bold, but as overly aggressive. If they're assertive, they become words that people like Rush Limbaugh may shout out on the radio. These are the kinds of oppositions that too easily get played out when a person is encouraged by their context to shut out a part of him/herself because it's not considered to be appropriate to the type to which they belong. For example, how do we categorize a sensitive new age guy, or a metrosexual man who pays attention to his appearance in a way that has nothing to do with his sexuality?

Rose Mary. A society inevitably interferes with any human being, and its categories determine how a male and a female act. According to what you're saying, then, our public culture is oppressing who we really are.

You could frame it like that, or you could consider that, though you may not be limited in the sense that you *can* choose, the number of choices that are available to you might be limited. That's another way to frame it. For example, if our society is limited in its ideas of what gendered possibilities are out there—whether through law, education, religion, or any institutions that forms family—if there are only two, then your experience buffet includes two. But what if we were to imagine the kind of space where more options were available?

I think that's actually truer now that in the past. I think about these new kinds of identities that people have begun to embrace, particularly younger people. Or about the radical fairies of earlier decades, people who didn't doubt that they were men, but embraced this kind of larger sense of what being a man might be. We also have a broader range of masculinities now, at least among gay men. Sometimes this is embraced in a kind of hyper-masculinity, with the fur and the muscles and the tattoos. They work out in the country with their tractors and go back to the city to earn money. To say that it's all oppressive is in some ways a misnomer because people have a number of opportunities set out in front of them to be used as models. But then, what are the consequences of those choices? We don't understand how to frame our desires without it doing so in conversation with these options that are available in the world. So, how do I know that my desire to dress in high heels, for example, is not normative if I am not instructed in that?

Rose Mary. In your opinion, how has the patriarchal system affected the feminine in both men and women in our society?

Patriarchy is a difficult word to talk about in the twenty-first century, partially because things have definitely changed in our time, and will continue to change. If the basic idea of patriarchy is that men have, on the whole, a disproportionate advantage in access to resources and command of other people, then that remains true. But when people can point to Oprah, Madonna, Hillary Clinton, it changes the way people hear the claim that men still have disproportionate power with respect to women. It becomes shriller. It becomes more paranoid. There are people who might say, "Hey, there's still a power imbalance."

Two examples come to mind. One, there was a recent conversation on *Meet the Press* between Rachel Maddow and Alex Castellanos, in which Rachel Maddow had just interviewed a woman who works with the Institute for Women's Policy and Research on her own show. This woman had the hard economic data that in the U.S., women earn seventy-seven cents to every dollar that men earn. She had just come from the interview with the hard data, and David Gregory gives her the floor on *Meet the Press.* The minute that she references the statistic, Alex Castellanos interrupts her right in the middle of her talk and says, "No, you've got your facts wrong."

Brian Riedel

Not only is this a gender performance between an out lesbian anchor and a male Republican commentator, but it also reshapes Rachel's rhetorical space, lending it a shrill tone that cries, "Let me have my space to speak." Alex Castellanos, in his realm, is able to sit back and be the guy who is graciously allowing the irrational woman to have her say. That was the performative space of that interaction. There are two pieces to this interaction. One, Rachel Maddow's facts were just dismissed, making the rational level of argument unavailable. Secondly, the emotional level of the argument was also unavailable to her in a way that could be seen as comparable, despite the fact that many people would say that she was right.

The second example is the problem of "the king of the hill." If masculinity and femininity were defined by dominance and submission, which many people may think might be the dynamic between them; if the rhetoric of the masculine defines it as the hard, the winner, the giver, the provider; then anytime you have two people who *both* claim the masculine, one of them has to win over the other. If you think about it in those terms, there can only be one king of the hill, one "real man." I think that's a really impoverished vision of what human capacity to relate might be, especially if you put yourself in the position of the person who becomes king of the hill knowing that others who want that position too will assail them on all sides. What might it look like if, instead of having this setup where only the top of the hill is the masculine and everything else is feminized to some degree or other, it was instead something more fertile, like a plain, where you can actually grow things, where we are able to communicate about the facts without dismissing them?

Rose Mary. Generally speaking, in terms of Western culture, have patriarchal values in the workforce taken a toll on people's feminine side?

There are a lot of different arguments about that. Some would say that there's no room for the feminine in the ranks of higher order success. We talk about the glass ceiling and about the kinds of attributes that are required to succeed in the business world. People think about needing to be aggressive, needing to get there first, to be a winner, a dominator, in order to beat the competition. This is a masculine framework that some would say leaves no room for the feminine. In terms of the behavior of people who do succeed—who rise to the level of Hillary Clinton, Oprah, Madeleine Albright, or Margaret Thatcher—all these women achieved a high level of power and success and were constantly criticized about the degree to which they were successfully feminine. Hillary Clinton was described as being too aggressive and too dominating, when these are the attributes that are often associated with success elsewhere.

Rose Mary. How do you think this intolerance towards not only the feminine, but even the masculine, is affecting the LGBT communities?

The way that sexuality has become a subject of conversation does a disservice because it puts the focus on sexual orientation. Sexuality is about a relationship between human beings regardless of their identities of those beings. Hidden within this issue is this idea that being in a relationship with somebody involves power. When relationships between people are about mutual support and understanding, the power is assumed to be equal. That may or may not be true, whether it's a heterosexual, homosexual, multigenerational, you-name-it relationship.

In terms of what it means for the LGBT communities, the idea of gender has not in itself become politically separable from sexual orientation, and I think it is damaging to LGBT rights. For example, look at the Employment Discrimination Act. The Human Rights campaign and several national leaders like Barney Frank and Tami Baldwin have wrestled twice on the national stage with the degree to which gender identity and its expression should also be incorporated alongside sexual orientation. This bill has come up in various forms in many of the last congresses since the one hundred sixth. In each and every one, I understand, there was debate about including transgender, and in the nineties the debate's result was "No." There was a huge backlash against that. Many of the organizations around the nation got involved in the ENDA United movement to support a trans-inclusive Employment Non-Discrimination Act at the federal level. In the most recent iteration, we ran into a problem framed as political expediency yet again. The logic went, "We want to get employment nondiscrimination for all, but let's get half a loaf now because the other half is too hard."

This is problematic because, by saying that gays and lesbians are just like everybody else except with regard to sexual orientation, it pushes all gender variance off into the realm of the "transgender." Look at the ways people define others on the street in terms of their orientation. What are the cues they look for? They're gendered cues. "They move in a way that doesn't seem feminine. They move in a way that doesn't seem masculine. They dress differently. They express in a way that's not butch enough or not femme enough." Those gender cues then become the proxies by which we socially predict other people's sexual orientations. To say somehow, that LGB is different from the T, gets away from the part of the problem that deals with sexuality. Our social being is gendered. The way we see each other is gendered. So, I think you can really see the impact that gender norms have on LGBT politics. In many cases, however, the transgender community has been thrown under the bus as a sacrifice to make lesbians and gays and some bisexuals look more mainstream because they're gender-normative.

Rose Mary. It comes to mind that this country is very sexually conscious; everything is about sex. As a human being, you get categorized just by your sexual inclinations. Our point of view is so black and white. Why can't we look at the other as she/he is? It's really bad. In an interview with Dr. James Hollis, he said that we're like teenagers with this black and white mentality.

Let's expand the scale a little bit. When we say society, we have to be careful about what we actually mean. Do we mean local friendship group? Do we mean where we work? Do we mean the state of Texas? Do we mean the United States? Do we mean the world? Do we mean NAFTA? What do we mean? I think part of the problem with how we frame this is that we forget that we are a species. We are an animal. I don't want to reduce the conversation to the drive to reproduce, but the fact that we sexualize our lives is completely unavoidable. It's part of what we do. Some people will use that to claim that anything that goes against the reproduction of the species over time is therefore unnatural. Other people will look for examples of natural deviants from that idea, like the Bonobos grooming each other in same sex pairings that look homo-sexualized to us. In that case, it's a projection, similar to a projection of one culture onto another. I think we have to be careful of marching out to the world looking for examples to support our position. We already picked our position; we're just looking for the facts to bolster it. That's the real trouble.

You asked about this question of embracing the other—whether it be the feminine, the masculine, the capital "Other," my next door neighbor, or another country, another species—and actually under-standing it on its own terms. You just have to go there. It's not just about an open mind, because the open mind can still have stuff in it that prevents other things, like the real world, from making it inside. A Buddhist might frame what's needed as an empty mind, a no-mind, so that there is actually space for that real encounter between yourself and that other person. That empty mind is it not going to walk in assuming that it will win, as if it were a competition; or that it will be right, as if there were something wrong about the other person, or the other culture from the start. In our own cultural framing, it's where gender is binary, either one or the other, these are the problems we wrestle with when we try to encounter someone else on their own terms.

Rose Mary. There is another section in the documentary that has to do with the body, that I think has to do with what you were talking about in seeing the Other and seeing yourself.
Lorís: There were two answers that were really interesting. One woman said that we are always living as if there is an imaginary eye looking at us. We are always seeing ourselves from an outside eye. Another woman said that, for

example, when we see a woman in a magazine, we see the woman with a man's eyes. We have internalized that the main judge in society is a white, heterosexual male. That's how we have learned to view and judge everything else.

There is a lot of power in recognizing that there are multiple perspectives, yet there is even more power in realizing that the value accorded to those perspectives is not necessarily the same. What would it mean to understand a hierarchy of perspectives, where some one person, or some one category is seen as more accurate, more powerful, more persuasive than the others? There was a great moment in advertisement criticism in the eighties where people looked at sexualized images of women and said that advertisement itself was pornographic. They said that somehow the perspective of a dominant, white, heterosexual male was embedded in that picture.

There was an interesting response to this, which said, what if we were to take account of what individual viewers bring to the moment of understanding that image, understanding that social encounter? It may well be that they know there is that white, heterocentric way of looking at it—a masculinist viewpoint, the Eye that looks at that image in a particular way and reads it. However, you could read it differently, you could embody it differently. You could say, "Well, that's one way. What about maybe saying that there is an empowerment there? What would it look like if…?" There is an opening there to kind of undermine the power that's just assumed to accrue around a white, heterocentric, masculinist viewpoint. That audience response, that opening up of interpretive capacity takes away the threatening power of the image to some extent. It's no longer a dominating image but an image that could be accepted or put to the side. It's an interesting problem though, because it's unstable. You can't fix the interpretation of the image in that point.

Rose Mary. It has gotten into the younger generations, however, especially today with all the technology. It's a very, very visual society. Everything is about images. How do I look to others? How am I going to be perceived? Somehow that devalues you inside.

The sense that we are aware that other people see us is not necessarily a new thing. It's magnified perhaps by having so many opportunities to encounter it, so many ways of capturing that moment of being seen by somebody else—whether it's the iPhone where we snap a picture at a party, the security camera watching us at the bank, or going to a party where someone happens to be looking at you from the other side of the room. In all of these occasions, you are being watched by somebody else, and you are mindful that when you are alone, you could be available to be seen by somebody. Maybe your room is bugged or you are eventually going to walk out of the room and be seen. That's not new, but our shock at how often we have the evidence of that might be new. The residual stuff—images, film, YouTube, Facebook, texting of images back and forth—it now seems to have turned up the volume, increased the speed, created more stuff for us to look at. But it has always been part of being human, as long as we have taken a look at each other and a look at ourselves through the eyes that other people use to see us. I like that, I have comfort from knowing that it's not new. We have evolved to be able to handle it. We have tools for that.

Rose Mary. This year there have been a lot of conversations going on about women's rights, but in order to reach true equity, there needs to be an understanding from both genders. What are some expectations and pressures that you think are imposed on men? Can you give some examples?

I want to start answering that question by going back to mentioning some of the ideas that we were talking about earlier with respect to undoing this "both genders" idea. I think there could be a better understanding of how we think about the issue of control, family planning, and sex education. These three things are very closely related.

We sell Viagra on TV, Cialis. We talk about this in such an open way. It's all there. It's part of the daily texture of our lives, the way we want to be engaged in these things. When you are young and you see this is a desirable space to be in intimacy, you think, "Great, why not do it?" Children play and experiment; we know this. How then, do you reconcile the economic and social impact of the truth of experimentation and play and desire with a set of rules that would take away the tools that allow young people to understand the outcomes and life-long impact of such behavior? If you're going to say, "Oh, boys will be boys. Let them play," then they should have the tools they need and the knowledge about how to use those tools. This means condoms and sex education. I think it's a very simple concatenation.

Rose Mary. When most of the world's population is made up of women, it's surprising to think we have not fought together for equity. What are some of the factors that you think are keeping us from coming together, and what we could do to change the situation?

Part of the history of feminist thinking, regardless of where that thinking has occurred—Europe, Africa, Asia, U.S.A.—is that whenever you run into identity politics as a solution, "come together as women," the consequence is the need to figure out who counts as a woman and which women are included. Much of the problem of third wave feminism in the United States and Western Europe, involved recognizing that the women in the United States and Western Europe are not all the women in the world; there were other women with other lives, and that there were differences even among those women in Western Europe and the United States. The impact of accepting that truth has been undoing some of the political assumptions of how organizing among women might work in the first place.

Nicholas Kristof and his wife, Sheryl WuDunn, came up with that famous book about trafficking, and asked what would happen if we took it seriously. When we start talking about coming together in the interest of protecting women, who is in that coalition? It's not necessarily going to be just women. It ought not to be just women. One of the key insights that people like bell hooks came to was that men are advocates of feminism, too, and they must be if feminism is to succeed.

How do you do this in ways that understand, value, and promote the differences that are meaningful among us? The women's movements of the United States look quite different from those in Mexico, or quite different if you are organizing on the border at a *maquiladora* versus organizing in the boardroom of PepsiCo. Yet those things can act in concert with each other as long as there are ways for them to communicate. I think that was one of the crucial insights of third wave feminism. After that, well then, it's all politics.

Rose Mary. Obama recently said that he agreed with the Same Sex Marriage Act. How will this affect not just the structure of public society—there will be a lot of gay couples who can marry—but also the internal psyche of the people? How will this change how communities see gay people?

Without a doubt it's a very pleasant historical development. For the first time in history a person at the pinnacle of the leading nations of the world has admitted that there is value to people taking care of people. Great! There's no question that it is a valuable development, but does it change anything? I would like to think about this on three levels. On the political level, nobody's mind is going to be changed by this. People who thought Obama supported it but was just hedging away from it for political reasons are right; he's still supportive. Whether you judge him or praise him for what he said, your mind about him has probably not changed. In addition, our ideas about same sex marriage have probably not changed. What can change minds, though, is what comes next. I think that's where the other two things that are on my mind about his statement come into play.

What happens to people who don't marry? I think that if our value is only measured through our pairing with other people, for that to be the standard by which we are judged, what does that mean for people who choose to stay single for one reason or another? Are they somehow lesser human beings? What happens to their rights? Who controls what happens to their money? What happens to their healthcare? What happens to their unemployment? There are basic aspects of being human that are not being taken care of through the institution of marriage. "Great, thank you for recognizing that these bonds matter, but what about the people who do not yet or ever engage in those bonds?" The next step is to ask how we are to think about their lives and their resources in a way that fosters social justice. That's the second question that comes to mind in at this stage in the marriage debate.

The third thing that comes to my mind is what I have heard people call the "argument of inevitability." Colonel Terrel Preston, affiliated with the Service Members Legal Defense Network, has recently retired from the military. He has had a great career and has also been involved in doing different policy and advocacy work for LGBT rights with Equality Texas. One of his arguments is that, as they move on, the generations are increasingly in favor of same sex marriage; so it follows that it will eventually be universally accepted. One of the problems I see with that argument is that, historically, we have seen backlashes on similar issues. We have seen this play out in the feminist movement and in the civil rights movement. We can't just assume that once you have had *Brown vs. Board of Education*, all education will be fine.

I do think the argument does good in that it gives people some hope for a future that will be better, because they can see that there is a trend and believe, "Yes, it will work." However, it makes it too easy for someone to say, "Well, if it's done, then I don't have to worry about it," and continue living in a bubble. They might not hear the issue about the North Carolina pastor who says it's appropriate to "beat the gay out of your son." They might not hear this kind of news.

Rose Mary. In his book, Under Saturn's Shadow, *the author Dr. James Hollis says that all men collude in a conspiracy of silence to suppress their emotional truth. Do you agree with this?*

I quibble with it. Not all men are the same, just as all women are not the same. Some men perceive that there is a value to be gained by adhering to a particular vision of the masculine, one that claims that emotions exist in a private realm, maybe not absent, maybe not taken out surgically, but private and not for public consumption. Wives get to see their husbands' emotions, daughters, maybe, mothers; but not co-workers, not the people you see out on the street. But that's only one vision of what masculinity might be; there are other examples that are easily accessible. Within the Christian tradition, you could look at Christ, whose emotional availability to the world was his exemplar for humankind. This is an exemplar of masculinity very different from the one that is emotionally cold and shut down. There are any number of other examples to which we could look—Buddha, for example.

There is another set of values, too, around the emotions that are vulnerable. Men showing anger in public is valued; you get a medal of honor in the military. Men showing cunning in business is valued. Remember in the eighties and the movie *Wall Street* when "greed was good?" There is a space for men showing vulnerable emotions, for a vision of masculinity as caretaking, as preserving. But it is a space that is somehow missed. I'm not sure I disagree or agree with the statement, but I quibble. I think it might be a narrow and focused interpretation of the kinds of masculinity that are available.

Rose Mary. What could we do as a community or as individuals to nurture our femininity?

It's really about nurturing the whole of us. If you are a woman and you find yourself to be angry about the way you're being treated, speak the anger in a way that's productive. If you find yourself emotionally moved, it's okay to cry in public. When it's about the nurturing of the whole person, it's about accepting that this is our emotional reality, whatever it is. The question is, what do you do with that reality? If your choice is to cut out that part of yourself and discard it as not you, regardless of who you are or what that part may be, that speaks to something. We are constantly in a project of self-creation, constantly in a project of trying to be, in this moment, the right person. If that person is to be whole, there are going to be some aggressive moments, some soft moments, some whole moments. I would start by questioning yourself if you start to feel the urge to edit. Where is that coming from and why? That's a question for each of us to consider on our own.

Rose Mary. For the most part, as human beings, we categorize by our inclination. Why can't we look at the Other as he/she is?

That's really tricky. Part of what happens when we talk about meeting someone where they are, or understanding someone as they are, is we talk about going there with an open mind. However, it's not enough just to have an open mind; you can have stuff in it that gets in the way of reality getting in. The Buddhist "no mind" is one that doesn't mistake the categories that it has inside of it for the real that is outside in the world. When it comes to gender, or race, or any of the other categories that we use to understand the world, so much of that is the pre-context, what you bring to it. Even with an open mind, you see and think, "Oh, this is a woman. This is a man." Those expectations then change what you actually interpret. When it comes to meeting the other, it's tricky territory.

We would like to think that we are capable of changing our minds. We would like to think that we are capable of growing. We would like to think we are capable of saying, "I had it wrong, I learned better, and now I have it right." What if things change and what was right at one time is not right in the present moment? The same could be true of gender. People attack this kind of thinking as cultural relativism. There is something uncomfortable about the position that says, "Anything is ok." Holding the moral argument at bay for a moment, the way we think about communication is gendered for a lot of people. Listening is a very feminine skill. However, talking, orating is a masculine skill. If the opportunity to engage is seen as somehow morally questionable because you have allowed yourself to become open to another person who might be wrong; well, so what if they are? That doesn't mean that you're wrong, too. It doesn't mean that having a conversation is wrong.

Rose Mary. It seems that we end up categorizing everything, but in the end, you're just a species. The truth is you can't control everything. I think it's also a product of how we rationalize things; they have to have a name, a category; but that's not how life is in the end.

Lorís. Well, it's all right to put a name to things; just don't hammer it down!

There's a word for that; it's called reification. It means making the word or the concept into the thing itself. We have gotten very good at mistaking the idea for the real in Western culture. It's the finger pointing to the moon.

Lorís. Yesterday, my brother was talking about how we sometimes try to pin point a problem, but we get lost in the process. You forget the problem and go off on a tangent, so that no one remembers what the problem was in the first place!

I fear that might have been some of my answers to your questions today! I think the really fascinating thing about the process you are engaged in is that you are gathering up all of this—I don't want to call it detritus, but this stuff. You then get to decide how to shape it. I don't know how the experience of sitting down and listening to it all is going to be for you.

Rose Mary. I think it will be pretty difficult.
Lorís. It's been pretty amazing. I feel like I'm on the completely opposite side from where I started.

"Opposite"! Really?

Lorís. Some days, on the dark days, I ask myself, why am I doing this? This doesn't even matter. I started out with a firm mission statement: "I want to give a space to that which is feminine for both men and women." That was very clear to me. I wasn't sure how I was going to do it, but I knew that's what I wanted to do. Now, with everything that I'm hearing, I begin to ask myself, "What was the feminine again?" People don't want to call it that anymore. They say it should be called something else. I find there is some kind of a space for it, then I see that there is not, and then I find that in some people there is. Right now, I am on the verge of not knowing what this film will be about anymore!

Some people would say that means you are ready to begin. In terms of the academic conversation, there are any number of people that you may find helpful, if not elucidating, depending on how you think of their use of language. Judith Butler is going to be a core figure, at least to know that she's out there and how her analysis is relevant. Her ideas about performativity came out in the nineties. She borrowed the idea from linguists and some others, not so much from the drama sense of a performance, but the sense of doing things with words. There are words that are performative; in saying them, an action is taken. For example, "I now pronounce you man and wife." Those words make you man and wife. So, Butler says that gender is like that also, and much of our social world as well. Maybe the whole texture of our life is a constantly repeated performance with no original. That was her insight. I think part of the key here, too, is to keep the focus global. Once you do that, you begin to see that these identity terms are make-believe stories that people organize themselves around in different ways in different settings; they aren't exponents of the real, somehow having emerged from our DNA.

There's a lot in this documentary that I think would be helpful for a lot of people if they're able to hear it. I think part of it is how you tell the story, who you show it to, and who is going to hear themselves in it. That's a big question.

Rose Mary. You mention that Butler speaks of performative words in gender. Could you elaborate more on this and how it plays its role in language?

In the late eighties and early nineties, Judith Butler was part of a really big revolution in the way we were thinking about what feminism was, what its goal was, and what it described. What does gender actually describe? There was a point in time when feminism wanted its unifying force to be grounded in the bodies of women. They wanted there to be a grounding, a solid foundation, whether it was biology, or social behavior, whatever it might be. One of the things she had some insight into was that there was a gap between the language that we use and the real that it describes—"women" for example—and the reality that it describes. Butler asked herself, "Where does gender actually live? Is it in our chromosomes? Is it in our bodies? Is it an essence deeply true about ourselves that some people have a female gender naturally embodied within them, and other people have some other gender, masculine perhaps?" What she came to see is that this was a trap, because the language and the real never quite map cohesively, no matter which way of framing it you choose. In order to escape out the framing problem of trying to ground gender in something physical, essential, biological, natural; she came to see that part of what made gender work was a repeated stylization of the body over time. The performative is this kind of sedimentation of practices and behaviors. If you behave one way one day, and again the next, and again the next, it becomes the real. That's the way gender became performative for Butler.

Rose Mary. What I am hearing is the sense that words have power. If someone pronounced the words, "You are now man and wife," those words have the power to keep them together for the rest of their lives, just by the priest pronouncing them on the altar.

That's the other part of the performative for Butler, words in and of themselves. She draws this from J.L. Austin's work, *How to Do Things with Words.* There is a category of words that make things happen because of the way they are. "I now pronounce you man and wife," makes that couple a man and wife. "I now pronounce you divorced," splits that coupling. "I now pronounce you of age to marry," a *quinceañera*; these are all performative acts. The words in and of themselves are those behaviors. They're social acts that make things real because they say it is that way. When you address someone as "Sir," that creates an authority for that person. When you address someone as "Ma'am," that genders them; it engenders them. It creates their gender in the moment.

Lorís. I have a question. I don't want to let go of my inner life. I want to keep developing who I am, finding out who I am not. On the other hand, I want to have a job that pays, and be successful, and all these other things. It seems that both of them require a lot of time. You have to meditate or read so much to find out everything about yourself, but then you basically have to become a workaholic if you want to have a luxurious life. I find that society promotes both things, depending on where you are. In this university, they promote personal development; but out there, you have to have all this money. I find it really difficult to balance both.

Rose Mary. Also, Lorís complains that no one ever told her that in all the years it might take her to be successful, she will probably have to take a few years off to raise her kids and her family, so how does she then catch up to the competition?

Lorís. Oh yes, there is also that matter.

There is a lot going on there, on multiple levels. How do you nurture yourself when so many of the demands of living in this world seem to call you away from that nurturing? How do you nurture others when, again, so many of the demands in this world seem to call us to pay attention to ourselves over other people? Make sure you provide it for yourself before you provide it for anyone else. I think at the base of this there is a misperception about what the relationship might be among these different things. What would it look like if we were to reframe it?

You can be mindful about how you make your money. You can be mindful about how you nurture yourself. So it's not so much a balancing act among multiple things, as it is a way of valuing time, a value placed on doing things in a purposeful way, so that you are not rushing to making the money, to make the dinner, to go to the gym and pick up the kids; not rushing through having a date with your partner or time with your friends. You never know where down the line these human bonds may turn into your next job, the next book project, the next film. Because these are the things we sing about. These are the things we make films about. These are the things that we teach each other about, how to be human with each other in a way that's sustainable and nurturing. The story that we see being sold time and again is that there is somehow a conflict between those, that in order to make money you have to sacrifice being human. In order to be successful you have to sacrifice time with your family. What would it look like if those were the same? It's a thought.

Lorís. How could someone have a better balance between their inner lives and their outer lives—turn up the volume of their own inner voice, and make it something they could think about on a daily basis?

When you notice yourself defining your success by comparing it to somebody else, that's always a good cue. "Oh, they got that TV. I have to get that TV"; or, "Look at the car they have! I need that car." "Look at that partner they have! He is so beautiful. She is so sexy. Is mine sexy enough? Is mine beautiful enough?" When you notice yourself playing that game, that's your cue that you have left a little bit of your inner life behind and you have not been listening to you! Here's the kicker though, the things that we think are valuable, we learn their value by seeing other people valuing them. If thousands of people surround one person, we assume that person is valuable because a thousand people are around them. What about the people that are around that person? What is their value? Do they get it from getting near that one person? Maybe they get it from somewhere else. Our inner value is not necessarily about our relationships to other people alone; it's about how we treat those relationships. That's where our real value lies.

Rose Mary. Is there something that you would like to add that we didn't mention?

I'm curious to know who your audience will be. With whom do you wish to share this story? There are a lot of people who would see this and say, "Great, fine." Whose minds do you want to change, and how? I don't think you're making this just to make a documentary. I think you're making it because you wish to change something. I actually have that question for anybody who's engaged in this project, "Whose minds are we trying to change? What is our strategy to do that?"

Lorís. I guess it would be the younger generations. In the environments I moved in, it seems to be more glamorous to say the right thing, or to be more open, accept more people; you hear it. But when I turn around and see what many people in my generation are doing—I get the feeling that their words and their actions do not match. One thing is talking about your beliefs but another thing is having the courage to act on them. If you say you are tolerant, or that you are accepting of your emotions, well, "Tolerate! Accept!" Or at least try to. I will have to find the audience slowly, after I see who is actually interested in this documentary.

We tend to say and do what we know until we learn something different; and then we change. There's a story I want to share with you of a graduate school friend of mine who, before she had children in her marriage, was very happy. However, right before she had her children, she started to say, "Well, I'm going to raise my children like this. I am going to be this kind of mother. I am going to be this kind of parent." Her first child is a boy. And all of the things that she had been really questioning about masculinity and femininity, she found replaying in this weird space of raising this new-to-her person, and he had a personality that started to look a lot like the things that were very traditionally masculine in the way that she had previously critiqued. She had wanted to raise a particular kind of son.

Then she had a daughter and it got even worse, because all of that work that she had done to undermine the one-or-the-other solid sense of gender began to flash in front of her eyes on a daily basis in ways that she could not avoid. How do you deal with it when your pre-lingual child acts in ways that are stereotypical to the gender? You think, "Where did that come from? Is that in her? Is that in him? What do I do with that when I have been trying to press up against those boundaries myself? Make space for people to be who they are! "Well," she thought, "this is who they are! Just because they are who they are, does this mean that the system that describes what they're doing is absolutely correct?" That's close to where she landed with her questioning.

I think it's a very powerful story, because even those of us who are very critical and reflexive are still living in the world, engaged in it. It comes up to us, it gives us this experience that we could choose to deny or we could choose to embrace. The question is, how does the embrace work? Do you embrace it through language that you don't like? Or do you ask yourself how to approach it differently? Now that her kids are older, my friend is able to talk about this with them in a way that she could not when she was a younger mother. That, too, is a different experience for her. So I think part of what you're seeing when you talk about your friends—who are saying one thing when they're in college and changing when they go off into the real world—is that they are reacting to the space that they are in. Maybe they, too, can change that over time a little bit. I don't know that they'll be the same person for the rest of their lives.

Loris. It's true. Studying at this university is like Disneyland compared to being "out there." By no means are we going to be rebellious and idealistic all of our lives. At some point we'll have to make a living and adapt to many things. However, I do believe there is a core essence in us that should be maintained, that should be left untouched. No matter what happens on the outside, you need to respect your essence. I feel that your backbone needs to remain your own, and no one else's. I think that's what got me the most, seeing others opening up and not paying attention to that essence anymore.

It's interesting how new that idea is, that there is a core self that encounters the world and then over time, changes. It's a very new idea. What if there were other models? There is an old Greek model in which the project of the self is always ongoing and there is never a core. It's not a diamond in the rough; it's an evolving muck. There are other models, too, like the constant state of becoming what Deleuze and Guattari might describe, where there is no beginning or end, but only a constant middle. I think that's also what our experience of the social is. It's been going on for a long time before we are injected into it. It's moving and changing, because we are moving and changing. It's all a moving target. That lifts the veil from gender claims—"This is what masculinity is, and this is what femininity is"—and shows them to be political claims that are about the here and now. They're shifting in and on themselves because that ground, too, has shifted.

Michelle Villalobos

Michelle Villalobos is the founder of The Women's Success Summit, Miami's largest business conference for entrepreneurial women, and co-founder of the online personal branding program, Make Them BEG, which won her the *Miami Herald* Business Plan Challenge in 2013. Two years earlier, *the Miami Herald* named Villalobos one of Miami's Top 20 Under 40. Villalobos's successful programs have been practiced and/or sponsored by American Express, Burger King, Gibraltar Private Bank & Trust, Frito-Lay, Constant Contact, LivingSocial, the National Association of Women Business Owners (NAWBO), and Brooks Brothers, among others.

I am a firm believer in the impact of first impressions, and Michelle gave me the impression she had it all: the job, the partner, the success, and most importantly to me,

the satisfaction. Her words came from a corporate background, but behind them I sensed a clear presence of the
feminine in her approach to business. With all this and
the gorgeous pops of bright colors in her presentations
and wardrobe, I was sold before the first introduction.

*Lorís. The feminist movement was a very strong and driven movement.
There were set goals, such as the right to vote. However, those goals seem to
be a bit diffuse, women in younger generations feel like the fight is over and
take everything for granted. What do you have to say about this?*

I know what you're talking about. What you say is really interesting
because I went to a liberal arts college, and it was the first time that I
was really exposed to the concept of women's studies or feminism. I
had studied about it theoretically in high school—the suffrage
movement to get women the right to vote—but I never really studied
how it applied to me. In college, I took all these feminist classes and
women's studies classes, which of course thrilled my parents, because
they were wondering what I was doing with the education they were
spending all that money on. They wanted to see that I was doing
something serious. Anyway, I took all these women's studies classes,
and I became quite the little feminist. I was seeing examples of
inequality everywhere—on TV, in the movies, especially in music
videos. I felt like I noticed there was a lot of inequity in college.

I graduated from a really good school, though, and when I got out
of college I thought there was a real even playing field and that there
would be the same opportunities available to me that there were for
the boys that I was graduating with. So we set off on our way, and I
spent five, six, seven, then ten years in my career path. I started
noticing as I got older that the guys seemed to pace ahead. They
seemed to be doing better overall. Not just over me; I could not take
myself as a good example since I moved around a lot. I noticed in
general the guys seemed to get ahead quicker. When I started
working in a more corporate environment, I noticed that it was easier
for the men to get ahead, especially when the boss and all the top-

level people were men, when the owner of the company was a man. You started to really see that the people at the top in this particular company were men and the worker bees were all women. So to answer your question, I feel that in college I noticed inequity. And then maybe ten to fifteen years later, I woke up to it.

Now, I am very aware of it, and in what I do now, which is helping women get ahead in business, I know the numbers. I know the statistics. I see some real disparities. People like to quote that there is unequal pay—"Women earn eighty cents on the dollar compared to men"—which is interesting and something to be addressed; but what I find even more interesting, more compelling and more disturbing, is that self-employed women only make fifty-five cents on the dollar compared to self-employed men. So, talk about the fact that women in jobs are earning less. Yes, they are, and that's unfair. Great, let's look at that figure and where it's coming from; but these women are in charge of their own businesses. They're self-employed. So, what's going on there? And that's what I'm out to try and figure out and fix.

Loris. I have a guy friend who always mentioned how in his company—it was an oil and gas company—everyone was equal. His boss was a man. But all the activities with the guys were very male-oriented. So, even if there were women working next to him, there was no way he could actually involve them. It was not because they didn't want to.

Are you going to go play football with the guys? Really? Because guys love it when women want to join in their football game, you know?

Loris. So it's also a social construct. It's not so much that they don't want to, but—

Exactly. Most of the time it's not on purpose; it's not conscious. If you think about it this way, the business world was built by men for other men. Women came knocking on the door, what, fifty years ago? We banged down the door; we got in; we're looking around, trying to change; but at the end of the day, it hasn't been that long. Really, it was men who built corporate America as well as the corporate culture worldwide. I don't know necessarily how we compare to all the other nations—there are some countries more gender equal than we are—but the fact is, we are making strides. We're getting ahead, and we know having women at the top works. We've learned from statistics and studies that companies who have more women in senior management positions are more profitable. We don't know if that is a cause-and-effect relationship. We don't know if it's because they have more women in senior leadership that they are successful, or if it's that more successful companies choose to have more women in senior leadership. We don't know, but the fact is the companies that are most profitable have more women at the top.

Although, you're right; there is a certain resistance. If a woman tries to go to the racket-ball club and play with the guys, it could actually hurt her chances more than help her because they'll say, "Who does she think she is?"

Lorís. Why do you think the phenomenon of the "Superwoman" image occurred in the first place? Do you think women got a double load of expectations since the feminist movement?

Yes! I mean I completely agree with that statement. It's tough because in the old days a woman competed for things like how well she raised her children, how beautiful her home looked, how well she cooked, and so on. There were all these things she was graded on that equated to being a good woman, a successful woman, an actualized woman. Today, on top of that, you have to add in career, salary, what she drives, does she have fancy labels, and a million other things. Yes, it's a double load of work. What's really important is for each woman to identify what is truly a priority, what is truly important for her. What happens is, if we let others decide what we're great at, and if we let the world tell us, then ultimately, we fall into this superwoman complex and it's impossible to live up to.

Most women cannot do it all, and if we do, it's going to wear on us, stress us out, bring us down, and shave years off of our lives. The key is to look inside of your own heart and say, "What is important to me? What do I want out of my life?" Then focus on that and to hell with everyone else who tries to tell you how you need to do something different. If that means you have to stay at home and raise your kids, then more power to you; focus on that. If that means go and work, if that means do it all, then, okay. However, you must be clear that not everything can be a priority.

Lorís. In the past, men had more heart disease. Now women are increasing in the statistics as well. It has been proven, the more stressed you are the more susceptible you are to diseases.

An issue of *Psychology Today* was dedicated to the differences between men and women, from birth. Brain differences, psychological, hormonal, everything. Women seem to handle continuous stress better. I don't know what the ultimate outcome of that is, if that means it wears on them more, if it's cumulative in the long-term. Nevertheless, women seem to be able to take on more stress. That isn't exciting because ultimately we will just take it on more and more. We'll see what happens with that.

Lorís. How can we lead more balanced lives in terms of our professional life and our personal life?

The point is what will make us happy? What is the goal here? If it's to make money, okay, that's one goal. If it's to be happy, that is another. What I find really fascinating is the reason women earn so much less when they are self-employed compared to when men go off on their own. This explanation is semi-anecdotal. Let's say a man is working his butt off in a job. He's getting overworked. He's doing ninety hour weeks, etc. He thinks, "If I can spend this much time and energy working for that guy, what could I do if I went off on my own? What could I build?" They think, "Alright, I've to make more money," because money is the major goal for men. They create something that is going to deliver money and make them look good. Status is important to men, cars and watches; they have to look good. So they create a business that is very viable. My brother just did it.

He went off on his own, created a business, and raised $300,000 in seed money.

On the other hand, a woman like me goes to work every day. Her boss is mean to her. She thinks, "I deserve better than this. I want to take Fridays off. I want to live my life. I want to be free. I want to have fun. I want to be creative. I want to help people."—because that's a big one for women. They all start non-profits. What happens is that men and women start on two completely different paths, just in the terms of their mindsets of the business that they're building. I don't want to be mean or generalize because not everybody falls into this category, but I certainly did. It's more of what Carl Wroth calls a "jobby." We create a "jobby." We start making cakes and we sell those cakes. We start making necklaces. It's things that are creative and fun and allow us to network. Men, they think, "This has to make me a ton of money because I cannot leave this job." Men still have that provider mindset. I think ultimately we go to business with two different sets of priorities. That's what it boils down to: What are your priorities. What are you really after?

A study was done on a graduating class out of business school. I believe the school was Carnegie Mellon University, Tepper Business School. Men ended up earning somewhere around four- to seven-thousand dollars more in their starting jobs—four- to seven-thousand dollars. Meanwhile, they're coming out with the same education and preparation. Everybody's thinking, "Oh my God, discrimination!" And that's what you first think, right? Well they dug a little deeper into this, and what they found was that a much higher percentage of women took the first offer that they were given and never negotiated that first offer. A much larger portion, 83 percent of the men, negotiated the first offer and ended up getting more money.

So, either the women accepted that they were worth less; or maybe they didn't know, because they didn't know what the men were being offered. They just thought, "They're being nice. They're offering me a job. I want the job." So they take it. Whereas the men would never take the first offer! "If they want me, they can pay more," they think.

But me, I've never negotiated a job offer. I'd say to myself, "Ok this is the offer; you're either going to accept it or decline it, but not ask for more." Do we women think we are worthless? I don't think that's the case; it's that nobody taught us how to negotiate. Nobody ever taught me! Nobody took me aside and said, "This is what you do."

The thing is, in schools, they don't teach you how to play the game. They don't teach men either, but I think men teach each other. It's sort of a father-to-son thing, or teacher to student. I don't know where men get it. Women, we mentor and nurture each other in a different way. However, we're not hard on each other the way men are, which pushes them forward. Men are more competitive; it's very different. I find it fascinating because what was said in that article in *Psychology Today* is that the biological differences are not as big as you think, considering how magnified they become through societal input and influence. A lot of it is nature; but a lot of it is nature interacting with the nurture. Think about this: According to one study, among female and male monkey babies, the male ones are more likely to reach for a truck and the female ones are more likely to reach for a doll. Monkeys, the same as human children! But the thing is that if the child continues to reach for the doll, and the child is more related to humans than to objects, then the way the environment starts to interact with that child is different, and this difference then becomes magnified and magnified and magnified. So it's like nature and nurture all merged together into one.

Jay. Talk to us about where you feel women stand in the business world. I heard that the discrimination isn't so much against the female sex, but against all the feminine qualities that a female carries, so that these qualities would be discriminated against in men as well. Some examples are the expression of emotions, having a more relational/social focus, and of course, parenting. What do you think?

Well, yes and no. I read a book by Lois Frankel that I find fascinating, in which she talked about the feminization of business. To some degree, there is discrimination against those feminine qualities, which is a true observation. Don't cry at the office. Don't show your soft side. Be tough. Negotiate. All that is true, but there seems to be a shift, at least in corporate America, toward valuing feminine qualities more. Why? Because we are moving toward a more collaborative, team-based, work environment. We are moving toward a more social interaction, even just with the online world. Women do really well on social media because we are really good relationship nurturers. So there is a movement toward accepting and valuing these feminine characteristics, more than ever.

There is more and more coming out about these "soft skills," which are more associated with women. The companies that are doing really well are the ones that are showing their soft side and having more personality and injecting business with emotion rather than being so rigid. In the business world, fifty, sixty, seventy years ago, it was much more like the military, very hierarchical, command-and-control style. Now, the organizations are broader, more flat, more fun and playful. Companies are starting to wake up and pay attention and realize they can have better employees if they support the whole female.

I've a lot of calls from companies like American Express or Burger King, and they say, "Hey, come speak to our women's leadership." They're all about trying to promote women, they're trying, but the women need to help. It's like, "We're trying to promote you but you have to grab it. You have to ask. You have to go for it."

Lorís. The business world is filled with women who think that in order to have success, you have to behave as a man or acquire masculine characteristics. Do you still find this to be true?

To some degree I think women do not need to acquire male characteristics, because a woman coming into the office dressed like a man, speaking like a man, acting like a man, often turns people off; men and women feel threatened. It's not about acquiring male characteristics; it's about learning specific skills and adapting those skills. For example, learning how to negotiate, something we talked about before. What we know about negotiation, we know from that study that women don't do it, so they don't earn as much. Yet we also know that when women try to negotiate like a man, they don't get as good a result. In fact, there can be backlash against her if she tries to negotiate that hard-nosed, boom, boom, boom! male style.

There has to be a female middle ground, knowing that you have to negotiate, and then understanding that you have to negotiate in your own fashion, in a way that is acceptable to whomever you are negotiating with. The beauty of all that, or the problem, is that you have to understand that when you are negotiating with a man it is one thing, and when you are negotiating with a woman it is another. I think women, we just have to be a lot more aware, a lot more intuitive about how to approach another person; we have to read people better. Luckily, that is in our skill set. It's sort of our natural, female skill set to be empathetic and intuitive, really to listen to other people. This is all really good, but ultimately we cannot just say, "Ok, I am going to don my male suit today and don my male characteristics today, and I am going to act like a man," because that backfires. So, it's not easy!

Lorís. I agree. Companies are becoming more flexible. If not, they're almost forced to become more flexible.

Yes! Good companies, bad companies, they're really putting money into training, education, empowering their women, educating the women, training the men, fostering teamwork, fostering communication skills. Things are changing. I really, really believe that. Ultimately, it's only been fifty years, or sixty.

Lorís. A woman once told me that when she started her first job, both her bosses were women. She began going to them for support, thinking that because they were women, they would help her out. In the end she told me her bosses did not react so well to that. They thought, "We have worked hard to get here, so now you have to work just as much as we did to get where we are. No short cuts." They had this attitude toward this woman like they saw her as someone who was coming in and trying to steal it all.

That's the typical Queen Bee mentality: "I had to work for it, so I am going to make you work for it." We get that a lot, and at the summit we actually address that topic, that women play dirty. It really is disturbing. It's not something that people have liked talking about. I've really wanted to bring it out into the open. I tried. I sent it to a lot of reporters and nobody really wants to talk about it because they have this idea that I'm perpetuating stereotypes. Even though there's data. You've seen it; it is sourced to the gills; I left no claim un-sourced or undocumented. Even so, they were thinking, "Well, we don't want to talk about that."

Lorís. It's harsh because it's one of the topics that needs the most attention and people turn away from it.

Well, even I want to turn away from it a little bit. Do you want to be the person who's saying that women stab each other in the back? You have to be careful. It's definitely not uplifting. I submitted a TED Talk about it; I tried everything. That was two years ago, I kind of gave up and moved forward in another direction. But every woman will talk about it one-on-one. Every woman will admit to it. Every woman will agree that she has been stabbed in the back. However, women will not say that they have done it to somebody else, which is interesting.

Lorís. Your business blends very strict masculine values along with feminine values. You get things done in a way our system wants them to be done, yet you still find a space to be a woman, to be feminine, creative, cheerful, and to nurture your own inspirations. How did you create this space? How can other women do this as well?

In my case—I have to be honest with you—I tried the other route. I tried to be more masculine. I tried to dress up in a serious suit, have a serious business card, have a serious website, and be a serious business consultant. Whether it's because I'm a woman or I am who I am personality wise, I wasn't authentic. It wasn't a fit for me. So what I decided to do was focus in on an audience I knew I resonated with, even when I was being myself, and that was other women. Therefore, I focused my business in a more female market; and that doesn't mean only women; it also means men who value female values, men who have no problem interacting with women, men who are drawn to women. From there I've been able to unleash who I am, my personality. I can be more creative, more feminine and all that. And what is interesting is that doing this has ended up drawing men back into the mix. If there's a lesson there, it's that if you're true to who you are what is naturally going to be attracted to you will be attracted to you, and from that will spring opportunities. So if you are a woman who's more masculine, like Jessica Kizorik, then being that way, authentic and true to yourself, is going to draw the right people.

Lorís. It goes back to the idea that if you let yourself be who you are, things will come to you.

It really does. I mean, you also want to have a solid plan and a vision and a strategy and action plan and to-do lists and all that stuff. But ultimately, if at the core of it you are getting to be you, things will be easier because you will not be fighting yourself all the time.

Lorís. Even though women in Western cultures pride themselves on being liberated, we're not that different from Eastern or Middle Eastern cultures. That is to say, our culture has a clear obsession with the female body, and this burdens girls and women. The cosmetic industry is huge, as well as the rising community of people with eating disorders. Many of these influences come from mass media. Can you talk a bit about how TV/advertisement/ magazines/etc., influence women and girls?

Oh my goodness. That reminds me of college. It's such a big topic; it's so schizophrenic. On the one hand, you open a magazine—let's say Marie Claire, Cosmo, or Vogue—and in the editorial they're all complaining about our obsession with being thin, but can't women be healthy and have a normal size on the page right there? There's a stick thin woman trying to sell you a handbag, you know? It's schizophrenic. You have to be skinny and beautiful and gorgeous and all this stuff, and by the way, you shouldn't be obsessed with your body and you shouldn't spend all your money on handbags and shoes, even though Hollywood is doing it. It's like this schizophrenic mass media. It boils down to somebody trying to sell you stuff; in order to sell you stuff, they portray the ideal woman. It's like this vicious cycle: What came first, the chicken or the egg? Is the ideal woman created by the mass media, or is it who we want to be, and so we feed into it, and they just tap into our secret desires?

It's scary stuff. I don't know where it's going to go because I get nervous when I see girls, young girls—and they've done studies on this, too—they're so depressed and not able to figure out who they are, what they want to do, how they are going to contribute to this world, how they are going to find fulfillment and happiness, because they're so focused on how boys see them and how other girls see them.

And the music that we listen to—the hip-hop stuff. I love dancing. I love hip-hop. I love music. I love going out. But sometimes I listen to this stuff and I think, "I can't dance to this!" It is like, "Ouch! Is this what you think of us?" The names they call us; that's such a deep dark topic, I don't even know where to begin. I did want to do an event, a girl-power kind of thing. We would not be teaching them or telling them; we would invite them to explore. "Let's listen to one song and break down those lyrics, let's listen to what that's really saying about you when you sing along to it." I'd love to do something like that.

Lorís. It's very difficult to fight an invisible demon that's always there, following you around. It becomes normal.

When I was in college we had a really high incidence of it because it's linked to upper-middle-class, high-performing, high achievers. They're good students, smart, athletes, a lot of extra-curricular activities. These girls are more likely to have an eating disorder, possibly because it's all about being perfect, or being the best. I've been told that control is another issue. It's very pervasive. And then you've got the flip side to it, more obesity than ever, heart diseases linked to obesity. There are so many things going on.

Lorís. Women who decide to stay at home are seen as weak and as if they haven't achieved their ultimate goals in life. In a highly-valued economic society, why are women denying other women their right to stay at home?

Yes, I've heard that. Again, it isn't a part of my personal experience, and we briefly touched on it before when I said you have to figure out what your priority is, what matters to you in life. If getting ahead in business is important to you, and I get that, then go ahead and do that, and have your kids and figure it out. We're biologically programmed to want to take care of our children when we have them. I mean, it's like dictated to us in our genes, "You want to nurture this child. You want to take care of this child." What's wrong with staying at home with your kids and raising a better kid? That's awesome. If that's what you want to do, great!

Lorís. I don't think I've ever met a woman who has just stayed at home and has been genuinely happy.

But, do you see the judgment that you have implied in what you said? You made a judgment, because you said, "I've never met a woman who has just stayed at home to watch her children," implying it's less. So you have to be careful, too, because you're making the assumption that it's less. And think about what values she brings to her children's lives and to the world by being a mother who's there. We know it's better to have a mom around than not to have a mom around, given the two options, right? It's better to have a mom around; therefore, there's a sacrifice implied in going away, and there's a sacrifice implied in staying home. Who's to say one sacrifice is better or worse than the other?

Jay. The interviewer is the most misogynist of them all!

I didn't say she was a misogynist. The thing is, we fall into the same traps. We just have to be monitoring and aware, because you don't want to be that way.

Lorís. I have to play the devil's advocate from time to time! It's a cultural bias that you inherit.

It's interesting, though, that your bias is very recent, because fifty, eighty years ago, the concept of women working outside the home, people would have said, "Oh, she has to go out and work? My god!" And now we say, "Oh, she wants to stay home!" It's flipped!

Lorís. To reach a balance between the sexes, both men and women need to be understanding of each other. What do you think are some men's issues that women have failed to address?

I don't know if this is exactly what you are aiming for, but we try to take sex out of the workplace; we try to pretend it does not exist. Our sexual roles—male, female, the dynamic between men and women—we try to pretend it isn't there. But what I've witnessed in the last couple of years in the male-female dynamic is that what men seek in personal relationships isn't necessarily nurturing or love, somebody to cook for them or clean for them; what men really need in a personal relationship is respect, above all. He needs the woman or the wife or whomever to respect him.

A woman needs all sorts of things, and we're not going to get into that. But I can go into the workplace with the understanding that when I deal with a man, the fundamental thing that he wants from a woman in a personal sense is respect. When I have approached business that way, with the attitude of giving men the respect that they need, I've found that I've gotten much, much more positive results. As opposed to approaching it saying, "I'm a man, too, and we're up against each other competing." I've decided to assume the feminine role: "I'm a woman, so what's wrong with that?" It's sort of a taboo. I'm not flirting. It isn't as if I'm taking a romantic approach, but what I'm saying is, "Well, if this is the way the dynamic works in an intimate personal relationship, why not approach business and give men who I'm dealing with the same respect they need."

And it works! I believe that women, instead of trying to negate their femininity or negate their womanhood, should instead just accept that there are certain gender roles. Maybe they're inborn; maybe they're not. Does it matter? Not really. At the end of the day what you want are results. You want to be able to make a deal. You want to be able to sell what you are selling. You want to be able to accomplish any number of things. Why not take what we know about the way men and women work best together and apply that? That's something I think women might have a tough time with. I think it might not be the most popular approach, but is it such a bad idea to give somebody else respect and let them assume the masculine role and assume the feminine role? Always bearing in mind what you are after, what your goals are, what you are up to.

Lorís. There is some truth in that. Even though we put a mask on at work, there are underlying social codes that inevitably exist.

Ultimately, what we're after is successful outcomes. If it yields a more successful outcome, great! I will give you an anecdotal example. We were talking about this very subject, two summits ago, and it was controversial to say the least. I got emails afterwards from women. One of the women on the stage said, "Men love to be the hero. They love to be able to rescue a woman if she is in trouble. If a woman needs something, it makes men feel really good to step in and fix it. Fix the situation." She said she does whatever is possible to take advantage of that. "If I need help, if I need something, I find that if I come to a man and say, 'Hey, I'm in trouble here, I could really use your help.' They usually step in and they take care of it." The other woman on the panel was just flabbergasted. She said, "I can't believe you do that! That is so unacceptable. You're weakening yourself."

So it's a polemic issue. Do you? Don't you? Is it somewhere in between? Each of us has to find our own happy medium in order to find the successful outcome we want. What it boils down to is, I think we have to work a little harder than men do when it comes to getting ahead. Most of the time, we're really the ones who have to make the adaptation, have to adjust, have to learn, you know? At the end of the day, I think we have to work harder at it.

Jay. I'm curious to know what your thoughts are about what is traditionally considered to be feminine by society—something like having certain feelings or attitudes, as opposed to being a woman. Do you think there's a separation between those two things? For example, childbirth, that's something that is related to being a woman. Nurturing or creating is considered feminine, but is found in both men and women. I have this thing where I think the word should be changed.

Well, like what we talked before about with you! With your personality style, you have a nurturing quality, which could be considered feminine. And no man wants to be considered feminine, right?

Lorís. And with that confusion of what is feminine and what is masculine we go into a society that discriminates against women because they discriminate against those qualities. In fact, this documentary was originally meant for women, but then we found that what was really being neglected were these feminine qualities. And to our surprise, men were the ones who suffered most from this because they were the ones who were being the most deprived of their femininity.

So they deny it in themselves, and then they try to control it in women. Since I do personality type work, I often find that the men who have a natural preference toward being nurturing, choose or self-type away from it. They don't want to admit it. They don't want to own it, or they get upset if that's how their type comes out because they think that being nurturing makes them feminine, and there's this rejection of those feminine characteristics, which in business are often discussed in terms of the difference between being aggressive and being submissive. It's a very masculine/feminine dichotomy. Under the aggressive type is the decisive, direct, commanding leadership style. That's the aggressive. The passive qualities are submissive, indecisive, and quiet, letting other people speak. Those are all associated with being bad in business. The aggressive side is associated with being good in business.

The thing is, there's a movement away from that toward a feminization of business, toward the idea that maybe all these feminine qualities, empathy and nurturing, they're not so bad, that they can be good for business too. We're starting to see a movement into the middle, but while women are embracing and learning, the men seem to resist those feminine qualities a lot. However, I do think you are right, there's a rejection by males of those female characteristics. It might be interesting to label it what it is instead of calling it feminine or associating it on the feminine.

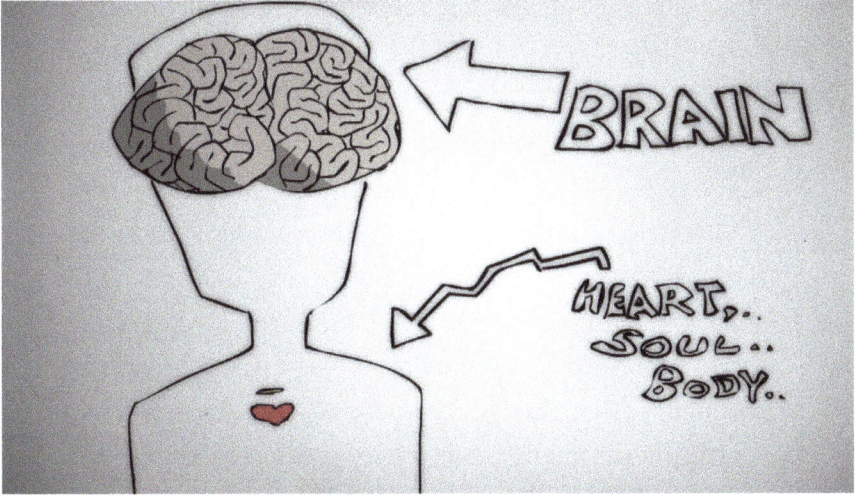

Terry Fassihi

Theresa Fassihi earned her undergraduate degree from Stanford University and her doctorate from the University of Tulsa. She is a licensed clinical psychologist with fifteen years' experience in treating eating disorders in in-patient and out-patient settings. She is a certified eating disorders specialist with the International Association of Eating Disorders Professionals. From 2005 to 2008, Dr. Fassihi worked in the Menninger Clinic's eating disorder program. In 2010, she founded the Houston Eating Disorders Center with Dr. Ovidio Bermudez and currently serves as president. A former assistant professor in the department of psychiatry at Baylor College of Medicine, she continues to serve as voluntary faculty. She also worked for the National Health Service in the United Kingdom in an outpatient clinic for eating disorder patients. Dr. Fassihi is the co-chair of the Research

Practice Committee and active member of the Scientific Committee at the Academy for Eating Disorders.

The first time I consciously accepted that I did not have the best relationship with my body was the year I lived overseas during my college years. I sought clinical help, scared I would not be able to do resolve my problems on my own, but only fell deeper and deeper into my own mental labyrinths. When I returned, I searched for someone who understood this daunting problem, and that is when I found Dr. Fassihi. She showed me how our society had normalized the quench for unattainable perfection, making it harder to recognize it as a problem. In opening my eyes to the greater social context of my struggles, she gave me the key I needed to open my own self-imposed cage and walk freely in my body.

Lorís. Can you speak to us in depth about eating disorders in the United States?

Yes, I would be happy to. It's a topic that is dear to my heart, and I am very concerned about it. Currently, we believe that at least ten million Americans suffer from eating disorders in this country, and we know that the numbers are growing, and they are growing fast. Anorexia nervosa is the most lethal psychiatric illness in the books. The fact that the numbers are so high, and increasing, is a serious concern. One worrisome problem is that it takes a long time for people to get diagnosed and treated for their eating disorders, and only a fraction of people with diagnosed eating disorders are getting the treatment they need.

Lorís. When a large portion of our young population is suffering from eating disorders, why do they face so much trouble with insurance companies?

Well, part of the reason that people have difficulty accessing treatment for eating disorders is that there has been a problem for a long time with mental health and insurance coverage. Across the spectrum of mental illnesses, there has been difficulty getting adequate treatment and coverage from insurance companies, so eating disorders are just a part of that. Also, eating disorders specifically have only been recognized and understood for the illness that they are for the past twenty years or so. So in a way, they are a new psychiatric illness and getting a full understanding from insurance companies is a developing process as well. The difficulty with the fact that people have trouble getting access to care is that delaying access to treatment only makes the illnesses more difficult to treat, and the prognosis gets poorer the longer someone stays in an eating disorder without treatment.

Lorís. What is the difference between an eating disorder and just dieting? How can a person know if they need help with this issue?

Those are a lot of questions! First of all, thinking about the thin ideal in our culture, the average American woman today is 5'4" and weighs 140lbs. This is the healthy size and weight. The average model that we see in the fashion magazines and on television is 5'11" and weighs 117lbs. The model is actually in the anorexic weight range, and our standard of beauty is in reality a sick ideal. Also, only 1-2% of Caucasian women would naturally fit into that beauty ideal. The majority of us would only achieve that look by doing something like dieting, under-eating, compulsive exercise, unhealthy behaviors. It's no surprise that many women feel that they need to do something about the way they look and start dieting.

Eating disorder specialists make a distinction between disordered eating and an eating disorder. We consider dieting to be disordered eating because you are fighting your body's natural appetites and natural shape and size in order to achieve a beauty ideal that really is not what you're meant to be. The result of that is that you stay on some diet if you can tolerate it or until you reach your goal, and then you stop that diet and your body gradually goes back to its normal self. You start this yo-yo cycling pattern of dieting, re-gaining the weight, losing it and regaining it again. Over time, this is not healthy for your body, it starts to mess up your natural metabolism, and a lot of people start to get to higher and higher weights in this yo-yo pattern. You actually end up gaining weight, not losing weight from dieting.

Lorís. This probably makes it better for the dieting industries. I was telling a friend that you spend your whole life trying to be a functional person, but this society is completely dysfunctional. When you finally become functional, you actually cease to function in society because this society is made for dysfunctional people. Thinking about this issue, I'm remembering that in ancient history, the one thing we praised in women was their fertility.

Fertility was treasured, yet here we are killing the fertility. One of the symptoms of anorexia is amenorrhea, which means you're not having your period and you're not fertile.

Lorís. Exactly. To me, it seems like women's models used to be strong, someone who could keep a community together. Now, even physically, it's like you're thinning so much that you are disappearing.

Taking away what is probably one of the most valuable things in ourselves and in our bodies.

Lorís. How can someone come to realize that they need help with this issue?

How to make the distinction between disordered eating and an eating disorder? An eating disorder is, as I mention earlier, a complex illness in which genetics plays a factor. What tends to happen is that people start with a diet and that diet triggers neurobiological changes in the brain of a person who has that genetic vulnerability so that they become caught up in a driven need to restrict and engage in other compensatory behaviors. While most of us cannot wait to get out of a diet or stop dieting, people with an eating disorder get completely pulled in, and they get into almost an addiction or an obsession with that diet. They can't stop. They get way beyond their goals and just keep going with their dieting and weight loss efforts. We believe though, that many people put themselves at risk of developing this eating disorder when they diet. They may not really know that they have a genetic vulnerability until it gets triggered through dieting.

Lorís. Are you saying that they're predisposed? Is it just a tendency that they have? Do they tend to be perfectionists or have type A personalities? How would you characterize the personality type? Is it similar to exposure to an addiction like alcoholism?

Those are complicated questions. What do we see in these individuals? If we wanted to predict, who could we identify as the most vulnerable to developing an eating disorder? We do tend to see certain character traits or personality types that are more vulnerable to eating disorders. Certainly perfectionism is a common trait of people with eating disorders. A tendency to other types of addictions is also common. A high percentage of people with eating disorders—approximately 40%—have addictions that need to be treated and addressed. Those are the other personality traits or vulnerabilities that I see. When someone who is perfectionist decides to go on a diet, you could say that's risky.

Lorís. If someone tells you that a person with an eating disorder can only blame his or herself, how would you respond as a clinician?

I would say that no one chooses to have an eating disorder. People with eating disorders suffer greatly and we never choose this lifestyle for ourselves. The majority of Americans, both male and female, are not satisfied with their appearance to begin with, and many of them try dieting. They never have the intention of getting sick. Often, their intention is to look better, feel better, get healthier. The problem is that these illnesses are biopsychosocial. There is a biological or genetic vulnerability to developing illness that nobody knows they have until it is triggered. Once it is, they are caught up in a cycle that they would never choose. It's not helpful to blame someone for their illness.

Lorís. How does self-image play into the matter of eating disorders?

As we all know, we live in a consumer culture, and one of the most powerful tools advertisers have to convince us to buy their products is to make us feel inadequate, like we should be more in some way, or like we need to change ourselves in order to find happiness. So what we find is that four out of five advertisements carry an attractiveness message: "Buy our product and you will look better"—or "younger," or whatever the case may be. "You will be more admired if you change your figure, if you look younger." These are the messages that we are bombarded with thousands and thousands and thousands of times a day. Even commercials for products like cars will put some photoshopped, attractive figure next to the car to convince us to buy it. They are using these messages every which way all day long. With photoshopping and other techniques for changing and perfecting these people that we see in the advertisements, the ideal becomes more and more unattainable. So that appreciating natural, healthy beauty is almost a thing of the past now.

Lorís. Why is our country so obsessed with the female body?

You know, I'm not sure I would agree that it is just our country. I think we live in a global culture now where the beauty ideal of our country is being disseminated all over the globe. With the Internet and other forms of media, our advertisement, movies and music are spreading all over, so that I think that we can't even say it's just our country anymore.

Why are we obsessed with the female body? I think that it's just a great vehicle for marketing, as I was saying earlier. When we're focused on an ideal female body, we're much more likely to buy what they are selling if we think it's going to help us reach those ideals. Really, it's a sad time for us women, to be objectified to the extent probably that we would have never dreamed possible.

Lorís. It seems to me that such knowledge has permeated Western society; we all know that marketing is made to target your insecurities, but no one does anything about it. To know something is different than actually acting on it. Two completely different worlds.

Lorís. Taking a broader look at things, women in Western cultures like to say they are liberated compared to other countries, but it seems to me that we're not as liberated as we think we are. Would you agree?

That is really an interesting question, with respect to internal obstacles. But I think there are a lot of external obstacles to women in Western cultures being fully liberated. Some feminist theorists believe that as women gain more rights in a society, the cultural beauty ideal becomes more unattainable as a sort of backlash to the fact that they are attaining more rights. Pursuing this beauty ideal becomes more and more challenging, almost distracting us from pursuing our new opportunities and goals. A couple of researchers and writers who have talked about this are Margo Maine[11], Susan Faludi[12], Naomi Wolf[13]. What they say is that the more time we have to spend on diets, surgeries, cosmetics, the less time we are going to spend empowering ourselves and utilizing our newly found rights. I do want to quote Jean Kilbourne[14] if I can. She has written, "The obsession with thinness is most deeply about cutting girls and women down to size. It is only a symbol, albeit a very powerful and destructive one, of the tremendous fear of female power" (1999, pg. 137). I really believe that this is true, and I think it does contribute to disordered eating and eating disorders.

Lorís. The more rights we get the more focused on body size we become?

They have actually done some research, and as you know, beauty ideals change over time. Back in the turn of the century it was the Gibson girl, very hour glass shaped, a little waist but very curvy. Then came the twenties, which was a period of liberation and

---

[11] Margo Maine is an American psychologist that focuses on eating disorders. She is the co-founder of Maine & Weinstein Specialty Group.
[12] Susan Faludi is an American Pulitzer Prize author, journalist and humanist focused on the human costs of high finance.
[13] Naomi Wolf is an American author and feminist activist best known for her bestselling books, *The Beauty Myth* and *The End of America*.
[14] Jean Kilbourne is an American author, speaker and filmmaker best known for her research on women's image in advertising.

freedom, and then the flapper was very skinny and kind of small. In the fifties, when women were very much staying at home raising kids in traditional nuclear families, women were curvy again; we had the Marilyn Monroe ideal. Then in the sixties, seventies, eighties, the women's movement comes back and the beauty ideal shrinks again. These are trends that some of these feminist theorists have studied and identified. That's what I was talking about.

Lorís. Do they ever explain why?

They speak of the backlash. Is it not interesting that they want a skinnier woman when we are starting to have more rights and power? Remember, in the twenties women were getting the vote as well, and so all of the sudden the beauty ideal shrinks. I don't think there's anyone out there making it happen; it's just an interesting trend, and it is disempowering.

Lorís. Eve Ensler[15], the playwright, also speaks about the power of the inner girl, and how that may frighten some.

We don't even say, "Oh, men are afraid of our power." It's just like the whole society is afraid of the shift.

Lorís. Women have been having conversations about their bodies for some time now, but men have not been heard yet. What do you believe this reveals about our society, with individuals who have such weakened relationships with their bodies?

It sounds like you are wondering—as we see an increasing pressure on women to achieve an unattainable beauty ideal that is more and more removed from what most of us would look like in normal conditions—you are wondering, "What about men? Are they also under some pressure to look ways that are hard to achieve for them?" I would say, yes. Men are under more and more pressure to strive for physical perfection. If you look at men's magazines, you see increased

---

[15] Eve Ensler is an American playwright and feminist activist. She is best known for her 1996 play *The Vagina Monologues.*

photoshopping and demands for them to look ways that are impossible unless they're spending hours and hours at the gym or dieting. And, more and more, they are using cosmetics to get to this look. I would add that the ratio of ads that focus on weight in women's magazines relative to men's magazines is 10.5 to 1. Which is about the same ratio of how many females relative to men have eating disorders. Isn't that interesting? Thus, we are under ten times more pressure as them to lose weight, and we have eating disorders about ten times as often. That's an interesting point.

Now the pressure that men experience is just a little bit different. About as many men are trying to gain weight as trying to lose weight because they're trying to get more muscular, big and strong. So a lot of men are aiming to get bigger and buffer. What we are also finding is a bit of difference between the heterosexual male community and the homosexual male community. Homosexual men tend to be under more pressure to get that sort of lean look, and so they are more at risk for developing the eating disorders of anorexia and bulimia than heterosexual men. Also, there are certain types of male athletes that are more vulnerable to developing eating disorders, particularly ones with certain weight limits or weight ranges that they need to be in to do their sport. In terms of what we know about what works for men in treatment of eating disorders, our knowledge is more limited because there are fewer that we have been able to study.

Loris. Are there fewer men in the studies because not so many of them are open about it?

That is a very good question. A final point to make about male eating disorders is that it's harder for them to come forward. It's mostly women who suffer from eating disorders, and most of the time in our culture we think of it as a woman's illness. If a man recognizes that he has some symptoms or that he is suffering from an eating disorder, there is an additional shame associated with that. They may be embarrassed to come forward and say, "I have an eating disorder." Also, it might not have been identified as readily by their doctors or therapists because the doctors and therapists also look for it more in women than they do in men.

Lorís. What about men's connection with their body? It seems they don't really have one.

Men with eating disorders do have some physical signs that they could recognize. For one, their testosterone levels do go down if they are malnourished, so they're libido and functioning go down. They get some warning signs pretty quickly as well that would concern them and cause them to want to seek help.

Lorís. Do you think it's important for people to develop strong and healthy relationships with their bodies from a young age? Do you think our society provides that type of education? Would you say the mass media holds some degree of responsibility?

Definitely. It's important for young people to develop a healthy, accepting, caring relationship with their bodies from an early age. Our society does not do enough to help with this. If anything, we are finding that at an earlier and earlier age, young people—both girls and boys—are receiving images from the media, from our culture, that contradict this message. Children as young as three, four, and five years old are worrying about being fat now. They're going on diets by age ten, or younger, at alarming rates. We have started to collect some data that shows that we're not doing enough to protect our children and to help them develop a healthy relationship with their bodies. We have a lot of work to do to turn this around.

Lorís. Do you think our society provides that type of education?

We're starting to. As you were mentioning earlier, Lorís, we all think we're media savvy, and we all know that advertising can harm us, but we're not so sure what to do about it from day to day. I think people are aware that we need to figure that out, especially our children. I'm actually really impressed with that aspect of Michelle Obama's campaign to promote health and well-being in children. The campaign aims to educate children about healthy nutrition and about being active and de-emphasizes the focus on weight as much as possible. I think that's going to be key to us challenging the focus on attractiveness and its narrow definition.

Lorís. I think one of the challenges is that every time we go into a new space, we always tend to fall back on what we already know. We seem to fall into tradition in the face of new territories; we tend to do what we know how to do. I think that's part of the challenge, to say, "This is a new space; therefore, it calls for new actions." It's difficult to come up with an appropriate response for a new experience. We just fall back on what we know.

Right, right. And what do we know? We know what the 7,000 media advertisements we see per day tell us. It's very hard to come up with a new paradigm right away. One thing that those of us who advocate for the prevention and treatment of eating disorders focus on is critical awareness. Critical awareness is a difficult, ongoing process that takes constant effort and work. It's really hard work, to look at every advertisement on a regular basis and think about how it's affecting you, why it's affecting you that way, whose agenda it's supporting, and whether or not it's in your best interest. How do you challenge that? It's an ongoing effort.

Lorís. Girls are getting eating disorders at much younger ages than before, is there any hope for the future generations to perceive themselves as both healthy *and* beautiful?

I never give up hope that future generations can believe that they are healthy and beautiful. I hope that projects like the one you're working on right now can help, along with a more pervasive effort by all of us as parents or teachers of our young generation to promote critical awareness and also to encourage people to spend less time with the media. Right now, approximately 40% of our time is spent in front of some sort of electronic media, whether it be our computers, our televisions, or our cellphones—40% of our day spent with these machines. I think one source of hope is to help people spend less time in front of electronic media and more time with each other (unless they are watching a movie like this).

Lorís. What changes would you suggest we make, both as a society and as individuals, in order to have healthier relationships with our bodies and lead happier and more fulfilling lives?

The same thing that would help us encourage our young children or future generations to have a healthy relationship with themselves will also help us. That is, less time with the media, more time with each other.

Lorís. Are eating disorders as prominent in other countries as they are here? If not, could it be that rates are lower where people spend more time with each other, being more communal?

You know, unfortunately we don't have such accurate data to distinguish the exact prevalence rates in other cultures. What we do know from studies of other cultures is that the more emphasis on electronic media, the more vulnerability and risk there is for eating disorders. Even though we would not say that mass media is the cause of eating disorders, it is definitely a risk factor. For example, a famous study called the Fiji study was done about fifteen years ago by Dr. Ann Becker, in which she looked at the beauty ideal and women's relationships with their bodies before and after television was brought to that country. She found that the beauty ideal there was actually a voluptuous, curvaceous one. After American shows like *Melrose Place* or *Beverly Hills 90210* became popular there, they found that people started going on diets. Once that started happening, a certain percentage of them began to develop eating disorders in a place where there were none before. So certainly, the beauty ideal is a factor.

Here is something Jean Kilbourne wrote about the Fiji study, "The influence of the media is strikingly illustrated in the recent study"—of course, it is not so recent anymore—"of young women in Fiji soon after the introduction of television to the culture. Before television was available, there was little talk of dieting in Fiji. 'You gained weight,' was a traditional compliment. And going thin, a sign of a problem." How about that! "Then, in '95, television came into the island. Within three years, the number of teenagers with risk of eating disorders more than doubled. Seventy-four percent of the teens in the study said they felt too big or fat,"—that's about what our data is—"and 62% said they had dieted in the past month." If that doesn't speak to the influence of culture!

But then of course, she explains, "This does not provide a direct causal link between television and eating disorders." We call it "a contributing factor," because one thing we can say is that ninety or a hundred girls may go on a diet, but only two develop an eating disorder. They have all watched the shows and seen the magazines; only two or three develop an eating disorder. That's why we have to be careful not to blame it all on the media. Can I add that? It's important to include this observation.

Lorís. Don't you have to be your own person? No one is pointing a gun at you and telling you to do something.

Well, it's not just that you have to be your own person. Although most of us are affected by the culture and the media and we get that message that we should do something about our appearance, most of us don't develop eating disorders. It's very important for us to realize that these are biopsychosocial illnesses; they are illnesses. Only a certain percentage of people are at risk of actually developing them. So those of us who treat eating disorders don't really think that the culture is the cause, but it is a factor, and it can put people who are already genetically vulnerable at risk. And it certainly makes the rest of us less content and happy with ourselves than we could be. Nevertheless, we don't say, "Advertisement and the media are the cause of eating disorders," and that's important to remember.

Lorís. Would you like to add anything else?

Yes, about First Lady Obama. Usually a first lady has a mission, and when Barack Obama was first elected, Michelle's mission was to fight childhood obesity. Those of us who treat eating disorders were very concerned that talking and talking about childhood obesity was going to shame and stigmatize children who are overweight, and trigger children, who are not overweight but who are afraid of becoming overweight, into eating disorders. Therefore, we in the eating disorder field wrote to her and said, "We know that shaming people will not work. What we really want to promote is health in our children, not thinness."

She has shifted a lot more, and we actually just wrote a press release with the Academy for Eating Disorders this week saying, "Thank you, First Lady Obama, for talking more about health and wellness." She knew what behaviors had to change: access to healthy food, playing outdoors more, being active. Now, she is just focusing on children's health and healthy lifestyles for children.

Lorís. "Health" is a very nice, neutral word. I feel that whenever you use more specific terms, people go to extremes, and you can't get them balanced. For some, "health" might mean playing outside, for others, reading more.

Balance. Are you spending too much time on the computer? It's not that you're not supposed to spend time on the computer, but should it really take up 40% of your day? It's balance. There's nothing wrong with a donut as long as you are not eating donuts for breakfast every day. Balance. I think that's the way her message is evolving.

James Hollis

Dr. James Hollis, author of several books, including *Finding Meaning in the Second Half of Life* and *What Matters Most: Living a More Considered Life,* was a professor of the humanities for twenty-six years in multiple universities. After training as a Jungian analyst in Zurich, Switzerland. He established his private practice in Houston, Texas, where he also served as executive director of the Jung Educational Center of Houston until 2008. Dr. Hollis is a retired senior training analyst for the Inter-Regional Society of Jungian Analysts and is vice president emeritus of the Jungian Philemon Foundation. Currently, he serves as a professor of Jungian studies at Saybrook University and Pacifica Graduate Institute.

I could sense my mother's anxiety in the car on the way to Dr. Hollis's interview session. When I tried to calm her down, asking, "What's the big deal?" she answered half-jokingly, "You don't understand. You don't understand who he is." When we arrived and he greeted us like any other polite person would, I glanced over to my mother, trying to speak through my eyes, "See? No big deal." Then we set up and asked the first question. When he began to speak, I was shocked, flabbergasted, in absolute awe, jaw-dropped for the entire hour. The deeper we got into the discussion, the more I stuttered and the more I worried about saying the wrong thing. At the end, we packed up and Dr. Hollis kindly helped us with our equipment. My mother glanced over to me, speaking through her eyes, "See?" My heart raced the whole way home.

Rose Mary. Could you describe the plight of men?

I think the central condition of men is of an extraordinary emotional isolation. I've seen it in so many of my patients and felt it in myself as a man. The way I've expressed that to women's groups when I've been asked to speak to them is to imagine three things: First of all, your closest circle of friends, those friends who you would talk to about your children, your marriage, your family, your body, your hopes, your disappointments is severed and you never have a chance to talk to them again. Secondly, imagine disconnecting from whatever the source is that you consider your guiding center: call it your intuition, your instincts, whatever. Imagine that, too, is broken forever. Thirdly, imagine that your worth as a human being significantly depends on your capacity to meet external standards of production, defined by strangers and has nothing to do with your personal life or your soul. You can see how those conditions would lead to an extraordinary isolation, and most likely self-alienation. That is the basic condition of most men. Most men are raised in a context in which those things are true. It means they dwell in shame and alienation, uneasiness, confusion, a lack of affirmation, and obviously, a lack of support and community as well.

Rose Mary. In that sense, society is built up in a way that does not allow men to express.

As horrific as sexual discrimination has been for women, it's been bad for men as well, because it has produced this one-sidedness of our personalities. Whatever we value about the human being is already truncated, already contained and constrained. Everybody suffers that way. One thing I know psychologically is that when any aspect of our personality is oppressed or repressed, it doesn't go away. It pathologizes in some way. It can pathologize through addictions, through violence, or through depression. Together, we see that wherever we suppress the living spirit of a person in whatever form— social, economic, political, or psychological—the human psyche reacts by pathologizing. I often work with people who are trying in a very personal way to deal with wherever their suffering has been. It comes not just from family origin, but also from those social constructs and constrictions within which all of us work.

Rose Mary. Why haven't men fought against this?

Many years ago, I was asked in Philadelphia to give a talk on the psychology of men, and I agreed to do so. I found myself un-characteristically resisting preparing for it, and I waited till the last minute, which is not my normal pattern. Then I had to ask myself about that resistance, "Why are you resisting?" I asked myself. And a voice responded, "Well, because this is shameful. This is risky. It exposes me to possible criticism or ridicule." Therefore, it occurred to me that what I had been doing all my life was sharing my secret with other men. All men are enlisted as little boys in that conspiracy of secrecy. One of the things you swear to is not to reveal yourself to others, because if you do, then you will be vulnerable and shamed. Every little boy is shamed, as girls too often are; and as a result, he learns to keep his mouth shut and to repress his own emotions, not to risk speaking to other people.

Now, one of the interesting things I found is that when I started my practice thirty-five years ago, I was seeing nine women to one man because it was at that point still a cultural inhibition for men to go into psychotherapy to explore what was going on in their lives. I don't advertise. People come here just because they find their way here, and today I am seeing seven men for every three women. That percentage has completely flipped to the other direction. I think it's a good sign. On the one hand, it means more men are in trouble psychologically, but it also means there is a greater permission for thoughtful people to address what is going on in their life.

Rose Mary. When you were talking about shame, it reminded me of Robert Bly[16]. What is the relationship between men and shame?

I think most men swim in shame, and it shows up in two profound ways. One is a lack of permission to be who one really is, because we feel we have to meet those standards that have been made for us. Secondly, you see it in grandiosity. The whole macho culture is an overcompensation for inner shame. Where you see boastful attitudes and where you see people investing in status symbols, what you are seeing psychologically is a compensation for what you are not seeing inside. There's a poem by a Swedish poet in which a person is being shown around a new city. He's supposed to be impressed by the exterior of all these great buildings and their façades, and the poem ends by him saying, "I see, and I am impressed by all this, but then I have to conclude that the slum is inside of you."

I think for most men there is a whole series of painful, secret feelings of inadequacy; and of course part of the conspiracy is to hide these feelings from the world and to hide it from yourself as best you can. But the psyche knows better, and sooner or later it shows up.

---

[16] Robert Bly is an American poet and activist. He was the leader of the mythopoetic men's movement, and he is best known for his book essays, *Iron John: A Book About Men.*

Most men come into therapy with feelings of failure. In other words, a woman would approach therapy by saying, "Well, it's a natural thing for me to talk this over with someone." But for a man, it's already a sense of personal failure, "If you were competent, if you were on top of your own situation, you would have solved this on your own. Since you didn't, you're having to consult some stranger to do it." That's already a confession of the trap of shame.

Rose Mary. Would you say that there is a feminine part of us that is not being allowed to express itself in men?

Yes. I am not comfortable with the terms *masculine* and *feminine* because I think they have been too tied to socialized roles and social constructions in the past. At the same time, what we have historically called the *feminine* is something that exists within men as well. And if men are in some way shamed for accessing that and living it, then we are driven toward more self-control and repression. That leads to an emotional disconnect. That is why I asked you to imagine a person who has cut his link to his own guiding source within. You realize that that person has depended entirely on external parameters for who he is, how valuable he is as a human being, and what he is supposed to be doing with his life. What Jung called the *"anima"*[17] is the inner feminine of the man. Jung's work in the nineteen twenties was revolutionary in that he recognized the so-called "contrasexual" within each person: the masculine dimension in the female psyche and the feminine dimension in the male's psyche. Those terms have since been critiqued and deconstructed repeatedly because they were rather gender-bound, yet there is a truth to the concept. "Anima" is, after all, the Latin word for "soul," so it has to do with a man's relation to his

---

[17] In C.G. Jung's school of analytical psychology, the Latin terms of *anima* and *animus* are used as archetypes of the unconscious mind. *Anima* represents the inner feminine side in males, whereas *animus* represents the inner masculine side in females.

own soul. And if that is a troubled or distanced relationship, then he is literally without guidance.

Rose Mary. In Spanish, "alma," the word for "soul"—like the Latin "anima"—is also feminine. Would you say that the relationship of the soul to the feminine is the reason why it is being attacked?

What I have said to men is that, "Your soul is not feminine; it is part of who you are as a man." Perhaps because it is experienced from the standpoint of consciousness as an "other," its otherness is construed as the feminine because that is the "other" for most men. The anima, again, is an image of soul. We need to ask what soul means. Soul is that part of us that longs for meaning, the part that suffers in its absence, and looks for it often in vicarious ways. It is always at work within us, and when it is violated, something terrible happens in the body, in our emotional tenor, or in our external life. Often the violation of the soul is what leads to outer violence as well.

Rose Mary. How has the patriarchal system affected men and women?

A patriarchal system is by definition one-sided. Jung's simplest definition of a neurosis was "the one-sidedness of a personality." We are actually rewarded for being one-sided in terms of our economic systems, so patriarchy would be any system that emphasizes hierarchy at the cost of equality, or that emphasizes roles at the cost of flexibility and sets unofficial standards by which everyone has to be evaluated or judged. There are places where those values are necessary and important, but when they are one-sided they are not compensated by the alternative value. Many people do not find in their families or places of business the kind of easy acceptance and psychological support that is so necessary to be healthy.

Rose Mary. In your book you talk about men's rites of passage. How does modern life express such transitions?

Our ancestors understood that the passage of the human psyche from its overdependence in childhood into the rigors and independence required in adulthood was a formidable task, so they developed very elaborate rights of separation. Typically, these had six stages. The first was a physical separation from the parents, often by way of ritual kidnapping. Second, came the symbolic "death" of the child's identity, because what is dying is the psychology of infantile perspective and of dependence. The third stage involved a ceremony of rebirth, because a new being is emerging. The fourth stage, the "teachings," usually involved three different layers: one, the archetypal teachings, involving who one's people are, where we have come from, who the gods are, and what the end of time is about; two, the rights, privileges, duties, and the polity in that particular culture; and three, the specific tasks of hunting, child bearing, defense, fishing and agriculture, etc. The fifth stage was typically an ordeal in which the most important characteristic was isolation, so that each person might learn, "I have resources within that I have to draw upon in service to functioning in the world." After an extended absence, the sixth and final stage was a return to the culture as a psychologically separated person. Generally speaking, except perhaps for things like the military, in our time we mostly have uninitiated adults walking around in large bodies but often governed by the psychology of childhood.

We can talk about our whole culture having an adolescent tinge to it. When you think of an adolescent, you think of a short attention span, black/white values, high distractibility, impatience, and avoidance of sustained rigors and expectations. Multiply that by millions, and you have an entire culture that is narcissistic, easily diverted, and looking for the next sensation of the hour. In the helping professions, adolescents used to be defined as roughly twelve to eighteen years old. Today, the age during which people are still considered psychologically adolescent is more like ten to twenty-eight.

Rose Mary. In your opinion, does the men's movement attempt to recover the feminine side?

I don't think there is much of a men's movement. I think it was popular for a few years, and my feeling at the time was that it would be short lived; it had a certain faddish quality to it. That isn't a criticism; I think the movement was honest and sincere. I also felt, however, that the majority of men would never be associated with it, again because of that shaming dimension we have talked about. I also saw that within most groups, hierarchies immediately began to form. In the land of the equal, some are more equal than others. In the long run, that dynamic just reconstitutes some of the old patriarchal values. I think that the men's movement, while still technically alive, is basically psychologically dead in our time.

Rose Mary. In Under Saturn's Shadow, *you state that the power of the feminine is in men's economy of the psyche (1994, pg 11). Could you elaborate on that?*

If a man does not realize that his inner source is his best guide, then he is going to be at the mercy of whatever is happening outside of him. Now, to call that source "the feminine" is to fall again into those gender definitions that are perhaps not the best way to approach this idea. To recognize this source is to realize, as I mentioned before, that your value won't be judged by your bank account, or your status in life, or your children; such judgment would be a devaluation of the soul in the individual.

The power, the insurgency of that inner life is terrifying in a man. I had a client who came to me once and reflexively ridiculed the fact that I had a box of tissues in my office, which is sort of standard for therapists. I said, "What's the issue here?" He said, "I would never cry." I said, "Don't you think there are tears locked up inside of you?" He said, "Oh no, we have better ways of dealing with things than that." Well, I knew that his prognosis for therapy was not very good, because he was so threatened by that inner life that a box of tissues was something he had to distance himself from, and he had to repress what was most powerful within him. Of course he was there at the insistence of his wife, and that well-intended coercion lasted only a few times, and he drifted away.

Whatever gets repressed systematically, particularly from generation to generation, builds up a tremendous pressure inside. That's one of the reasons why you see so much rabid homophobia, for example. This is particularly true among adolescent youth, because they're the ones whose hold on their emerging masculinity is so fragile that it is threatened by literally anything. That rejection of the so-called "feminine," which they see outside of themselves, is part of the continual restraining of the emergent self, which is thereby isolated and pathologized. Anytime you ask an individual to fit a role, you are already truncating that human being's possibilities. This happened to women, and of course women have rightly protested it and gained a greater consciousness. The men's movement represents a belated response to these limiting roles, and it has not been sustained efficiently.

I do think our popular culture is evolving a bit. Ideas are available to men today that were not available to our fathers, and this is beginning to change the climate. As I mentioned, my own practice has altered significantly. Without my advertising in any way, these men have found their way here to consider their lives in perhaps a new way.

Rose Mary. Could you speak a little about how all of this plays out in romantic relationships?

I have a book on romance where I discuss these ideas (1998). Romance is a popular fantasy that holds that one can find oneself through the other. The earlier a person is in the process—the younger a person is psychologically—the more likely that person will be to look for completion through the other. If a man is drawn to a particular woman, he is perhaps driven unconsciously by his desire for her to compensate what he needs to address himself. Genuine maturation obliges us to ask the question, "What am I asking from that person that I need to ask of myself?" This is quite contrary to a romantic fantasy because a romantic fantasy believes, "I am an incomplete person; you are incomplete; but by fusion, we will become a whole person." That is very seductive, very powerful, and after a while leads to stultification and dependency, and usually dissatisfaction. The irony is that the more loving way to treat a partner is to be able to state, "My emotional well-being is in my hands. My emotional development is something I am accountable for." This is to lift the expectations about one's own emotional and personal growth off of the shoulders of the beloved.

Rose Mary. You mention in one part of your book: "When we remember the patriarchies as a cultural contrivance, an invention to compensate for power-lessness, we realize that men, contrary to widespread opinion, are more often the dependent sex" (1994, pg. 48). *Can you elaborate on that?*

Any one-sided system is going to be threatened by its opposite. A patriarchal system is inherently based on power. Whoever is on top oppresses whoever is below them, whether it be women or other men. Men also get enlisted in hierarchical struggles. As Joseph Campbell[18] once said, a person can spend an entire lifetime climbing the corporate ladder, only to realize that it is placed against the wrong wall. Ultimately, this leads to delusional emptiness. That kind of external ambition has the power to dominate a person's life and dominate his or her emotional development. Of course, women in the corporate world are experiencing those same kinds of pressures. Increasingly, they are finding that the rat race—which demands that they sacrifice aspects of their personality—is the way to advance in the company or the only way to get more competitive than the people they are competing against. The psychic cost to any hierarchical structure will weigh on both genders.

---

[18] Joseph Campbell is an American mythologist and author. He is best known for his concept of the "Hero's Journey."

Rose Mary. Do you find that the lack of the feminine has been detrimental to our environment?

What we have historically called "the feminine" has been a respect for "relatedness." Archetypally, we speak of the earth as a kind of collective image of the "Mother." The personal repository we have of that archetype is our body. Most men think of the body as a machine that wears out. If you can't get a replacement for it, you're just dead or thrown onto the junk heap. Wherever there is a diminution of relatedness there is going to be a cost. Our treatment of the environment is symptomatic of a diminution of the so-called "feminine." From the beginning in the book of Genesis, you find the whole patriarchal fantasy of assuming domination over the earth instead of living in harmony with it, controlling and dominating it. Sooner or later, the repressed values are going to revolt. One of the central ideas of analytical psychology is *the principle of compensation*, by which we mean, whatever is one-sided in the conscious culture exerts pressure on the unconscious and will show up somewhere else. Our impending ecological crisis is an example of the pressure building in nature itself, which will seek to restore balance at our cost. Wherever there is unbalance, a price will be paid, and that repressed material will gather enough energy to exact its revenge sooner or later.

Rose Mary. It's common for people to confuse "the feminine" with "feminism." Could you comment on this?

I think any one of those terms quickly becomes associated to other ideas in a limiting way. I would like to get rid of the terms "masculine" and "feminine." However, we also have to account for the different kinds of energies and values that they were perhaps pointing toward historically. Irene de Castillejo was a Spanish analyst who talked about the difference between "focused awareness," which is task-oriented; and "diffusive awareness," which is relational (1997). She pointed out that we need both, whether you are a man or a woman, in order to be a full person in relationship with others. We can also say that every human being has two basic needs: nurturance and empowerment. Historically, we assigned nurturance to the feminine and empowerment to the masculine. Well, women need nurturance and empowerment, and men need nurturance and empowerment. The question is, "What nurtures me emotionally? What gives me a sense of permission to take who I am into the world?" Wherever there are obstacles, these become the impediment to realizing one's fuller humanity. In that regard, both men and women are ultimately accountable for both nurturance and empowerment. I don't think those are necessarily replacement terms, but I think they are trying to get at what the terms "masculine" and "feminine" once pointed toward

Rose Mary. What changes would we need to enact in order to transform into a society that embodied both nurturance and empowerment?

First of all, we would have to have more flexible social and economic systems that allowed the interchange of roles and duties among men and women. We would also have to provide things like childcare, for example, equal opportunity, equal pay, rights that represent values that our society claims to be addressing but is still doing so in a very haphazard way. Our social, economic, and political structures would have to reflect these values. For example, I know two men in particular who don't want to be out there in the rat race, who want to stay at home and take care of the children; but they're subject to ridicule from their friends, including women friends, as if there were something inadequate in them. These are people who would consider themselves enlightened and modern, and this sort of reverse discrimination is present even with them. We are a long way from the kind of changes that I think individuals need to go through.

This raises a question about the dynamics of change. I do believe change comes primarily from individuals. We can make social changes, but what brings the public awareness to the level necessary to realize those social changes is a situation in which enough individuals are dealing with the issues in their own lives. Individual work leads in turn to changes in social attitude, which then lead to changes in legislation, and so forth. Simple questions like equal pay for equal work, which I think is part of our law now, are still not practiced. Therefore, there is much work to be done yet.

Lorís. You mentioned in your book that the more we are able to disentangle something from the feminine, the more we will be able to relate to it. Sometimes we need to take out a part of ourselves and look at it face to face so we can recognize it. Can you elaborate on that please?

A basic principle of all relationships is that a relationship with another person is no more evolved than the degree to which the relationship with oneself has developed. "Whatever is neglected within me, I am unwittingly dumping on my children or on my partner. If I can lay claim to what needs to be addressed and developed within me, then I am going to present a more complete person to my partner and my community." Again, it requires a measure of maturity, accountability, and courage to take that on rather than expecting someone else to do it for us. I think we can reserve the word "love" for the person who is able to say, "I have to work on my own stuff and take on my own developmental assignments." Then you may say, "What is the purpose of a relationship?" Well, it serves to support the growth and development of each party, and when that happens relationship is a wonderful thing. When that is opposed, when people's growth and development are threatened, it can be a horrific constriction. One could say that the function of a relationship is to support the growth of each party toward becoming a complete human being. Once in a while you can actually see those kinds of models. However, I think the younger we are, or the more psycho-logically undeveloped we are, the more we're going to expect the other take care of us, or compensate for us, or cover those bases that we're not covering ourselves. I cannot split off and say, "I will take care of the economics; my wife will care of relationships."

Marie-Louise von Franz joked once about the pure thinking type who comes home and says, "Hi honey, I'm home—but it's none of your business."[19] She was using it as an example, of course, of a very split individual. We have had split roles to live up to for millennia. Fortunately, those roles are being deconstructed, and with them comes the challenge—again—of nurturance and empowerment. I am accountable for facing that challenge. The value of "the other" is that it pulls me out of my narcissistic circle, and in encountering the otherness of the other, I am enlarged. It becomes a dialectical, developmental relationship. The other is not here to confirm me; the other is here to be an "other." If I am capable of tolerating that, then I grow. We grow because, together, we are forming a third, and more evolved, relationship that results from internalizing the otherness of the other.

---

[19] Marie-Louise von Franz (1915-1998) is a Swiss Jungian scholar best known for her work on the psychology of fairy tales.

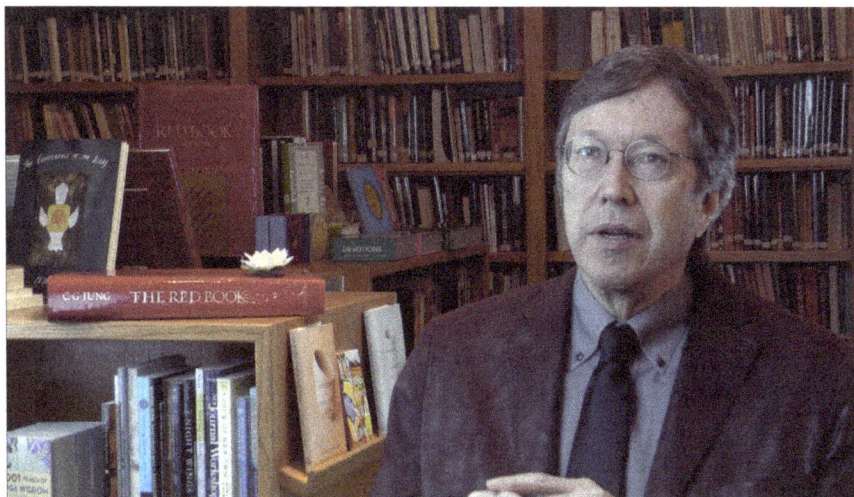

Jerry Ruhl

Dr. Jerry M. Ruhl, co-author of *Contentment: A Way to True Happiness*, *Balancing Heaven and Earth*, and *Living Your Unlived Life* along with Jungian analyst Robert A. Johnson, is a lecturer and clinical psychologist living in Houston, Texas. Dr. Ruhl is the executive director of the Jung Center of Houston and a faculty member in the Saybrook University graduate studies program in Jungian studies. Dr. Ruhl sees patients in private practice, facilitates dream groups, and presents seminars around the nation.

Sometimes life changing events divide your life into before and after a particular event. A conversation I had with Jerry was one of those events for me. I was telling him about a particular dream that disturbed me, a dream I have not forgotten to this day, and while I wasn't exactly waiting for him to decipher what it meant, part of me was hoping for a hint. What I received was a comment, just a brief sentence, "So, you're like a warrior. You always need to be fighting for something." With that observation, Dr. Ruhl named something within me that I had always known, but hadn't understood. That afternoon I met a dangerous little girl, and I decided to take her under my wing and test her capabilities, this time with love. Thus, post-conversation-with-Jerry life began.

Lorís. In your opinion, how might we reach a balance between masculine and feminine principles?

That's a big question. I'd to break it down into two pieces. The first question is, "What is 'masculine,' and what is 'feminine'?" Swiss psychiatrist Carl Jung had the idea that every person, regardless of whether they are a man or a woman, has the spectrum of masculinity and femininity within. He argued that gender differences can have profound effects on the unconscious psychology of men and women. Recent studies from evolutionary psychology, neuroscience, and neuroaffective research support Jung's ideas. Both genders have elements of both the masculine and the feminine; the difference is a question of emphasis.

Males have significantly larger neuronal densities in the preoptic area of the brain that is involved in sexual activity. The nucleus is triple the size in males. The anterior cingulate gyrus—responsible for attachment, bonding, and the panic system—is more active in females. These scientific findings relate to observed nurturant and social behaviors in females and higher aggression and dominance in males. Female brains have a proportionally larger corpus callosum than males; this is the structure that connects the more "emotional" right brain with the more "rational" left brain, and could explain less facility with emotional and holistic processing in males. Female brains show greater hemispheric coordination and use both hemispheres in speech. Whereas males typically use only the left brain for speech.

These basic biological differences in gender temperament are highly resistant to socialization.

I am not advocating for the validity of gender stereotypes, but such studies are interesting because they suggest how "male" and "female" distinctions are innately recognized by the human brain. Men and women should be free to explore the masculine and feminine aspects of themselves without prejudice or negative judgment. The point is that the terms "masculine" and "feminine" are not arbitrary social constructs, but biologically based, innate ideas—however abstract and thematic—that shape the way we make symbols. As a result of the conscious processing present in both sexes, we can reflect upon these tendencies and ignore or modify them to some extent. There are not rigid boundaries between the sexes, but rather "soft" boundaries. The relative degree of differentiation between genders is only partial, and there will always be overlap. The degree of masculinization or feminization of the brain probably determines the degree to which people identify with either "essence" in themselves.

Jung used the term *anima*, Latin for "soul," to represent "femininity" as men come to understand it through their development into adulthood. Nature provides men a way of recognizing and understanding "feminine beings" through the inner image of an ideal feminine; and she symbolizes all sorts of entanglements and heartaches, but also the promise of bliss and redemption. This archetypal image contains "feminine" aspects of a man's psychological makeup, and expresses that which is archetypally feminine—i.e., the feminine tendencies that are less differentiated within his masculinized brain.

The brain can generate all sorts of female images innately. When this imagery is used to symbolize a part of a man's mind, she has all the qualities of a goddess: She is powerful, timeless, ubiquitous, and protean. A man projects this onto the woman he falls in love with, and then is disappointed when, after a few months, the projections dissolve and he realizes he is in relationship with a mere mortal woman. The American pastime is then to blame your partner and move on to look for someone else who might heal your childhood wounds, fill in your missing pieces, and bring you the ecstasy and wholeness that can only truly come from your spiritual life. We call that romance.

Just as men have an innate internal image of woman as part of the perceptual-conceptual system, women have an innate image of man, which Jung called the *animus*. Often, it is related to the father, the first experience of the masculine. This impacts women's relationships. However, men and women have different value systems. Unlike men, who appear to have a consistent system designed to seek out a particular kind of female all the time, women have a system designed to detect essentially different kinds of partners. Cross-culturally, mate value for women is largely determined by status, prestige, current resource holdings, long-term ambition, intelligence, interpersonal dominance, social popularity, sense of humor, reputation for kindness, maturity, height, and strength. So, men and women both carry an inner image of the feminine and a feminine ideal within them that plays a major role in relationships and who we are attracted to. We look for that ideal. This is tricky business, talking about definitions of masculine and feminine. They're not necessarily identified with one gender or another from a psychological perspective.

Then we have this other issue of the patriarchy. The patriarchy has to do with power. That's why the Western male ego has such trouble coping with feelings and love. These make a man feel out of control, because they are secretly what every man most needs—to be ecstatic and lifted out of the sterile confines of our tight little ego worlds. The feminine has historically threatened this drive for power and control, and so has been suppressed, at great cost, not only to women, but to all of society. Our feeling life is in great poverty. Patriarchy has produced wonders of materialism and technology, but our inner life has been sacrificed. I don't think happiness is something we can just order up, though it is in the U.S. Declaration of Independence that we have the right to the pursuit of happiness. Americans in Western culture increasingly think that happiness is something that can be provided through material goods or positions of power. People think that hate is the opposite of love; actually, the opposite of love is power. If I really love you, we share an identity. In power, I want to control you for my own ego needs. Both men and women live this way, and the result is tragic.

Part of the problem of patriarchy, is that it is one-sided. Our economy is based on material production, the pursuit of money and power. That is the tail that wags the dog. This approach does not ultimately produce happiness. What happens to feeling? What happens to empathy? As a depth psychologist, I was once asked to give a talk at an exclusive all-boys private school in Ohio about the archetype of masculinity. I struggled for days trying to understand what is archetypally masculine. The best I could come up with is that the masculine—remember, this is found in both men and women—has something to do with a heroic attitude, a heroic quest. We can see this in masculine stories from ancient times. Odysseus, Parsifal, Luke Skywalker, Harry Potter—these are examples of going out in quest for something and being tested along the way. The classic hero learns how to fight dragons and rescue a fair maiden. There is also a theme of winning a prize of some kind, or building something such as a new perspective, a new idea, a new religion. Patriarchy is one of those institutions built by masculine questing. The masculine institutionalizes these prizes, sets boundaries around them, such as the Church or the Corporation. The sky gods who reside on high and make rules are masculine. Along the way, the feminine and the earthly were diminished by patriarchy. The feminine is always pulling us into life because, after all, women carry life.

Lorís. Patriarchal society doesn't really give us space for language that relates to feeling. Could you elaborate on that? Do you think we should include more of that language?

Language will tell you a lot about how a society values a particular faculty. When we don't have feeling and relatedness, our lives become very one-sided. We have fine differentiation of "things" such as a hundred words for different kinds of nuts and bolts, but less than a handful of words to help us understand love. We are far less adapted in our relationships. Look at the divorce rate. Half of all marriages will end in divorce. Clearly, patriarchal society has valued progress, power, materialism, expansion. We have wonderful technology and poverty of feeling. I struggle to come up with language to talk about feeling. I recently taught a class on yearning, for example, trying to differentiate it from other types of emotions. Yearning contains desire; it contains an awareness of loss and even death, an awareness that the moment is precious because it will not last. You can hear yearning in French impressionistic music. Debussy could layer chords together with a genius for knowing how certain tones could evoke certain emotions in us. His music is filled with yearning. We have that language, music, to help us understand feeling.

Today, so many of our social institutions are in crisis. They're too one-sided. We've become fascinated with power and filled with God-almightiness. The rise of the feminine is a necessary corrective to patriarchal institutions. I see this in the medical field. The increase in the number of women doctors is changing the way medicine is practiced. They don't want to operate like cogs on an assembly line. They want to balance family with career. They want to have relatedness with their patients. They are fighting an uphill battle, however, because big medicine is big business. The institution is more about money and power, and the feminine is concerned with healing, which we have lost because it requires that you spend more than seven minutes talking technology and dispensing pills. Patriarchal institutions are entrenched, but feminine energies are essential to reforming and revitalizing them. This must continue. There is no stopping it, even though society will go through times of backlash.

Lorís. There is almost no talk about the relationship between men and their bodies. Why do you think men have been so distanced from creating this relationship? Do you believe this could have an effect on men's psyche?

Absolutely. This goes back to Judeo-Christian traditions that are so strong in our culture, in which the body is viewed as sinful. We probably have Paul to thank for that. Under patriarchy, the body is either viewed as a sexual instrument, which of course is played up in our culture; or as an instrument for work. Many men relate to the body as a pack animal that they boss around and force to do certain things until it no longer responds and starts to break down. This is an embodiment of patriarchy, power over nature. We think of our bodies as being somehow other. We think, "My body is rebelling against me," as opposed to the more integrated, "My body is I."

Look at the sad evolution of sports. Professional sports are not about play anymore. They're really organized brutality, expressions of power using hired combatants whom we passively watch and maybe identify with. You see that increasingly in college sports, college athletes as pawns in a game of big money and big power. Sadly, it has filtered down to high school sports, which used to be the last domain where we could use the body as an expression of the spirit. The body should be a sacred and inspirational place to test the limits of your strength. I think our alienation from it has been generated in patriarchy.

Lorís. Has the feminine been associated too much with women? Does this end up penalizing men so that they don't want to be associated with the feminine?

As I said before, we have to be careful about stereotypes. Both men and women have access to feeling. I think the masculine is associated with the creation of hierarchies, while the feminine questions the old forms. Both are necessary and both coexist in men and women. The problems arise when we get too far one-sided, both individually and collectively. That's the problem of patriarchy, a one-sidedness that then gets rigid and lacks the flexibility to bring in new energy, new ideas, new creativity.

Lorís. How do you believe an ordinary individual could reach a better balance between the masculine and the feminine? How could he or she start?

While some of our institutions need to break down, I am optimistic. As the feminine rises, hopefully we will have a more balanced relationship to the earth, to our own bodies, and to the divine. It all has to do with a change in consciousness, and that begins with the individual. Regardless of how our institutions, whether the government or the church, try to defend the old status quo, things must change. The Internet is a great example. Look at the freedom that has been unleashed with the Internet. Now intelligence agencies are shown to be using it to shut down our freedoms, to control our lives. But despite those efforts to control, the new energy finds a way. The promise is a wonderful marriage of the two, the masculine and the feminine, don't you think?

Lorís. I never thought about it that way. But the Internet is so chaotic; I guess it is a feminine space.

I equate the feminine to the uncertainty principle. There is something about the feminine that does not like too much order. When things get too structured, too hierarchical, the feminine comes in and shakes it up. That is what makes life interesting!

Lorís. And frustrating! Taking everything to a very personal level, how could an individual reach a balanced life?

To achieve balance between the masculine and the feminine, listen to your inner life. It will tell you when you're getting out of balance. Listen to your dreams, listen to your bodily symptoms, listen to the people who drive you crazy. Those are all bits of information that tell you about how you are out of balance in some way. Jung famously said: "I call God all those things that cross my willful path that upset my plans, that turn my life around unexpectedly, for better or for worse." He is suggesting that we listen to the unexpected, the so-called chance events that pop up in our lives instead of trying to push through our willful agenda all the time. To keep your life in order in our culture, you need to have a strong ego, to pay your taxes and balance your checkbook, to go to school, to get accredited in some career, all those things that are necessary. But don't forget to listen to your inner life.

Estela Seale

Psychologist and social worker Estela Seale studied clinical psychology and philosophy at the Universidad Pontífica of Mexico. She has worked at the Starlight Hospital since 1998 and is the coauthor of the collection of short stories *Vitrales*. Seale has been a lecturer for psychology symposiums worldwide.

I wish I could present this next interview through an audio file, just so you could hear her speak. Although to receive the full effect, you would have to listen to her speak in her mother tongue, Spanish. I've listened to Estela's voice and observed her move ever since I was young. Every time I heard, "Estela is coming for coffee this afternoon," two things would pop into my head: cigarettes, and the sound of her velvety rasping voice. The way she speaks would get me every time, her words playing with the cigarette smoke dragging out of her lips. I've always told my mother that I wanted to speak like Estela, and I'm still working on it. Maybe one day.

Lorís. To you, what is the feminine?

That is a very smart and intriguing question; precisely because even to this day, many people associate femininity with passiveness and submission. Most people consider the feminine or femininity to be passive and tolerant, and to some extent, subtly aggressive. For me, femininity has nothing to do with that. On the contrary, for me, femininity consists of the capacity to receive not only life, but livelihood; the capacity to create and generate atmospheres of warmth and nurturance. It can show itself in an intellectual arena, in creativity and the arts, in a domestic atmosphere, in friendship and the sharing of emotions, in job communication and motivation, anywhere.

Lorís. Can you talk about how women have been premised with a fractured paradigm of what we call the feminine?

Since the old days, we have been permeated and bombarded with the sad and gloomy passages of St. Augustine through St. Thomas Aquinas, describing women as nature's frustrated attempt to create a whole being, which would be realized in man. Therefore, since childhood, women were considered defective, pseudo-males who failed to generate the best self. As a result, women were considered by many cultures to be incompetent, suffering from a congenital mishap and they needed to ask for forgiveness by working hard, behaving properly, and aligning their norms with the establishment in order to be validated and accepted. They start the run, so to speak, with a tremendous handicap, because as Octavio Paz used to say, they had existence before discovering their own essence. For me, that was the rudest form of abuse women have suffered throughout the generations.

Lorís. How do these problems affect women with their relationships in life?

Terms like "the opposite sex" or "the opposite gender" generate such confusion. We are not "opposite" to anybody; we are complementary. We belong to the same species; so, to denigrate the role of women is to minimize the role of men as an entity. We are partners in the enterprise of generating life, not necessarily in the form of a human—another baby, a marriage, and so on—but in mutual enterprises that will create the world as a better place to live in. To develop a full human experience, it is necessary to accept one's identity, to identify the gender orientation of each of us as a gratifying, happy enterprise for individuals evolved in the most common and modest partnership that exists, a human couple.

Lorís. There is a constant demonization of the female body that started with the ascetics, before Christians. Today, we find it in the media, the entertainment world, and religion. Can you elaborate on this?

Sadly, we did some research at the hospital on this. In the past, women were held captive to keep them from communicating with their lovers and generating all kinds of evil to their offspring and to their spouses. Therefore, they needed some sort of intervention when their spouses were at war. Any number of instruments were used, physical objects, like shields and binding shoes that caused so much pain in women's feet that they were doomed to be seated, captive at home. Chastity belts, used to impose chastity and modesty, were tremendously abusive to women's bodies—as if modesty were something that needed to be provided externally and not born out of genuine conviction. Women have always been told who they needed to be and what they needed to do without having the opportunity to discover who they were and where they wanted to orientate their energy in order to become the best person that they were meant to become. Women are deprived of that right. They are told they need to be obedient, to be submissive to their spouses, to clean, to cook, not to laugh publicly or dress provocatively.

Historically, even today, in several cultures—in Africa, for instance—the shapely body of a woman attracts men. Neuroscience has demonstrated that men were attracted not only to symmetric features, but to shapely forms, roundly forms in women, because they were the ones more likely to conceive, to keep the baby and the pregnancy healthy, and even to survive in times of wild hunger and starvation after delivery. These women were more fertile and more adapted to survive in adverse conditions.

Presently, women are told to work to deform their bodies, to hurt their feet, for example, with horrendous platforms that put them at risk for bone fractures and spinal defects and malformations. They are told that this intense mechanism that is perceived even instinctually by primitive cultures, is not okay; they need to not have a feminine shape, to resign their physical femininity because it's not "trendy." This self-denigrating attitude has permeated our culture to the point of generating brutal distortions of self-perception, so that a woman thinks, "If I'm a little bit overweight or shapely, I'm not okay. It's not the world that imposes this distorted expectation on me," she thinks, "the problem is me because I'm eating too much or not working out hard enough, or not exercising, or undergoing surgery, liposuction or whatever cosmetic procedure will allow me to look less and less and less feminine and less and less human." It's important to reflect upon and explore the deep motivations for this kind of attitude.

Lorís. To ask us to stop eating would be like asking us to stop breathing.
It absolutely goes against survival. We are permeated by a culture that is alienating and self-destructive. Probably the worst form of self-destruction is the one that pushes a little girl, a young woman, a young adult, to stop eating; in other words, to stop being. It is to ask a person to be nonexistent. People realize this but continue to practice these compulsive behaviors, because they are looking to fulfill one of the three basic human needs: the sense of belonging, to be needed, to be validated and loved. "In order to be loved and accepted," the logic

goes, "I am going to need to stop eating, even if I have to pay for the consequences of that action." They are ready to pay the cost for it without realizing the torment they're going to go through, the alienation and nothingness.

Lorís. We have spoken before about how the worst thing that has happened to a woman is the idea that she should not accept herself, the feeling that there is something not right about her. Can you elaborate on that?

In an over-populated world, many governments are interested in natal control. So when a little girl is born, in many cultures it is seen by the family as a catastrophic event. Women are sometimes traded for cattle or hens, or for a little money. In these situations, women essentially are taught from day one they are second-rate, third-rate citizens wherever they belong.

There are some countries in which equality of the genders has been taken on through the painstaking efforts of their citizen women. Even though I hated the extremism of women walking through Times Square with bras in their hands, I really do subscribe with Marguerite Yourcenar, that women constituted a new form of slavery.

Presently, we are charged with the duty to maintain the family, to raise the offspring, to look beautiful, to pretend and appear as if we are forever and always twenty-one. We are told to be intelligent, but not to the point of exhibiting it or making the man around us insecure, to provide financially for our families, and to keep the house impeccable. All these things are contradictory in and of themselves and demand lots of energy drain and waste on the part of women.

Lorís. Where or when do you think femininity started to be perceived as inferior to masculinity?

Well I think that in many cosmological myths of creation—those of ancient Sumer, for example—women introduced evil into the world. Among the ancient Greeks, we find the myth of Pandora. In the Judeo-Christian cosmic creation myth, Lilith at first, and then Eve lead men to the Fall. Even for the Greeks, women were considered a necessary evil. Though Plato held that some of them, privileged beings, belonged in the academy, those were only symbolic aspects of femininity. In practice, they were excluded. They were not competitive in any arena that required scientific or intellectual elaboration. Women have been working to lift this sense of guilt and shame for centuries. It has required tremendous analysis as a group, as a team—from the silence and isolation of a living room, of a master bedroom, of a shack—for each individual woman to realize that she does not need to live someone else's life, to live fulfilling the expectations that have been imposed on her. This has been a genuine victory, and it needs to be validated.

Lorís. In this movement in which the particular strengths of women are identified, are men denied their emotional sense of being?

To some extent, yes, what is considered feminine is to share emotions, to experience sympathy and empathy, an ability to be moved by the feelings of another, and it is an ability that women have, undeniably. I don't know if it is a multigenerational learned or imposed behavior, but it is a fact. If that is seen as feminine, and men are forced to suppress whatever feminine trait they might have: it's socially unacceptable for a man to cry, to manifest sadness, even to be chronically depressed is considered a sort of treason to the group. Therefore, if you attack anything you consider a feminine trait, if you demonize it and put it on the back burner of the social strata, without knowing it, you are diminishing the role and dignity of men as well.

Lorís. Why are women the victims of so many the eating disorders?

As we mentioned before, being born a woman makes you a defective, incomplete human being from day one, and women are the first to be blamed. In my day, British-European couture—European couture as a whole—was to blame for asking and demanding smaller sizes in order to spend less on fabric and materials, so that their products would be cheaper to make and their fares more profitable. Later on, it was insinuated that women photograph better with less weight. These kinds of things result in the brutal tendency that has been imposed on women, asking them to work toward contradictory goals. Work out; study hard; work enough to be self-sufficient, and even to earn a living for you and your family; and at the same time, deprive yourself totally of fat nutrients. At the end, it is kind of like asking women not to be fertile, not to reproduce, not to be alive, like those movable hangers that have been described as the "ideal" by many famous designers in many cultures. I think this is one of the crimes against humanity that has gone unpunished in our days. I have treated many people, from ages fourteen up to twenty-five with several severe eating disorders. These people are lacking teeth, they're losing their hair, they have osteoporosis, they were unable to maintain a pregnancy or delivered prematurely, all because of the anguish of being rejected. It wasn't an egomaniacal obsession that forced them to become so self-destructive, but the desperate need for acceptance and belonging. I think that kind of self-destructiveness is always based on shame, guilt and fear, which do not allow them to be present in their own lives.

Lorís. You mentioned something about how thin women photograph better, and now people's lives are based on the images presented in the media. In today's world, it seems that it is more important to look a specific way than to be.

Exactly, I could not agree with you more. We live in an appearance-oriented world in which to appear is more relevant than to be. I recently read an article that suggested that, before our economic crisis, we experienced a moral and axiological crisis. The author is absolutely right in his description of a world in which the goal is to appear ethereal, without any focus on thinking better or acting better, it is absolutely ridiculous. Elongated figures, like the gothic cathedrals are so absolutely breathtaking because elongated and slim always suggests eternity, something that attends and points to the heavens. Humankind is not composed of spiritual beings trying to become human, nor animals trying to become spiritual; we are simultaneously a body and a soul incarnated.

We need to accept the fact that we fulfill and follow the laws of gravity. We need to have some sort of body mass and fat in order to survive. Basically the brain is nourished with glucose and is constituted by fat and water. Therefore, if you deprive the brain from fat—fatty acids for instance, and glucose—you are dooming yourself to dementia. Cultures that have been forced into malnourishment through food deprivation are generationally less and less intellectually oriented and tend to have learning disabilities. It is related to nutrition. Now then, if I bought the message that in order to be loved, approved of, and validated, I needed to look twenty years younger, perfect like a picture on Facebook, I would literally need to be drowning myself into psychosis. Psychosis is an altered perception of self. If I need to weigh eighty pounds in order to feel accepted, and I'm convinced of that pseudo-reality and accept it; I will live in an altered state of perception. I'll always think of myself as fat when in reality I'm a genuine living skeleton. Well, it's not only normal to be a healthy weight; it's desirable for me in order to have a fulfilled and healthy life.

Lorís. If change is always a product surging from the inside out, what has stopped women from achieving the internal change necessary to change society?

Basically, I would say it is fear. Fear to take chances, fear of rejection, and fear of their own potential. It is a behavior learned across generations. Neuroscience has proven that little girls, when exposed to toys like guns, cars, and trucks; and little boys who are exposed to dolls, little dresses, and makeup; they all play indiscriminately, proving that gender preferences in play are the result of a learned behavior. It's an imposed role model.

Whenever a little boy exhibits what is considered to be a "girlish" trait, he's punished, mocked, bullied by his friends, even by his own parents. Little boys are not supposed to feel or act out emotions. They aren't supposed to experience fear. It isn't socially tolerable. This creates tremendous anxiety disorders in them. Diminishing the feminine role and its value doesn't go without consequences for humankind as a whole, including men and boys. In order to be respected and integrated, men need to respect women as their equals, as their partners.

During the Crusades of the Middle Ages, women were left at home alone taking care of the goods of the kingdom, while their husbands and lovers left for war. These women spent their lives productively generating art without precedent in history. They created poetry, troubadour writing, and all kinds of handmade artifacts still seen in cathedrals, all by women. In the Second World War, women in the United States of America were the ones left at home, and the economy didn't collapse. Women put aside their fears about being productive or rejected by their spouses, by their parents or grandparents or even siblings; and they took the risk to enter not only the universities and colleges, but also industry. They generated a high level of pro-ductivity that made this country the recognized leader of the Western world.

Women need the credit that they deserve. If a woman decides to search her soul to discover her true self, not what others want her to be; and to take chances, even if it means risking rejection and judgment, she should be able to do it without the experience of being ostracized. This is a hard price she must pay in some cultures, but she will be rewarded—absolutely rewarded because she will then discover that it's not fair or decent to be forced to live someone else's life.

Debra Andrist

Dr. Debra D. Andrist is the chair of foreign languages at Sam Houston State University and winner of several grants and awards for service, teaching and administration. She focuses her sociological research on class and gender in literature. Her scholarly work includes international presentations, books, translations, articles, reviews, interviews, and movie guides. Dr. Andrist has directed study abroad programs in Mexico, Spain, and Ireland, and was an exchange professor in Chile and Canada and a Fulbright-Hayes scholar in Morocco.

Because of circumstances and her perfect Spanish, every time I had spoken to Dr. Andrist previous to our interview had been in my mother tongue, Spanish. She always interested me because her clothes always matched perfectly, sometimes even with her jewelry.

She seemed sweet, but I could never get a full view of who she was. I went to lunch with her and my mother one day to invite her to participate in my film, and we brought up the topic of the feminine and women. That's the first time I heard Dr. Andrist speak in English, and that was the first time I really saw the strength and the experience she carried within. I finally understood who she was and why she was. It was like meeting her for the first time, and I loved it.

Rose Mary. You wrote an article about Marianism. In ancient societies, women had a place. What happened? Or what happened that caused women to become second-class citizens?

I believe biology was a factor, initially. I base this on a lot of readings, particularly Gerda Lerner[20], who wrote on the birth of patriarchy. Initially, it makes sense that, if a woman had a child to care for, she wasn't as free to go out and hunt. Yet women were always the gatherers and did the main part of the maintenance of the family. Men, because they didn't have that attachment they had to protect, could have more freedom. There was a little bit of biology early on, but of course that's not very applicable at this point. According to a lot of the reading I have done—and one of the books I really like is *When God Was a Woman* (Stone, 1976)—I honestly think that patriarchy came with monotheism. My article about Marianism traces how things changed in the Roman Catholic Church in order to give precedence to men and to the replacement of female gods and gods of fertility and so on, with male gods, and then, with one male god.

Rose Mary. Do you find it detrimental to the development of a person to deny attributes considered feminine?

---

[20] Gerda Lerner American author and historian best known for her work in the field of women's history.

It would be detrimental to both sexes to have femininity defined in a very strict way that sets it as inferior to masculinity, because it plays into all those nasty tendencies to power that we *homo sapiens* suffer from. Sometimes I say to students, "Whatever happened that kept us from getting above chickens and pecking orders?" So, it's bad for men; and naturally, it's bad for women.

Rose Mary. I have another question about religion. In your perception, how did we end up conceiving that divinity was purely masculine? Do you think it had to do with wars, with which side got the power in the end?

I think it does. There are a number of works that explore how we make God in our own image. According to biblical tradition, it's not only that we were made in God's image, but that we made God in our own image. Those with the power get to define the terms!

Rose Mary. Why has our inner and outer femininity shrunk to the point that women are not valued in the labor force or the sacred sphere?

As a supervisor, as a department chair in a university, I have to admit that part of this has to do with the concern about whether or not people will be able to fulfill their job requirements when children get sick. If the responsibility were equally divided, it would be different. But there is still a tendency—and I see this in my own life, in my sister's life, and in my friends' lives—for childcare to be the major responsibility of the woman. I think our society has started to change in terms of men taking equal responsibility for their children, recognizing men as equally nurturing. But we've got to hit some kind of a center point with both of the sexes.

Women have contributed to this problem just as much as men, in that some of us are lazy; some of us are comfortable; some of us are too well-socialized. Women who don't carry their part of the workload have to take some of the blame, as it were, for others who are doing more. It's not that I think we ought to demand rights, because that seldom works, to demand; but, just like in the social movements of the sixties, somebody has to say, "Hey wait a minute!"

just to call attention to the fact that things are not as they should be. It's not just about equality, not just about being fair. Things are not as they should be for the best psychological health of men and women, the best economic, or other health of society.

Rose Mary. Why is it that in our society we're still denying women their equity and men their femininity?

You know, this is something that I go through a whole lot. I used to be an absolute Skinnerian; everything was environment. The older I've gotten, the more reading I have done, the more studies that have been done, I really see a factor in biology and brain chemistry. We can't deny that. It's a situation in which something gets going in a society and everybody buys into it because somebody is getting something out of it, either negative or positive. The main thing, I believe, is comfort level. It's easier, and I am going to admit this too, it's easier to manipulate a situation, because it's faster. To bat your eyelashes and be cute and need help, and you get what you want faster than if you are just plain assertive and an equal. That's the problem. How can we find, as women, a balance between saying, "I am your equal; I deserve equality," and at the same time work toward that equality with maybe a little bit of assertiveness, "Hey, you will and you must."

Rose Mary. Why do you think the majority of women have not joined together to work towards equality?

It's a combination of things. There are women who want to be the queen bee. They want to be the only one, the exception in a society that does not have equality according to sex. However, as I mentioned before, the opposite also occurs, those women who see an easier route in the traditional ways. Even those among us who have been activists for a long time are torn because we have been socialized in a certain way, and it is underlined by society. As I have gotten older I have thought to myself, "Gee, some of my friends were a lot smarter to be ladies who lunched, because they are supported financially; they don't have to go to work. They can be at home with their kids."

In social movements you can never get everybody onboard. You've got to have a loud bunch that calls attention, together with those who just applaud along, in order to get things changed. It's not very dramatic, and it's not very pretty, but that's how things happen in a society. Screaming certainly doesn't work, because then everybody writes you off. While I really have a problem with the whole idea that a woman has to be twice as good to get twice as far, that's what has taken us farther than those who yell louder, and certainly than those who just settle in comfortably with the way it's always been.

Rose Mary. If change is always a product surging from the inside out, what would you say will change society?

That's a problem because the inside is so effectively socialized by the outside, and as long as the outside is still given over to tradition, as it is in almost every society in terms of inequality of the sexes; the inside is going to be torn. My generation would be emblematic of that. The Betty Friedans of the world are my mother's age or a little older. We are the ones who are torn between what is comfortable, what works, what we have been socialized for; and the freedom we were also socialized for—was to have careers, to have options, to make our own decisions, and to be able to self-define. I think that some younger women have made strides and not known it, particularly in childcare. It is now just a given for women that the men are going to be equally responsible for nurturing and in the home. But it's not all ok, yet. It's going to happen on the inside and on the outside, but because each feeds the other back and forth, it's just going to take time.

Loris. Do you think it's getting better for younger generations or is it just a catch-22?

Oh, it's unbelievably better. A few years ago, during the Clarence Thomas / Anita Hill situation, I was steaming at the implication that women have to say "No" by not saying it outright. A friend of mine, a professor at Baylor, said to me, "Hold on just a second here." He said, "my wife," who is a little older than I am, "thought that she could go to college, but that she would be a nurse or a teacher; that was pretty much what you did. "It never occurred to my daughter that she couldn't do anything she was intellectually capable of, and she's a big-time crusading prosecutor in New York City." That really brought it home for me. Things have changed enormously, not enough, not widespread enough, but certainly in terms of careers and attitudes.

The thing I worry about is the backlash. Lots of women who then want to have it all can, but they have to have help to do it. So they fall into traditional ways, because those are their models. They fall into being stay at home mothers, if they can afford it; or they take a sabbatical, if they are academics; or they take time from their careers. Very few men do that, but it is happening. I would use my older son as an example. He had his dream job. He was a sports commentator on television. He went all over the world. When he and his wife decided to have a baby, he changed. He went into news production so he could be home with their little daughter three days a week, and they only have to have the nanny two days a week. This was practically unheard of before, but every once in a while, there's a guy who does that. You see a number of younger men, possibly motivated by their wives' expectations, sometimes because of their mothers, who have been socialized differently.

Lorís. Is there anything else you would like to add?

I think this is a really important project. This is the kind of thing that helps make change because it's an educational tool. It's not threatening; it's not plotting; but people are going to listen to it. I think it's the kind of thing that moves things forward. We need more projects like this because we have a lot of people thinking it's all okay now because women can be astronauts. It's not all okay now. It's better, but there is still a long way to go.

Patricia Gras and Aurora Losada

Patricia Gras is a passionate storyteller and journalist, and the recipient of over 170 journalism awards including six regional Emmy Awards and seventeen national Tellys. With five languages and three master's degrees, her work has been recognized with honors from many organizations, including American Women in Journalism, American Women in Radio and Television, the Texas Medical Association, and many, many more. She has also been inducted into *Who's Who of American Women*, *Who's Who in the Media*, and *Oxford's International Biography*. She joined Houston PBS (KUHT-TV) in 1990 to host the respected public affairs program *Almanac*, followed by the award-winning, nationally syndicated series *Living Smart with Patricia Gras*, which aired on over 200 PBS channels. In her twenty-four-year career, Patricia has interviewed such notables as former President Jimmy Carter and President George H.W. Bush,

Secretaries of State Madeleine Albright and Jim Baker, best-selling authors Alice Walker, Isabel Allende, and Daniel Yergin, and many other intellectuals, international personalities, and celebrities. Currently, Patricia is the founder and director of Gras Productions.

Aurora Losada is a Columbia University graduate with two master's degrees in journalism and public affairs. She was a financial editor with Reuters in Miami, an editor of the *Wall Street Journal Americas* in New York, and the Washington, DC, correspondent for one of the most influential newspapers in Spain, *El Mundo*. Presently, Aurora is the editor of the award-winning Spanish-language publication *La Voz de Houston* and lavoztx.com, as well as one of the *Houston Chronicle*'s editorial managers. She is a panelist on the Houston Public Media radio show *Houston Matters* and one of four judges in the South Regional Committee of the Marshall Scholarships granted by the UK government. Her areas of study include Latinos in the USA, women's issues, and coding.

I look up to Patti and Aurora. In fact, my brother and I thought we might adopt them as honorary aunts. I have never experienced a single moment of boredom in their presence. They don't talk about insignificant things. They talk about the world, politics, women, and economics, and they find the space to laugh about it. I invited them to interview for my film in exchange for dinner and wine. I think Patti accepted because of the dinner, and Aurora because of the wine. Nonetheless, they both happily agreed. I wish I could have turned my camera on sooner when the time came to sit down and talk, because the conversation and jokes that went back and forth between them before the start of the interview was priceless. The instant I mentioned we were recording, they snapped back into their professional selves. What you are about to read is only an edited version of a typical night with Patti and Aurora.

Lorís. What is femininity or the feminine?

Aurora. I think you can say femininity, the feminine, is both strength and delicacy, both firmness and love, a very different understanding of life in general. When you are a woman, everyone thinks that to be feminine you have to answer to very specific standards or stereotypes, and I don't think that's the case. I think that you're basically nurturing others in a different way, understanding others in a different way.

Patricia. I would add that feminine means nurturing power, strength, intuition, love, compassion, all the right-brain emotional characteristics of a woman, and of course the sensuality of a woman, that a man does not have.

Lorís. Do you think your definition is in line with what is presented in the media?

Patricia. I think in the media you have more sexual overtones. When you say "media" you're not just talking news, but also television, right? I think in the media there are sexual overtones and the woman is often seen as an object. I don't consider that to be the feminine at all. I see the feminine as something sacred.

Aurora. I agree, and I also think that to some extent, there is some perversion in the way the media and TV play with two different stereotypes. One of them is the sexual object that you can definitely see all around, but then the other one is the supposedly smarter, more knowledgeable woman who can have an articulate conversation and can convey a very strong and deep message. The way the media presents that, TV in particular, is that it has to be either/or. You rarely see a woman on TV playing an important role in the news, for instance, or saying something that is strongly compelling, while at the same time being sexual. The same is true of the reverse. For the most part, all the women who are supposed to be compelling and knowledgeable are not attractive or not young. I think that's really perverse, because it completely distorts what a woman is.

Lorís. In your opinion, what triggered this portrayal of women in the media?

Patricia. Ratings. When you're talking about the media, you're talking about ratings, and usually you get ratings through two things: sex and conflict. It works to have the violence against women, which I am totally against, especially in the media. Again, conflict and sexuality are the things people want to watch, unfortunately. It must have to do something with the instinctive, the survival of the fittest. I don't know why, but I see it a lot and I think it's quite upsetting.

Aurora. I think part of it is because there are very few women at the helm of media companies. I'd like to think that if there were more, things would change, even if only a bit. There is a lot of testosterone in the meeting room where decisions are made in the media realm. Having said all that, however, I think part of the reason is because women—and I should include myself here—usually don't speak up about these things. The media just reflects "what people want," based on ratings. Again, I think it's related to the fact that women are rarely at the head of those companies.

Patricia. I agree somewhat that there are not enough women in positions of power; but unfortunately, the women who are in positions of power act like men, and that's another subject altogether. The feminine has to come back and has to make a difference in that area. We blame men a lot but some men are balanced between the masculine and the feminine. But some women, the kind of women who run companies, they lose their balance and become more like the male energy, because they think that's what works to get ahead or to be at the helm of a corporation or company.

Aurora. I agree. I was watching an interview with Hillary Clinton today, and it was so absurd because it had to do with the fact that she has been showing herself in different public events lately with no makeup and with her glasses on—and those are thick glasses. So, the interview was about some sort of criticism about this, and her reaction was like, "I don't give a damn about this." That's the kind of personality or attitude from women, particularly when they are on TV, that conveys to other women, "Hey! What's the fuss about it? I am who I am, and I don't care if millions of people in the world are watching me with no makeup and glasses. Because you know what? I have a huge brain. I have a top position, and, really, I know what I'm doing."

Patricia. We're starting to see a shift toward more women who are going to be running corporations. Theirs are the kind of management skills that are needed. You no longer see the authoritarian type of system, the more male, patriarchal style. You're going to have a more nurturing, listening, compassionate management style. That's what's going to succeed in the future. So, I think females are going to come into play if they value their femininity, because I do think we have to value our femininity in order to tap its strength use it without fear that it's not "manly" or "intellectual" enough. It goes back to balance. Men or women, I think there are few people running corporations whose female and male energy is balanced enough for them to do a good job. These people would be able to use both their intellect and their intuition.

Lorís. Both of you who come from the media environment, and in that context the way you think is different than most of the other women in the media. They are against these ideas. They want to look beautiful.

Patricia. There's no doubt that you have to look good to be in the media industry. If you're a woman who looks good, who makes herself up and looks pretty, feminine and sensual; if you're a woman like that who knows how to carry yourself, you're going to do better. And there's nothing wrong with that. What I see as wrong is that you're having to use those good looks in place of your intellect to get ahead. I do think you have to use both, but there is power in being able to declare: "No, we shouldn't have to look nice; men don't have to look nice, why do we?" There's a power in our beauty, but we shouldn't depend on our beauty to succeed. It's only a part of it.

Obviously, we are getting to a point in our lives, in our fifties, when we're getting older, and we don't see that many women in television or in the movies who are getting the best roles or the best anchoring jobs after the age of fifty. That's a problem with our society because we're supposed to be beautiful all the time and young all the time. I don't know that the problem is related more to women, or to the society of aging. We don't like to age, we want to look young all the time, when, in reality, most of us are not young.

Aurora. And it's not just in the media, but in society in general. One of the things that has happened with women in the workplace is that there is no doubt about the advantage enjoyed by a woman who is beautiful or stylish or graceful. And to be completely honest, I think we know it and we sometimes use it. The problem is that there comes a point at which you're trading something away. Instead of being yourself in addition to whatever beauty you possess, whatever grace and good manners, you should also make a strong showing of your intellect, your knowledge, your capabilities and your skills. That's not negotiable. That's not tradable.

I think that's a problem in general with women, particularly in media, because it's an environment that makes you feel more insecure; you're totally exposed all the time, though more so in TV than in other media outlets. But the same thing happens in print, and probably in radio, and online in the social media era. Once a woman has a position and some sort of leverage in a company, it's going to be incredibly hard for her to go places if she lets herself be trapped by the beauty factor. At some point, she needs to be willing to let go and say, "Hey, you know what? I want to do this and we're going to do this no matter what." At that point it doesn't matter if you're beautiful or not, or if you're an angel or not; what matters is what you want. And honestly, I think we have a long way to go. We are the first ones who need to understand that nobody is going to come and do that for us.

Patricia. I totally agree. If I were to stop and think, "Oh I'm fifty-something. I can't do anything because it's over for me. My career is over because I'm too old"; if I think that way, that's what's going to happen. A man never questions whether he's going to be able to make it at fifty. He thinks, "Okay, this is what I want. I don't care how old I am." That's what we can gain from the male energy, the ability to go ahead without thinking, "I'm a woman. I'm conditioned to think that no one wants to see me anymore." We have to train ourselves in that area to be more like them. If you think about all these stereotypes start asking yourself, "What are they thinking? How am I doing?" you can go crazy.

Aurora. I think part of the problem is that, in general, women try to avoid conflict—not every woman, but in general. We're always looking for ways to get along and to make things smooth. Conflict is part of day-to-day life, but it's also part of any position in any company. The conflict is generated with both men and other women, by the way, not only with men. But once you start coming into conflict with men in particular, particularly a man in a high position, it's even harder. You start trying to back off because you understand that it's going to be really tough.

I think this can only change when this generation or future generations of women start educating younger women in a different way. We must convey to our daughters that it's okay to stand up for yourself, to pursue whatever you believe is good even if you make a mistake. Believe in yourself. I don't think that's been the message from one generation of women to the next. It's not about men being terrible because they rule the world, or the media and the industries we're talking about. The problem has more to do with women not understanding that the only way to cut the vicious cycle is to do something about the next generation of women. Until we do that, nothing is going to change, really.

Lorís. The media is also a part of that education, so how can you change it? To me it's like women have been misrepresented for many years in the media. Media is an exhibition of society's unconscious belief that women are objects.

Patricia. Well, I think we've come a long way. I mean, my God, even in the last ten years you've seen an improvement. You see female characters in the movies and in television who are strong and sure of themselves, who are feminine, and use their power in a positive way. So, I think we've come a long way. And as Aurora said, once women start owning their own companies, the change will continue gradually, and our daughters will be raised differently than the way we were raised. You may try to teach your daughter what you learned from your mother and find that it's not working anymore. Their peers are a lot more confident. They're savvier and a lot more international, because they have access to more news and they've seen strong women all around the world. Now, you don't just see Hillary Clinton; you see Leymah Gbowee[21] from Liberia, and other women in all these other parts of the world, patriarchal societies where you wouldn't think they'd have the strength, and still they're forging ahead.

Aurora. I agree, and I also think the question of representation has to do with who makes the editorial decisions. Let's not forget, everything you see on TV, everything you read in the paper or anything you listen to on the radio, has been previously discussed, agreed upon, and edited. So, someone, or a group, has decided, "This is what we're going to serve you as our news menu today." When more women—and hopefully, women who agree with the ideas that we're talking about here—have higher positions in these editorial meetings, they can have a more authoritative, stronger voice about what exactly goes into tomorrow's paper, what exactly will be shown in today's news shows.

Patricia. Yes, it's changing already.

---

[21] Leymah Gbowee is a Liberian Noble Peace Prize winner who led a women's peace movement to end the Second Liberian Civil War in 2003. She is the central character in Abigail Disney's documentary film *Pray the Devil Back to Hell.*

Loris. It's been changing. But there are still very few women behind the decision-making positions in the media.[22]

Patricia. Yes, we still have a long way to go.

Aurora. It's in media and in other industries as well. On the one hand, it's been very hard for women to break through, although I agree with Patricia that we've come a long way. There's definitely still a long way to go, and not just in the media. Just to give you an example, look at the top one hundred companies here in Houston. There's probably one woman heading one of those companies. And it's not because there are not enough women prepared for it in terms of the skills, the academic preparation, and the expertise; it's because we're still having a hard time breaking the glass ceiling. You can blame the many years of patriarchy, or you can blame a corporate environment that is still harsh toward women in companies, because these things are true. Or you can blame men; you can blame your background; you can blame many, many things. But the truth of the matter is, when we stop blaming and we start acting then things will change. In the media and in any other industry.

Patricia. You also have to consider the women who have children and families and therefore so many more responsibilities than men. I don't think that's ever going to change. So, do we measure the success or the happiness of women by what percentage of them are running companies? That's another philosophical question to be addressed. To me, running a company isn't necessarily the greatest thing you can do. Maybe it's not what makes us happier, or more productive, or producers of quality work. That's another issue.

---

[22] According to a research study done by The Women's Media Center called "The Status of Women in the U.S. Media 2013," females only owned 6.8 percent of 1,348 commercial television stations in 2011. Men are also given preference in covering important political issues such as the presidential election in 2012. For example, a bar graph showing sourcing by gender during the presidential election between January 1, 2012 to November 6, 2012 shows renowned news organizations such as CNN: State of the Union with Candy Crowly with to source 84.7 percent males, 13.8 females and 1.5 percent unknown.

Aurora. I agree with you. The truth of the matter is that companies will benefit from having more women, and so will society in general because women manage in a totally different way, and that's also being feminine. It involves more compassion and creates more synergies with others. And once you feel like you're secure in your position, you tend to listen more. That's not only good for the companies, but also for the world.

Lorís. By the same token, I see the same lack of feminine values in the media. You can see that through the objectification of the female body. All you see in the media are women with huge breasts and huge rear-ends. Women and even men are being looked at exclusively from the masculine perspective. The media doesn't care about anything else.

Rose Mary. But this is also a cycle, because that is what the consumers buy. So, where does the responsibility of the consumer lie in relation to the media? I don't think consumers are even conscious of it. People just go out there and buy what they want. The three of us have seen this. If you bring something that is visually attractive to men, it sells more. With Literal Magazine's website, I get more hits on the nude or suggestive covers. Have you found this to be true?

Patricia. Well, sex sells, right? I think there is a different value system for men and for women in the media. For example, I notice that newswomen in Spanish-language media have to wear low-cut dresses and stand in a certain way. They're doing it because men want women to be sensual. They don't want to think of women as professional and doing their job. My theory is that this is part of a cultural tradition of machismo in the Hispanic world, where the woman is supposed to serve the man, be there for her man and do whatever he wants. Women are still saying, "Yeah, okay. Let's go ahead and look that way, because that's what sells." They don't understand what they're doing. They're just accepting a paradigm in which they are property and others decide what they will look like and how they're going to sell, and as women, we aren't saying no. I see that this happens more in Hispanic media than in American media, and personally, I refuse to do it as a journalist.

Aurora. It's pretty evident that women are objectified, particularly on TV. I don't know to what extent this is a question of what the consumer asks for. There's an ongoing dilemma about this issue: Is this what people are asking for? Some of the newspapers I worked at took this attitude, "This is what people ask for." I would respond by asking them to define for me the term "people." "People" in this context is a very abstract thing floating in the air; but really, who are these "people"?

Having said that, I believe part of the problem is that TV is constantly competing with itself. When you have a woman with brains who is also beautiful here, and a woman with brains who is not so beautiful there, you're always going to pick the one with brains and beauty. That's a default response that is unavoidable. I'm not sure about this, but it's very likely that it happens the same way with men. Just look at CNN. Some of their anchors and reporters could be Calvin Klein models. We're not just talking about women here. This doesn't mean that the anchors aren't good journalists; it's that they were picked for a very specific reason: they were one among twenty-five who not only knew how to do their job, but also had amazing looks.

Again, it's also important to consider content. I remember the recent case of a girl who was gang-raped. A group of football players drugged her till she was comatose. The kids were very young; I think the number one tragedy was that they didn't even know what they were doing. Obviously, they were all found guilty, and in CNN's trial coverage, when they read the verdict CNN was expressing so much pity for these boys who had ruined their lives at a very young age because of what they did on a crazy night; and I remember thinking that it was outrageous that nobody mentioned the victim. Not once. So, it's not just about what you see on screen or the appearance of the anchors or the reporters; it's also about the content. I think women who are working for big networks, newspapers, or websites like Huffington Post—and I would include myself here—should take responsibility for enacting change from their different positions. Because really, if we don't fight for change, nobody will.

Lorís. Aren't women the majority of the public watching TV? Who benefits from those women on TV showing their breasts?

Patricia. Well maybe I think it's because that's a standard. The standard is, "Oh, if you have nice boobs and you look sexual, then you're going to get more men." So women look at other women on TV and say, "I want to look like that so that I can get more men."

Aurora. It also goes back to education. It always goes back to education. About 0.5 percent of the population is uneducated but brilliant and gifted with a bright mind and personality; everyone else needs an education to understand certain things. If you're lucky enough or privileged enough to have an education and say, "I really don't want to watch this; I don't feel related to these women showing boobs and wearing short skirts and high heels with their long brown hair"; you'll probably change the channel. But let's not forget that there are many women out there who have no education and probably identify with those women. It's terrible because it perpetuates the stereotype, but that's the way it is. And of course, the TV outlets know that.

Patricia. I mean it's definitely ratings. But I always wonder if the ratings would go down if they didn't dress that way. I don't know.

Aurora. Let's talk about Spanish TV in Spain for a minute. Every time I go, it's not only these sexual messages and images I see, but even worse. They're picking the dumbest women they can find to run TV shows. Why are they doing that? It's almost like an act of violence against women. They're insulting all female viewers because they're conveying that this girl was the best one they could find, when it's absolutely not true. There are sure to be many women who are better prepared and more experienced, who can put on a better show, but they intentionally pick the dumbest girl they can find. It's laughable, and people consume it, and it's kind of cruel. They want to see a stupid woman running a show. I think, to some extent, that "violence" is the word.

Patricia. It's a type of violence.

Aurora. Yes, it is.

Patricia. I think it's really important for us to be balanced in our own lives, to have the male and the female parts of us in balance, and not to think all the male stuff is bad and all the female is good, or vice versa. Women do tend to approach things differently because of the fact that we have children and the fact that we have to multitask, but if you and your partner are balanced, then that is the ideal. Right now, the world is unbalanced in patriarchy, and it's a mess. I think once we can get more women involved in bringing balance, things are going to get better. I'm very hopeful.

Aurora. It comes down to knowing who you are and what you want, and believing in yourself. We cannot expect change to come from outside. We cannot expect others to do this for us. We need to find a way to be successful in the workplace and successful as mothers or fathers, while taking care of ourselves, believing in ourselves enough to know what we want and convey that to others effectively. It's all about self-confidence.

Patricia. Brilliant answer.

Lorís. In a more concrete way, how would you change the workforce to make it more balanced?

Aurora. That's a very good question. In the first place, I think you need to have more men and women working together at an executive level, because whether you like it or not, that's where the decisions are made. Everything that is decided at that level comes down to affect the rest of the workforce. Secondly, I believe that it has to do with the natural relationship between men and women. If I trust you, no matter whether you are a man or a woman, I am going to have a good relationship with you, personally and professionally. We need to trust each other more. We need to see each other with different eyes. Women need to start looking at men not from the point of view of extreme feminists, but simply as people you want to work with because you have things to learn from them, because they are your colleagues. Men need to do the same. They need to understand and acknowledge that women are able to do many things for which they traditionally were not recognized.

We have been talking about how the world is changing, how businesses and the economy are changing, and we haven't yet mentioned that women—both from third world countries and also here in the United States and in Europe have themselves been a very powerful engine for change. Women in India, for instance, are building up small businesses through micro-credits, or microloans. Here in the United States, women multi-task like crazy, and this is one of the most valued skills in the workforce. Women tend to care for their family, for their elders, for whomever is suffering, and we have time no matter what for friends, for spouses, for children. You can translate those skills to the workforce. Also, as Patricia was saying, we are much more collaborative. I think it's part of what we are. We can provide more understanding in the workforce. Women can be stern when they need to be stern, yet at the same time always look at every single aspect of a situation. They have a more comprehensive and more global view of what is going on. They come up with different solutions.

Patricia. As the economy changes, as we change our roles and men become more feminine while women become more masculine, I believe that companies who value the female paradigm—collaboration, understanding, and compassion—these companies will do better. If this happens, more women will automatically become a part of the workforce. If I had a daughter, I would want her to be an entre-preneur. I would want her to start her own company, to be the decision-maker. I wouldn't encourage her to go into the corporate world, because the corporate world is going to take a long time to change. However, we women are highly entrepreneurial, period. Especially Latino women.

The world is changing and I think we are shifting to a more feminine paradigm. We're not there yet, far from it, but we can create change by being entrepreneurs, owning our own companies, and hiring the people who we want to hire. If I had my own company, I would hire 50 percent men and 50 percent women. However, the men would have to be in tune with their feminine side, and the women would have to be in tune with their masculine side. It goes back to the yin and yang. We can't keep bashing men for the imbalance, because we have allowed it to happen. Maybe the male paradigm in ourselves is allowing men to take over. How do we stop that? I think you have to own your own business, or start your own business. It's happening already, though I don't think it's changing in the corporate world as fast as it is in the other world, where you have people starting their own businesses.

Aurora. If a woman isn't an entrepreneur, the only way to change things in the workplace and to bring more of the feminine in, is to be in a situation of power. When you're in a position of power, you can just say, "Things are going to be this way." That's something I think women need to know how to do. Sometimes, we're apologizing even before we make a decision, lest someone doesn't agree with it. It's interesting to watch all these women who are coming into positions of power in very specific high technology companies, as they try to incorporate the feminine in the workplace. It's not just a grassroots movement going on in the workplace. Somebody with a lot of power and a lot of decision-making is saying, "This is how things are going to be from now on, whether you like it or not, because this is what I want you to do."

Patricia. Think about it, the guys who are running Facebook and Google, they are in touch with their feminine side. They're allowing all kinds of changes to facilitate bringing more women in. We have to work with men to change things; we can't do it ourselves. There are men who will work with us to unite the two paradigms.

Lorís. If change is always something that comes from the inside out, what has impeded women from achieving this change?

Aurora. I think we've made a lot of changes, but even in the Western world we still have a lot to put up with. Patricia was mentioning women with children before. And there's nothing harder for a woman than having to deal with being a good mom, a good employee, a good professional, a good wife or a good partner, a good friend, and a good daughter. Part of what we still need to work out that was left undone after the feminism wave of the sixties and seventies is that we're not superwomen. How to do you work that out? I have no idea. But it's very strenuous, and I don't think the next generation will put up with it.

Patricia. But isn't that the male paradigm? To say that to be successful you need to have money and run a company. Maybe that's not the paradigm that we need to look at. Maybe a woman can be just as happy being a good mom and being a good wife. That's not happening anymore because the economy is changing, but who's to say that we need to have power and money to be happy? As women, we can balance that male ideal of having more power. The power paradigm is what society views as positive and good, but maybe a mom should be a mom and not necessarily a professional if that's what makes her happy. It's a very complicated issue. It comes down to what makes people happy and free, able to fulfill their needs and wishes.

Lorís. In a way you are inviting the feminine paradigm to come into the dialogue.

Patricia. Absolutely. It's absent because most societies place greater value on the male paradigm.

Lorís. After graduating, you're supposed to follow a ten-year plan and end up where you want to be, but nobody takes into account that somewhere in those ten years you have to get married and have kids. They're not educating us correctly, but purely by men's standards. It has nothing to do with what I want to do.

Aurora. And the thing is, even if you choose to pursue a career but then somewhere along the way decide to marry and have kids; 90

percent of the responsibility of that domestic situation is going to be on your shoulders. And nobody tells you that. I feel that schools should be educating both boys and girls about what's coming their way in the future, and how to confront specific responsibilities. Let's not forget that men are also being educated in a very specific way. They are experiencing their own transition and they're kind of lost in translation

Lorís. Following the wisdom that most change starts from within, what do you think men and women should do to give femininity its place, not only in society but also within each of us as individuals?

Aurora. Well, you need very brave men for that, and women.

Patricia. Yes, you have to start with self-confidence. You have to start with a little girl, making sure that you build character through actions so that you create females who are more confident as children. You do that through activities where they feel more confident, and then grow in confidence. They learn to embrace their femininity as something positive and not as something that needs to be repressed or hidden for fear.

Take the issue you mentioned of dumbing girls down, for example. If a girl is intelligent, a lot of times she is rejected by the boys. Well, girls have to believe that, sooner or later, the man they want will accept them for who they are; but first they have to accept themselves. So it does start with children and teaching girls how to grow up and how to be strong, feminine women.

Aurora. I would add that you also need to start educating boys.

Patricia. I agree, the boys need to be taught just as much as the girls. We need to teach children and adults balance. We need the feminine and we need the masculine. One is not better than the other; they complement each other. When one tries to take the other over, there is dysfunction. There is dysfunction when there's too much intuition too much compassion and nurturing; and the same is true with too much intellect, too much force and power. We need both. It's the happiest combination. The Chinese call it the yin and yang.

Patriarchy sees each side as something good or something bad, but neither is true. They need to work together to reach the best outcome.

Lorís. Is there anything else you would like to mention?

Aurora. Just to wrap it up, I really believe in the power of friendship among women, support groups created by women and for women. This may sound counterintuitive, because we've been speaking all this time about how important it is to balance feminine and masculine in order to create healthy relationships. But having said all that, when women come together to support each other, there is an unexplainable feeling and energy going on that only happens among women. We're all in the same boat, because we're all women and we all have to go through the same issues that we are talking about. A very important reality of becoming a woman is that you may become a mother at some point. You can give life. I think that is something that every woman, whether she becomes a mother or not, carries with her. And that creates a current of energy among women. I strongly believe that if women come together, they can create a very intense, powerful context for change. But as women, we all need to believe in this, too.

Patricia. I think that we are the creative energy, and in this new century, we need to be the ones who make that change. We have the power. That's why it's called the "sacred feminine." We have divine creative energy, and we are the ones who can change the world. We are the ones that can improve it. We are the ones who have to stop the destruction of the planet and violence against women.

Aurora. Sisterhood.

Patricia. Sisterhood.

Brandon Mack

Brandon Mack is an educator and activist working in Houston, Texas. He received his bachelor's of sociology at Rice University, a master's of science in sociology from Texas A&M University, and a master's of education from the University of Houston. His research interests include the intersectionality of race, gender, and sexuality, and his work on effemmiphobia has been profiled in the GLAAD media award-winning article, "Why Can't You Just Butch Up? Gay Men, Effeminacy, and Our War with Ourselves." He has also given workshops on the topic of effemiphobia at national conferences, including the National Gay and Lesbian Task Force: Creating Change conference.

I was lucky to be at the right time and in the right place when Professor Mack gave a talk in a class at Rice University. I ran after him after he finished and begged him for an interview. I don't think he had any idea who I was or what I was up to, but he generously accepted, only half knowing what he was getting into. I had never heard of effemiphobia, nor had I been very exposed to LGBT theory, but what I came to understand from Mack's same-sex dynamics encouraged me to continue my quest for the feminine. I found how the rules and hierarchies that applied to relationships between homosexual male couples were almost identical to heterosexual couples. There was attraction and power in all of these relationships, love in the best of them. Once again, gender and sex was almost irrelevant. This conversation has stayed with me since.

Lorís. To you, what is the feminine?

In general, people think that the feminine are things we associate with being a woman. Unfortunately, that's more of a subjugated sense of what the feminine is. In our country we seem to understand the masculine as those qualities that are dominant, prevalent, known, and forceful, to a certain extent. Whereas the feminine would be the opposite of that, qualities that are viewed as being lesser, more subjugated, docile. Those are the ideas that can really come into play when you think about the feminine. I think there is a fear sometimes because people don't want to be associated with "weakness" and qualities that are attributed to the feminine. You see people not fully embracing the feminine, but wanting to shy away from what they perceive as feminine.

Lorís. It's strange because everyone has both parts.

Everyone has both a feminine and a masculine side. You have to accept that everyone has a duality within them.

Lorís. Could you explain to us what effemiphobia is, where it comes from, and why you think it came about?

Effemiphobia, specifically the way I look at it, is about the fear of effeminacy from gay men towards other gay men. It deals with the fear that certain men feel when they are associated with men who are gay, those men who act in what is considered to be a stereotypical "gay" way. They're very flamboyant, and their presentation can be viewed as feminine. They wear clothing that is associated with women, and they present themselves in what would be considered to be a feminine style. Some men don't choose to associate with gay men because of those links. That's where effemiphobia plays out.

I feel like the height and surge of the phenomenon has come as a result of many different things. J.L. King wrote a book called *On the Down Low* (2005), which discusses African American men who have sex with other men while also having female relationships. That particular book was used to explain the rise in occurrence of HIV and AIDS among African American women. It sparked people to ask themselves, "Is this guy gay? How do we figure out if he's gay? Oh, if he acts effeminate then he must be gay." "Down Low" men don't want to be associated with a gay identity because they lose all the privileges associated with masculinity. They lose their positions within their community because they're now demonized for being "gay." So there was a heightened awareness as a result of that book. Then, other people began trying to figure out, "Who is gay, and who is not gay?" The need to seek out who exactly is and isn't gay has only fractured the gay community as well as the entire community of us as a people.

Lorís. Can you speak about the different hierarchies in the gay community and their relationship with effeminacy? What does it say about our biases as a culture?

It's very interesting that within the gay community there are a lot of different stereotypes. One book that has looked into the various stereotypes and how they relate to effeminacy is called *Faeries, Bears, and Leathermen,* by Peter Hennen (2008). The remarkable thing is that if you look specifically at the three categories from the title, they each have a different stereotype and a different response to effeminacy. "Faeries" really praise femininity. They have communities where they actually go out into the woods and embrace their feminine side. They will dress up in women's clothing. They have nicknames that are very feminine, like "cupcake." It's really about embracing both the masculine and the feminine side.

Then you have the "bears." Bears are about being "real men." They emphasize being natural. You'll see that they have a lot of hair; they're very masculine-presenting, and they hang out with other masculine-presenting men to take away that notion that you have to be effeminate in order to be gay. They show that you can still be a masculine-presenting male and carry on a loving relationship with gay men. Next, you have the "leathermen," who punish effeminacy. They call men derogatory names while also engaging in erotic behavior dealing with leather and bondage and other type of sexual activity where they really punish effeminacy and forbid acting in effeminate ways.

So, within the community you do see a hierarchy in which those men who are considered to behave more "straight" are privileged over those men who are considered to act effeminately. In the study that I work with, I consistently see the phrase "no fats no fems" on men's online profiles. They really don't want someone who is overweight, and they don't want someone who acts in a feminine way. Weaved within that phrase you see a hierarchy. There is a preference for men to act straight, because then they won't be locked in derogatory judgment. They're not going to be noticeable within society. That creates a hierarchy within the community in which the masculine-presenting men who you would not assume to be gay are highly-valued and praised; while the man who is very effeminate in his presentation is placed lower on the totem pole. He is already demonized by society, and now he is further demonized by his own community.

Lorís. It's shocking that society punishes a person more for being effeminate than for being gay, even though homosexuality is so targeted. What really terrifies people, then, is being effeminate. Even among women today, you see the desire to act like men. It seems the more masculine you are, the more validation you get everywhere.

Absolutely. It's really related to the whole notion of power. Who has the power? Because what is masculine and dominant is considered to be powerful, women are taking on masculine characteristics. They take on those characteristics that are considered masculine in order to show their control and prove their dominance. The same thing happens in the gay community. Men want to show that they don't lose their dominance by being gay.

There are a lot of associations here with the power dynamics within relationships, and the power dynamics related to sexual positioning. The top figure, or the person who is the giver, is considered to be the dominant figure. The person who is the receiver, or has the bottom position, is perceived to be the more docile, the more submissive person in the relationship. You will see these characteristics in how men interact with one another. They want their tops to be very dominant. They don't believe that a top could be a submissive person; and you also see that a dominant person could not be considered to be a bottom because of the submissive roles associated with it. Even within the gay community, then, you see a heteronormativity along the lines of, "A man must be this, and a woman must be that," in the associations related to sexual positioning.

Lorís. Do you think that Western culture denies men of their femininity? If so, how do you think men are affected by this when it comes to developing their personal identities? How are they affected when it comes to relationships with their partners?

I definitely think that Western culture feeds into these dynamics. Look at the Marlboro man, or John Wayne, the way we have privileged tough men in our community. Men aren't supposed to cry or show emotion. All those things that are associated with the effeminate make him "less of a man." Boys aren't supposed to cry. They're not supposed to show emotion. They're not supposed to be caring and nurturing individuals. That has really impacted the way we interact with one another.

If you have taken all this in and still believe in traditional notions of what a man is, this will impact how you view other men and how you relate to them. If, for example, you attach your manhood to your sexual positioning and you know you're a top, then you would want to feel that your top status is not going to be negated by someone who could be equally dominant. Consequently, these men sometimes try to go for a person who is a little more submissive. You see the same thing on the reverse side, too, men who think, "Because I am submissive, because I am effeminate, because I have accepted all these notions of what is against my manhood, I need someone who balances that out." This reflects a heteronormative belief that the receiver, or the "woman" in the relationship, has to have a "man" in his relationship. You see them seek out dominant, straight-acting partners to find that balance.

These notions related to the effeminate, and the struggle to accept the duality that exists in all men, really impact how they relate to each other and how they seek out partners. They're not just looking for the person who satisfies what they're looking for in a relationship, or who shares the same interests or seems a good match; instead, they really look to see what the persona of a potential partner is. They ask, "In what way does this man act in relation to his manliness and his effeminacy, and will that balance my perception of my own manhood and effeminacy?

Lorís. In many of the interviews that we have done, the issue of labeling comes up. It seems that society has only come up with a limited number of categories, and if you don't fit in them, you're out. So you see people trying to squish themselves into these categories so that they can be seen as something. People aren't allowed to claim conflicting categories. As you said, people should be whole; they shouldn't be looking for something else that completes them. Your thoughts can be applied to pretty much all categories.

Absolutely. One thing I like to say is that there is no love for the in-between. By that, I mean that there's no love for someone who doesn't completely, one hundred percent, fit a certain category. We want everybody to fit into these nice, neat categories so that we can instantly mark who they are, instantly assign all these assumptions to who they are. If they don't fit 100 percent, we throw them away or negate who they are. And I do agree that you see that among heterosexuals as well as among homosexuals. It frustrates me that a group of people who have already been demonized for their homosexuality, for innately being who they are, can now be negated because they don't fit into a nice, neat little box.

Lorís. It also goes back to negating the feminine, because it is very masculine to make something square and structured; as opposed to the feminine, which is a more diffuse energy, like creativity and intuition, more of an unknown territory.

Yes, absolutely. The "feminine mystique." Even that term shows that there is a mysterious quality that is associated with the effeminate, with the feminine; whereas, the masculine is known. It has very clear-cut definitions. Because masculinity and being a man is so dominant, we automatically know what it is. So whatever qualities oppose the masculine are considered to be "mystiques." They are feminine, and we put them into their own kind of category.

Lorís. There are currently many conversations going on about women's rights; but to reach full equity, we must also know the pressures or expectations that are imposed on men. What are they?

First, I will answer from the heterosexual perspective. I sometimes think that, because the women's rights movement has been defined as women taking their own action, there is a feeling that women who are involved with the movement hate men. Men who are heterosexual feel that they can't be a part of it because of the way its history has always been described. But this is about equal rights. If you're someone who believes in equal rights, you can participate in this movement.

I think many of the civil rights movements have not been defined as something that everyone can be a part of if they fundamentally believe in the equal rights of all people. Instead, the characteristics associated with the initial group involved have defined the movement and the participation. You hear heterosexual men say, "Oh, I can't be a part of that because innately those women don't like me. They view me as the enemy." So they are unable to see that if they really do support a woman's full right to inclusion and equality, it's their right to be a part of the movement. It's their right to do their part, to say they don't agree with what is going on. Looking at women's current struggles over reproductive rights, for example, we ask, "Why can't we participate in that struggle?" We should have every right to participate.

From the gay perspective, I find it interesting that, because the term "gay" has a sexual orientation as well as an effeminacy component; you will see the participation in the rights struggle to vary based on how men feel about these components. You'll see men engaging in same-sex relations, but because they don't self-identify as gay—they don't view themselves as gay because of their own relationship with effeminacy—they won't participate in the movement. They won't say anything, even though they are engaging in the same sexual activity, and those laws will still be used against them and their relationships. The participants who are involved in the movement are very, very effeminate; and because the men who don't view themselves as gay have not wrestled with their own feelings towards effeminacy, you will see them not participating in those movements. It goes back to the fundamental question of equal rights for everyone. Everyone should be able to participate in that struggle. Heterosexual people who feel that gay people should have equal rights should be able to participate in the gay rights movement just like men should be able to participate in the women's rights movement.

Loris. We were talking about that the other day, and Jay was saying, "Why is it called 'feminism'?" It's like the word only includes females. He suggested that, to him, the word "feminism" already excludes males, but I think it's appropriate because it's the counterpart to such a masculine environment.

The terminology definitely plays a part in terms of people's acceptance of the movement and in their own participation. Even in the gay rights movement, you see that gay marriage has now been framed as "marriage equality," instead of just using the term "gay marriage," which only refers to same-sex. When you use the term, "marriage equality," it can refer to same-sex marriage or interracial marriage, and you want all to be equally recognized. In addition, the term, "marriage equality," means anybody could be a part of it. Even the terms "feminism" or "women's movement" limit who is involved and who is actually benefitting. When it's "equal rights," everybody is a part of it.

Lorís. I also think the movement has evolved a little. It did start out with women, but it grew into more. It's important; language plays a huge role. Even the terms "masculine" and "feminine" are an example. Being feminine can include things like being vulnerable. Everyone is vulnerable, but when you say "feminine," it is reduced only to women, as if men could not be vulnerable.

Words have power. Just like you said, when you are labeled "feminine," you are automatically associated with things like being more docile or having less power. Whereas, if you are "masculine," you have power; you have the dominant position. When you use words such as "vulnerable," the associations that come up are feeling lesser, feeling open and laid bare right there. It's very, very important for people to think about the terms that we use towards one another and the words that we use against one another, because of all the associations that come with them. Sometimes the meaning is lost because of the words that are used.

Lorís. Our society as a whole tends to express the individual's attitudes. Do you think that by over-valuing masculine attributes, we are affecting our environment?

I think it's affecting us as a society. We associate so much with what we consider to be masculine and what we consider to be effeminate, but we don't see the crossing-over. This blindness reaffirms the definitions. What we really need to see in our society is more of that crossing-over, more awareness that "things that are masculine can also have a feminine side to them, and things that are feminine can also have a masculine side, and they're both equal and valid."

I think it becomes a problem when the perception of the feminine crossing into the masculine generates a punishment or a value judgment against it. That's wrong. The same thing happens when the masculine crosses over into the feminine. There is a value judgment once again, and a negation that says it's wrong. When we do that, we reaffirm the need for that separateness. Masculine must be this; feminine must be that. We think, "This is right." When we see the mixing, we think, "That is wrong." It needs to be the other way around; both are equal and valid.

Nevertheless, we are so conditioned to the idea that there are only two sides, and that those sides are not equal and not supposed to mix, that we instantly make those value judgments. Even at a young age, both notions are made to be separate; instead of saying, "Okay, the boys are playing with dolls at one moment. They're enjoying themselves. They're not hurting anyone. That's fine. Equal and valid." If we did that from the start, I think our society wouldn't maintain that dividing system where one is right and one is wrong.

Lorís. How could we change our actions or our behavior to create a more balanced collective psyche as a society?

We need to realize that equality is truly that; it's about being equal. We must realize that masculinity and femininity are equal, that they both exist, and that they're going to exist in every person. Individuals are going to have their masculine moments, and they're going to have their feminine moments. It's okay to have both; it's okay to express both, because innately that is a part of us as humans. Every single person, man or woman, has a masculine and a feminine dimension.

I think once we realize that it's okay within ourselves to have both the masculine and the feminine side, it will translate into social change so that, hopefully, it will be okay to be who you are innately.

Abigail Disney

Dr. Abigail E. Disney is a filmmaker, philanthropist, and activist, with degrees from Yale, Stanford, and Columbia. She is the president of the film production company, Fork Films, and has produced many documentaries, including *Pray the Devil Back to Hell* (2008), an award-winning documentary about the Liberian women who peacefully ended their country's fourteen-year civil war, and the executive producer of the PBS award-winning mini-series *Women, War & Peace*. Abigail cofounded the Daphne Foundation, dedicated to low-income communities in the five boroughs of New York City and founded Peace is Loud, which amplifies women's voices in the media. She serves as a board member for a number of organizations, including the Global Fund for Women and the Peace Research Endowment. Her justice and advocacy work has been recognized through numerous awards, including the International Advocate for Peace (IAP) award.

Back in 2011, my mom had asked me to help her perform a quick video interview with a film director that was coming to speak to Rice University after her film screening. I was a lazy student at the time and said I didn't want to do it, but my mom said I would regret it. Those words couldn't have been more true. When I arrived I saw Abigail Disney walking towards us while she laughed with someone else. I liked her right away, but when she started talking my eyes grew bigger and bigger. Before my mom finished asking her questions for her website, I jumped in with, "Can I ask you one last question that has nothing to do with what we are talking about right now?" Abby smiled and said, "Oh, it's the Disney question. Everyone asks the Disney question. Go ahead." I hadn't made the Disney connection yet, and my question went something like this, "Women in Western countries say they're liberated, but are we really?" The surprise on her face made me feel extremely proud of myself, and I immediately became her groupie. I asked her if she might participate in the interview project that I was contemplating / thinking about / possibly planning to maybe do. She agreed, and a year later I emailed her and soon thereafter found myself in her office in New York making sure I would never forget that moment with a wide-eyed presence and about a hundred selfies.

Lorís. To you, what is the feminine?
   I thought about this question for a long time, because I persist in dividing the world up between the things that women do and the things that men do. We all contain elements of both. Every

civilization, every thought system, thinks in terms of the same opposing forces or energies in the world. In China, they are yin and yang. It's larger than simply masculine and feminine. It's just that women tend toward one thing and men tend toward another. That's a more helpful way of thinking of it because if you think of it as "masculine" and "feminine," then you run into all this anxiety everybody has. "I'm a woman behaving like a male," or "I'm a man behaving like a female." I think it's effective to view those kinds of opposing forces as something so much larger than just sexuality or gender.

One force would be the left-brain, or the masculine, or the yin, or however you want to call it. Men tend to test better at sense of direction. They think in more systematic ways. They tend to be more logical, more aggressive. They tend to love risk and thrive on it. The feminine, or those things that women seem to embrace or embody in a more general way, are things like being more nurturing, being more intuitive, being bad at directions, being more verbal, being more into a story than a fact. I think that's the way, at a general level, people tend to divide up masculine and feminine.

Lorís. In ancient times, even before Greek civilizations, cultures praised goddesses that represented feminine aspects, such as nurturance, the power to create, introspection, or inspiration. As time has gone by, celebrities who represent sexuality have replaced such goddesses. How do you feel about this issue? Do you agree?

In our celebrity culture now, we have women who have in fact replaced the goddesses. Unfortunately, they have taken sexuality and they have boiled it down into something way less complex than it was for an Artemis or an Athena. The difference between pleasure and happiness is a matter of nuance and layers and complexity. That is the difference between the sexuality in a Kim Kardashian and the sexuality in Venus. It is a boiling down of sex to a physical act, when in fact it is so much richer, an interaction based in the spirit and in the heart.

The Greek goddesses are interesting because we remember them as being mostly about what we think of as feminine virtues, but they were actually not confined to those virtues. I mean, Diana was a hunter. Athena sprang from Zeus's head; she was about art and culture and thinking and writing and intellectuality. We have reduced a much more complex system to an idea of just Venus or Aphrodite, or these images we have of mothers nursing children and so forth. We have narrowed those goddesses down to simply "masculine" and "feminine," when they really were not all that simple.

However, between the Greek goddesses and now, before we got to the part where all we had was Paris Hilton and Beyoncé, came monotheism. That's a really big difference in systems of thinking, because in polytheism people were encouraged to think of the world as being very complex; female goddesses had intellectual capacities and embodied intellectual abilities, and a male god like Dionysius was able to embody losing it at a party and having too much to drink and not being rational at all. These are very complex ways of understanding the world. Monotheism boils all those forces down into two simple opposites: There are good things, and there are bad things. God embodies the good things, and Satan embodies the bad things. This is a simplistic way of understanding the forces of nature and the forces of intellectuality and the soul. You also reduce the world to a struggle for dominance between two simple forces. If you have eight or twelve or fifteen ideas, then you're not so quick to want one of them to be on top and one of them to be on bottom.

Therefore, we lost our ability to understand the world as an interdependent, nuanced system, and our need to see the world as a question of dominance or competitiveness became the principle way of understanding how these things operate. I believe this is our problem around gender. "If there are two systems," the logic goes, "then one has to be better than the other," or "one has to control the other." We privilege the masculine over the feminine.

Popular culture is interesting because we privilege the masculine, yet all you see are images of women. But of course all you really see are images of one woman. I mean, look at someone like Olivia Wilde. She is a very beautiful woman. She made it from television to film, and in the process her publicists and agents took charge of her hair and her makeup. I noticed that the photographs of her on the magazine covers started to change; she started looking less and less like a particular person, and more and more like this one universal ideal of beauty that's on every cover of every magazine. If you walk by the magazine stands, they're all starting to look the same, all reduced to a single idea of what a nose should be, what the eyes should be, what the size of the forehead should be.

While it looks like women have a lot of value and a lot of importance in popular culture, they have no control, they have no autonomy, and they certainly have no latitude in being something not right in the center of what is acceptable. In that system, everyone is feeling victimized. We have privileged the Paris Hiltons and the Beyoncés, and we have said, "Oh my god, look at their sexuality. They're amazing!" All we care about is their beauty. "Aren't they wonderful? Aren't they beautiful?" Those women are feeling victimized because they know that they inhabit this tiny little universe, and the ways in which they can violate all the rules are so many and so dangerous. The stakes are so high.

While they're feeling victimized, everyone else is feeling victimized in a way by them! I feel victimized! Why can't it be ok that I'm fifty-two years old, and I'm not perfectly thin? And men feel victimized because these women are what they are expected to be able to attain. They can't! The women decide whether or not the relationship goes forward, and the men feel victimized.

I think we've all lost something enormous in adopting this single idea of what women can be. It's one idea of a woman. It is something really important—our attractiveness, our sexuality, our beauty, all the ways in which we can look amazing and sound and feel amazing. That's a wonderful part of who we are, but it's only one piece of a much more complex whole. We have taken that one piece and we have lifted it up so high, that everyone is losing inside of the system.

Lorís. That's true. I never thought of it that way. Where polytheism can offer various models of a reality, monotheism only offers one.

Well, every faith system looks better from a distance.

Lorís. Do you believe that fractured paradigms of women produced by the media have commercialized the energy that femininity carries in both men and women?

Because popular culture is so subsumed with sexuality, and because popular culture is after all, a business—it's about consumption, about me creating a product that you want and will give me money for—the relationship of the commercial transaction to the interaction, which is sex, has turned the interaction into a transaction. The idea of consumption—of having, of owning—has so suffused our sense of sexuality that we really have lost something very important, particularly in your generation. It's really pandemic. You can't look at Facebook, at a music video, or even a commercial on the youngest children's stations without seeing some elements of pornography, even if it's just in the dance moves, little subtle things like that. The language has become suffused with it.

Lorís. Women today have access to almost any profession and are able to reach high positions in society. However, there seems to be something missing in the picture. Many women have been criticized for "becoming men" in the workforce or in politics in order to climb into higher positions, yet women who decide to stay at home are neglected for being weak somehow and not growing into their full potential. Our documentary plays with the idea that our society devalues feminine characteristics in both men and women, and this is a part of why women are always falling one step behind. It seems that some unspoken assumptions continue to flow through our psyche, such as "intuition is not as strong as reason," "emotions are a sign of weakness," or "receptiveness and uncertainty go in opposition to profitable results." How do you view this argument? Does it follow with your experience or with your observations? Would you share some examples?

I've seen time and time again how intuition gets devalued and intellect is privileged, though I don't want to live in a world where instinct is privileged over intellect one hundred percent of the time, either. The strength we should be shooting for is in balance. The culture we are living in right now has lost the capacity to balance these qualities. It undervalues the aspects of the heart and the mind that are loosely associated with femininity, like instinct and intuition, emotion, connectedness, and consensus-based decision-making. It has been to our detriment.

If you look at business, there are certain moments in which you can see the intellect has led everybody into a rabbit hole of failure. For me, the classic example is Coke. Many years ago, the company changed its recipe. They came out and said, "We have a new recipe!" but nobody wanted it, nobody liked it. The decision to change the recipe had come from a series of meetings and focus groups and studies and scientific analyses of the new recipe; but nobody had thought to ask about the people's emotional connectedness to the old Coke. Would they react rationally or would they react in an emotional way to this change? Of course, the reaction was emotional. Coke sales plummeted and the company was in real danger. It was really because of a hyper-attention to intellectuality that they almost sank the company.

Money is such an important value in the world that we now in-habit. Just look at the arguments around the 2012 presidential election and the common logic that Mitt Romney was going to be nominated because, "He made a lot of money; therefore, he's a smart guy." So we take the having and the getting of money to be a sign of character. We really look at money as a positive indicator of character, and we see an ability to dominate in the business world as a very important value. Business is business, and it's easy to say, "I've made more money than you've made," because I can just compare my revenues with your revenues. This is a very rational standard of judgment, and in the traditional ways of thinking that is thought of as a male quality.

But in business, people rely on intuition all of the time. The business that my grandfather and uncle built was obviously a business that was built on intuition, on art, on understanding and sensing what people wanted, understanding their emotional lives and the world. Disney was a company that blended rationality and science and math and all those things, with intuition and what you call feminine qualities. So yes, we have devalued what we have called feminine virtues, but we rely on them all of the time, and they suffuse our world in many, many ways.

The question is, how can a woman in a position of power be comfortable, and feel and look comfortable holding and owning that power, when power is ascribed to men more often than it is to women? How can the people underneath her and around her be comfortable with her in power when it is such an inversion of what we have been trained to think is okay? I think Hilary Clinton has done a really interesting thing in the last few years. Here is a woman who was married to the president, and there is no more feminine way to step into power than being married to the president. That's as traditional as it gets! But because she didn't want to inhabit that position in a traditional way she was really reviled. She was hated. She was the single most divisive figure in American politics during her husband's administration.

New York is a really interesting state. Here in the city it's predominantly Democrat. We went 96% for Kerry or something like that in Manhattan. But upstate, which is half of the state's population, is seriously Republican. You can't be a divisive figure and win this state; you have to be able to win independent voters and Republicans. Interestingly enough, when she decided to run for the Senate, she won those voters, and she did it in a very feminine way. She went town by town, meeting by meeting, hand shake by handshake, and she listened to people. She called it the "listening tour." I've never heard of a politician elevating listening as a value. I think that was really why she won that election so easily, and then the next election even more easily. When she retired, she was almost the most popular senator in our history, and it was because she elevated listening as a value. She never walked away from her feminine qualities. In fact, she embraced them, and she foregrounded them.

As secretary of state, she is just as tough and rough as everybody else. Frankly, I wish she was less traditionally male in some of her approaches, but you know we live in the time we live in and we have the president we have, and so we use force—a fair amount, as a country, we have a history of that. Where force is not involved, she has been a very adept negotiator, and I think this is because she is a listener. Very often, in rooms where the negotiations are happening, she is working with people who have not encountered a lot of listening in their histories. They are surprised by it and open to thinking in new ways about the negotiation. It took her a long time to be able to do all of this and still be liked by people, but I think it is very interesting that the American public at least has come to a point at which it now sees a woman who embraces all her femininity and still feels comfortable in power. They accept her.

The single most important thing about Hillary Clinton in the last few years is that she has started to let herself look terrible sometimes and nobody gives her a hard time about it. It's an interesting development. She showed up for a meeting—in China, I think—in a scrunchie. There was a little article about it, but when I think about the critique of her when she was running for president last time—every pantsuit, every hair clip, her cleavage, the wrinkles on her face, the highlights in her hair; everything was dissected and parsed—the fact that she could go into a meeting in a scrunchie and nobody made a big deal about it represents a huge progress. She has been able to win her power and be accepted by people, and in doing that, she has been able to push the way forward a bit for other women.

Loris. Absolutely. In terms of tradition, it seems that whenever we enter new territories we tend to fall back on what we already know, which makes it harder to move forward as a society.

With respect to this idea, there's a really important difference between hard prejudice and soft prejudice. Hard prejudice is, "Black people are bad, and I will never hire a Black person." That's a hard prejudice. It's out loud. It's obvious. It is what it is. It's racism. That's easy to describe, and it's easy to legislate against. The first part of any civil rights movement or human rights movement is to legislate and make these behaviors illegal. But then there are the soft prejudices, and I think this is what we are contending with in this country. It's also what we're dealing with around gender, and we will be for a long time. Soft prejudices are the unexamined assumptions, like, "When I get in the airplane and the pilot is a man, I feel a little safer." It's one of those deep things that you don't really look at or take out or examine. It's just a feeling, and we can't be blamed for those feelings. They get hardwired into us by culture, by our parents, by circumstance, and it's very unusual to take them out and hold our own feet to the fire about them.

Women's experiences around power are very much colored by soft prejudice. The White House Project did this amazing study of television ads for women who wanted to run for office. They conducted dial tests where people dialed up or down when they saw the candidate and they tested these neutral male and female candidates in different settings: wearing a jacket, not wearing a jacket, sitting in an office, walking through a field, all these different contexts. In every single one of these, men and women both dialed up the minute they saw the male candidate, and both men and women dialed down when they saw the female candidate. This means that gender alone was the first and strongest attribute that every single person reacted to when they were trying to assess whether or not this was an appropriate person to vote into a position of power. It's so set in us, and not just in men but in women, too, sometimes more so than men.

Lorís. In your documentary, Pray the Devil Back to Hell, *you tell the inspiring story of how Liberia came to be a better country through peace. Can you give us a brief summary of what your documentary was about?*

Pray the Devil Back to Hell is a story about a group of Christian and Muslim women in Liberia. There had been a really long and horrible civil war, and these women got together, worked out their differences, and started praying for peace. They wore white and sat outside on the president's route to work, and they prayed and fasted and sang for peace. Eventually, they were able to persuade him to go to peace talks that were being held in Ghana. They went to the peace talks and they sat outside there also, praying, fasting, and singing. Eventually, when the peace talks broke down, they took the whole event hostage and they basically forced a resolution. It's an incredible story. It was a totally unknown story at the time we made the film. The woman who led these women has gone to receive a Nobel peace prize.

Lorís. The women of Liberia, even though peaceful, were not pushovers. Many people mistake peace with passiveness. Part of the beauty in their story is that their battle was perfectly balanced between the feminine and the masculine; it had structure and direction, yet the power came from within. Their most effective weapon was the strength in their heart. In many ways, their story can be influential not only for social movements, but also for the inner battles that every individual faces. Can you speak to us about your experience with this aspect of the story? How could people like us in Western cultures learn to act similarly?

What I learned from the women in Liberia was that there definitely is a big difference between being passive and being non-violent. Being non-violent means you act without violence. That means you step forward, you put your life on the line, you speak, you resist, you protest, you organize. In many ways, non-violence is a more dangerous way to organize and to protest than violence.

There is enormous passivity in American culture, in particular, but also across the developed world. This is in part because we are generations removed from any kind of real discomfort. In Europe, you're still in a generation where your parents remember the war, remember the displacement and the fear; but in the United States, we have never had war on our doorsteps. We have not had the kind of suffering and poverty and deprivation that existed during the

Depression since the thirties. We are a little too fat and happy in this country. Unfortunately, popular culture doesn't help because it contributes to fatness, not to happiness. It's distracting. It makes people who act look foolish. If you watch the media and you see how activists are depicted, they tend to look silly. Everyone in this country is so invested in being acceptable to everyone else that there's a sort of allergy to taking a risk, to stepping out and protesting.

One of the things that Lama Bouie has taught me in the way she petitioned the women in our film, is that you have to be willing to be made fun of. You have to be willing not to be taken seriously. You have to be willing to look ridiculous and be hated if you want to fight hard for justice. Actually, that's why I really admire the Occupy protesters, because they have been much bigger, much stronger, and much more effective than the media has consistently painted them to be, and they have nevertheless continued forward. They really don't care how they are depicted; they're just going to keep doing what they are doing. It takes a willingness to throw away the need to be acceptable.

Lorís. More than half of the population is women, and we still haven't really fought together. Why haven't we?

There's a big difference between the fight for women's rights and other civil rights movements, like the movement for civil rights in the south in the fifties and sixties, because we are married, theoretically, to our oppressors. We're all put together in families. It's not as though Martin Luther King went to bed every night with Mrs. Bull Connor. He and his family and his community were all together, and therefore they could all put their weight behind something as a group. Women are asking for things that will occasionally cause families to change. They will ask something of the men they very much love and need, and it may be something the men are not willing to give. So, we're not so sure we want to fight for feminism if it risks our relationships. This is why we have consistently won ground and then lost it, why you can't always get women to support women's issues.

There are also very legitimate disagreements among women. The argument in our community around choice is a really important one that I don't think we're ever going to resolve. People can legitimately disagree on this one. What it means for the movement is that there are serious divisions that we will never really be able to bind. We are 51 percent of the population, but you will never get 51 percent of the vote, because there is just too much nuance and complexity. There's too much for everyone to lose.

Lorís: Women are fighting all over the place for their equality, yet men have remained silent about the oppression they face. Do you think there are many pressures that should be lifted from men's shoulders also? If so, which ones?
Are you saying men are silent about the pressures men face?

Lorís: Yes.
Okay, because men are also silent about the pressures that women face. There's that, and that's really important. Men have never really stood up for us. I don't think we will ever break through until men stand with us. No civil rights movement has ever broken through until the day people who had nothing to gain by the movement stood in solidarity with the lower power group. In the civil rights movement in the south, you had people from all over the north coming to the freedom riots and risking their lives with nothing to gain except that their country would be better and more decent if this movement prevailed. Women have never had men stand in solidarity with them. By that, I mean men have never really pushed back on each other about what it is they're asking from women in this culture.

Now, men have never really talked about the pressures they themselves face in part because one of the basic and most difficult pressures they face is the one to seem always strong and never vulnerable. As a mother of sons, I can see how they really take that one on in adolescence. I watch with pain as my sons step into their role as men and become alienated from their own feelings and their own sense of self. It breaks my heart really. Unless things change significantly, I don't know if we will ever see men talk about the difficulties of being men, precisely because they are not allowed to.

That's why I think bringing women into power is going to make such a difference. When you bring a few women into the room, they start kind of loosening the space up and bringing some unexpected skills and personality traits to the discourse. This gives more latitude to everyone else, particularly to the men in the room, to behave less stereotypically. Women enrich these spaces just by loosening them up. That's what I'm hoping to see.

Lorís. Many young women are excited to be able to follow their dreams of self-fulfillment without limitations, but they have not let go of the prince charming ideal. On the other hand, many young men are supporters of strong, independent women, yet they dislike the loss of manhood or control that a relationship with a woman like that may carry. How can we come to a better understanding in contemporary romantic relationships? What sacrifices should each gender make or not make?

I don't think romantic relationships are necessarily that different than they have ever been. Each one is a negotiation between two human beings. Everybody, since the beginning of time, has had the ideal against which they were struggling in forming the particular bond that is one marriage between two individual people. We are all shackled by stupid ideas that we have grown up with. When a woman has a prince charming in her imagination, it's not just that he is a nice guy, kind and generous, but there are all these ridiculous and irrelevant ideas that go with it. Maybe he is blond, and six feet three, and has a lot of money, all these external qualities that interfere with her ability actually to connect with that guy who might be Mr. Right. I'm in a thirty-three-year relationship and I'm married to a really hot, handsome guy; but that stops mattering in a big hurry. This is a marathon, not a sprint.

I think men are also being failed by the way the media guides them into the belief that they are a failure if they're not attached to a woman who asks nothing of them, who looks like a Barbie doll and is some kind of genie that grants all their sexual and emotional wishes. Honestly, a relationship with a person with no self is no more satisfying than being alone. Our challenge as mature people is to free ourselves from those shackles and to think for ourselves. If a man is feeling emasculated by being with a strong woman, then it's going to be up to the two them to figure out how to make that work, either by him giving up some of his expectations about how he is supposed to look in the world or what he needs to feel like a strong, legitimate man; or by her finding a way to accommodate him. Everything's a negotiation, everything, every step of the way. And that has never not been true. It really is up to each of us as individuals to find our way through this maze and make our own paths. Otherwise, if we go the way the media has been urging us to go, we are all lost.

I also really believe that another reason we have all lost in the new equation for romance is because many of us have seen a lot of pornography before we have even had a physical encounter with someone of the opposite sex. That can't be good for anyone, and not only for all the obvious reasons of exploitation, but also because of the way it kills the imagination. Imagination is essential to love and romance, and pornography has a way of narrowing down an idea of what is possible between two human beings. That's everybody's loss. Our current system is failing everyone, because we have been shackled to a series of really bad ideas that have narrowed down our sense of opportunity.

Lorís. This question about relationships always leads to a discussion about how the media permeates all aspects of life. It's not exclusive to relationships or self-image anymore; I think my idea of success has been influenced by the media. I'll see this fraction of a second in a movie or on TV, and of course what it represents involves effort and preparation, but it's that one image that makes me spend endless hours trying to be what I saw in that moment.

We blame a lot of things on the media, and that's not completely fair; we are each responsible for ourselves. There has never been a generation of people who have grown up so steeped in images that are imported from the public square. The amount of television, of film, of video games and magazines and internet activity—I didn't grow up with that nearly as much as you guys did. So you can't deny that this forms your expectations of the world; there are currents which are pretty consistent across all of them.

Lorís. In the end, the media is getting money from what we consume. In terms of responsibility, where do you draw the line between what they show us and what we buy?

Well the media represents two issues. In the first place, it's created by people out of intention and deliberate planning. While it's a profit-driven business, each person as an individual in that business should ask themselves, "Am I making the world a better place or not?" If everybody did, we would have a very different media. Secondly, the media is also a symptom. I think of our popular culture like this: If America, the whole country, fell asleep and had a dream; this is what our dream would look like. It is both a consequence and cause of the culture we have. Because these two things are constantly in a dance with each other, it's really difficult to blame any particular part of it, which is why it's so hard to get your hands wrapped around it.

Lorís: Given our society gives great value to profits, technology, and quick production, do you feel that the "ordinary" individual has suffered some side effects from these values?

Individuals have suffered enormously in the way that our American culture has gotten so very good at combining desire with consumption. The advertisement business in particular is very good at stimulating that part of you that needs a dress, or a pair of shoes or a perfume, an idea. In some important ways, they have taken desire—which is an enormous, untamable, amorphous thing in all of us, a giant driving force—and they've narrowed it down, and given us a lot of little objects to occupy ourselves with. They have diminished us. It took all those Greek gods to understand and describe desire, and they have narrowed it down to Selena Gomez's perfume.

The whole enormous apparatus that constitutes what we call the media is driven by profit. What benefits the people who create it is making you want more. Thus, most media is predicated on the idea that what you need when you walk out or turn off is a feeling of thirst or hunger for the next thing. And that's not true of advertising only. Look at films these days; there's always a sequel. It never really ends! There is always the next one coming. This is the problem; it interrupts our relationship with desire and our capacity to examine it willingly. It's like the dynamics of addiction. An addict will generally always be looking for the next thing, and the next thing, and the next. "Enough" is a receding horizon in front of us. Just like with the dynamics of addiction, the only way to break this cycle is for each of us to go into our hearts. It's unrealistic to think we can go out to Hollywood and yell from the rooftop of the Capitol Records building screaming, "Stop it you guys!" The profit motive is powerful; it has the inevitability of gravity.

It's going to be on each of us as individuals to choose to look into our hearts to understand what we truly need. We need to reflect on what it is to have enough. "Enough" is not an idea that gets looked at nearly as much as it should, either in the media or in our hearts. "Enough" is way short of what most people are shooting for. If we could take all the emotional energy that we continue to spend after we've gotten enough but are still shooting for more, and spend it instead on making our home lives and family lives better, attending to our own souls, and making the world a better place, imagine how much different the world would be. Imagine what it could be if each one of us could stop at whatever "enough" is.

Rose Mary. In a way, it also has to do with patriarchy, doesn't it? It's part of the same system.

Consider this: a naked woman on the cover of a magazine will sell to women and men, but a naked man on the cover of a magazine will only sell a certain number of copies. Women are accepting this. They have internalized a desire to see the naked female form. There is a dominant image of who desire is for and what it's about, and the observer as we imagine him is a heterosexual male. We have all internalized this notion of who the person of the center of the culture is. That really wreaks havoc on your sense of self if you're a woman. You grow and you're an adolescent in this culture and you're seeing this image of desire being a woman; and even though you, too, are a woman you're looking at her like a man. It plays havoc with your sense of identity as it develops.

Lorís. What about our environment? How have our attitudes affected our Earth, and why do you think we haven't taken enough action to nurture our planet?

To a large extent, the problems that we're having in terms of our environment are fairly simple. If all I really understand and care about are my profits over this next quarter, this next year, then I'm going to want oil. "Give me oil! Give me more oil!" I mean, if profits are what drive things, then oil is the answer. Our business culture has gotten faster. The omnipresence of the business media is highly competitive and the cycles are getting faster. Because of this, it's unfortunately really difficult for a business person to thrive unless they deliver on that need for profit and growth, quarter over quarter. So, until we change our business culture and our business cycles, we aren't going see any significant change in the understanding of the need to protect the environment.

Lorís. I've signed petitions for different issues, and they've answered back that they would lose their jobs if they complied. I thought it was silly to think of shareholders and jobs when, without the environment, there won't even be shareholders and jobs to deal with.

But without the shareholders and the jobs, you're not going to have a way to protect the environment either. That's the problem. It's really difficult to break this cycle. We need the shareholders, we need the profits, and we need the jobs, too. The spotted owl is important, but there are all these loggers in the northwest who need to feed their children. This is really complicated. Changing the way we're polluting the environment is going to involve a massive dislocation of a lot of people, and jobs. Unless we figure out how to do this in a way that respects what people need, it's never going to happen.

Lorís. If a society is only a reflection of the individuals who make it up, what changes could we enact in order to become a more balanced and whole society? What could each individual do to reach a more balanced sense of self?

Well that's the eternal question, isn't it? I think probably the trick is to learn how to listen to your heart. I think a lot of us have lost track of the sound of our inner Jiminy Cricket who is always saying, "Wait! Wait! That doesn't sound right! Don't go with all those boys! Don't go to that place!" We all have that inner voice; we're born with it. There are so many voices that appear as we grow up: peers, media, parents, general mores. When the inner voice says something that is the opposite of what's going on outside, it's really difficult to follow it. It's hard to push back at your parents or your peers or what you think is normal. If each of us listened to that inner voice, though, it would be easier to find the right path. It would be easier to find the place where you were meant to settle. We all still need to acknowledge the chorus outside of us, but give a little more authority to the voice inside of us.

In terms of enacting change in my own life, I look at it this way. I was born unique, as everyone else was, so I have a unique set of skills, abilities, and circumstances, and I'm going to deploy these to the best of my ability in order to enact change and make the world a better place. I think of it in terms of small, medium, and large. Small is my family, my world of friendships and relationships and everything that is close to me. I want to be the best possible person for everyone around me at that granular level. Medium is my city, my country, my people. I want to be the best possible neighbor, the best possible voter, taxpayer, citizen. I want to see that my country does the right thing and is good to each other and generous. Large is global and also cosmic. I want to be the best possible person to contribute to the goodness of the world. I want to be one brick in the wall that is good.

We are all infinite but also limited. We need to give up on the idea that, "I myself alone can fix the world." I think that is a very damaging belief because it causes despair; you can't ever change the world on your own. If you let go of that idea and you let yourself join this enormous mass of people who want to make the world a better place, just be one of those many, many people, the best one you can possibly be, then you realize, "Oh my god, it's good news! I'm not a hero, and I'm not the star of something. I'm just a bit player, just an extra, but look at me! Look at us in this galaxy of world-changers. This is a beautiful galaxy, and this is where I want to be." I just want to inhabit the world in the best way I can and then trust that all these other people who are also trying to enact change are pushing the world to a better, higher state.

Cynthia Eller

Dr. Cynthia Eller is an associate professor of philosophy and religion at Montclair State University in New Jersey and the author of *The Myth of Matriarchal Prehistory: Why an Invented Past Will Not Give Women a Future* and *Gentlemen and Amazons: The Myth of Matriarchal Prehistory, 1861-1900*. I first encountered Dr. Eller's work on the Internet in a discussion related to her book, *The Myth of Matriarchal Prehistory*. I remember a dynamic discussion in the comments section between a woman who did not agree with what she had read and Dr. Eller. The exchange piqued my curiosity, and I researched Dr. Eller's ideas about the origin of patriarchy even further.

When I first met her at her office in Montclair, I was impressed by everything about Dr. Eller, who she was, what she said, how she talked about her life and life in general. Her poised and intelligent air seemed like an incarnation of everything I was seeking out in my film. Everything she spoke of, she seemed to act upon. She genuinely lived by the words she preached. My favorite part of our conversation was the final discussion about integrating institutionalized religion with the complex impulses and tendencies of human nature. How could these two be reconciled without losing something essential, either faith or a part of yourself? Dr. Eller had lost neither, and she left nothing out. She had it all, and I wanted that. I still want that.

Rose Mary. From your experience, how would you define the feminine, or femininity? How would you characterize it?

I think of the feminine as mainly being a set of images that cultures create and associate with women. It's very culturally variable. What is considered feminine in one culture is not necessarily what is considered feminine somewhere else. So, in many ways I consider it to be an arbitrary collection of images that we line up with women. The image of the feminine in our culture is usually thought of as very maternal, very much about nurturing, and relationships, making things good between people, and so on. But what is considered feminine in one culture is not what is going to be considered feminine in another. The associations are kind of arbitrary from one culture to another. I think of femininity or the feminine as this cultural construct made up of all sorts of forces: social forces, religious forces, economic forces, and so on.

Rose Mary. Can you talk about how the matriarchy started in the first place?

I am completely fascinated by matriarchal myth. I spent years and years and years writing about this, so I have a lot to say on the subject. The idea of cultures where women are either in charge, or things are more centered around women, or around maternal values, is an idea that pops out around cultures all over the world. That idea is very old; the ancient Greeks talked about it. I think it is a natural impulse to imagine societies like that, especially when you are in male-dominated societies. It's natural to say, "Well, what would it be like if we swapped? How would people behave? Would the culture change? If so, would it be dramatically different? Would it be not so very different?" A lot of it is just a thought experiment in gender reversals. For that reason, it tends to arise, ironically, in male-dominated cultures. People want to experiment with the idea.

The first real upswing in the history of the matriarchal myth started in 1861 with a Swiss scholar named Johann Jakob Bachofen. He decided that pre-classical Greece was matriarchal. He really meant "matriarchal"; not just that it was goddess-worshipping or that it honored women, but that the women held the political power; they controlled the armies, and so on. He was the one who initially came up with the idea, but it really took off among British anthropologists. I think there are a couple of reasons why it did. I think they were exploring what was feminine, what was masculine, and what it would be like if we balanced those differently. They were also in the middle of their own feminist movement, so it was a time when it made sense to think about these things.

Another big part of the reason why they experimented with matriarchal ideas is that society as a whole had recently come to believe that human beings had been around for about 100,000 years. Prior to that, you were supposed to say—even if you weren't sure you believed it—that God created the world as told in Genesis, in seven days, 6,000 years ago. If you look at a 6,000-year time scale and you know that 3,000 years of them have been male-dominant, you don't have a lot of space to play with. What really happened in this huge upswing in the late nineteenth century is that people suddenly had this enormous prehistory, this enormous span of time. They could imagine whatever they wanted for it. Instead of saying, "Well, we know what human beings are like. We know what human societies are like. We have seen it. We have watched it. We have writings for most of it"; suddenly you had all this space in which human beings could have been anything. Societies could have been anything, and their religion could have been anything. People used that to come up with all sorts of interesting and novel ideas about what religion would have been like in prehistoric times.

That is really the genesis of matriarchal myth. I think it caught on very strongly with second wave feminists because it offered hope that things were possibly very different in the past and so they could be different in the future, especially looking at the very long timescale that this operates on. If you say, "The patriarchy arose in 3,000 BCE," which is a date that is usually given, that's actually 5,000 years of patriarchy. That is a tiny fraction of time if we have been here for 100,000 years. If we had been worshipping the goddess and treating nature well and honoring women, it makes the patriarchy seem like this small, bad accident that can be fixed, rather than something fundamental about human nature.

Of course its appeal in the late nineteenth century was very different because most of the men who built up the idea of this matriarchal past likened it to a boy growing up, "Well, he is attached to his mother when he is young, but then he becomes a man and that's when life really starts to happen." They would say, "Yes, women were more prominent; goddesses were more prominent; but we could never become civilized. We could have never become advanced with women running things. Men had to take over." They promoted this evolutionary sequence, of having gone from primitive and undeveloped to something much more wonderful, namely, male dominance and the worship of a male god. Some of their work, interestingly, had a bit of a feminist tone to it. They were hoping for a more egalitarian future. Nevertheless, the way they saw the story in general was that this matriarchal past, this infancy of the human race, had to yield to male dominance for progress to happen.

So, the myth of matriarchal prehistory holds that there were these original human societies that were matriarchal and goddess-worshipping, and then something terrible happened. There was a patriarchal revolution; everything has been awful since; and we can hope for something better in the future. I wouldn't say that the story is false. It can't be proven false, since there is so much we don't know about prehistory. But everything we do know, everything we can recover archeologically, and everything we can see from living cultures now; would lead us to believe that this never happened.

The fascinating question is, "Why was that story so fascinating for so many people?" It has been used not just by feminists, but by communists, by fascists of the Third Reich, by people with very different political positions to support. I think the matriarchal myth is so attractive because people need to play with reversals. They look at a society that is male-dominant and worships a male god, and they need to think, "How would it be *if*."

My personal opinion—this is not verified anywhere—is that it comes from male anxiety. Men know that they are given an advantage that their sisters are not. They do not know exactly why they got so lucky, or why they should be treated so differently. One way of thinking about that is to imagine things in the reverse and to show that they don't work, as we have seen in the logic appealed to by the nineteenth-century British anthropologists. In a way, it gave men an excuse to continue with their patterns of male dominance. Now, it's more a story of a golden era that was destroyed and to which we can hopefully return, for both women and men. I see it more as a thought experiment than anything else, and as such, it has been very fruitful for a lot of people. They really have imagined some wonderful things and they have been very innovative in their own spirituality, but I don't think there is any historical basis for really believing that it happened.

Rose Mary. When I started my undergrad, I had a professor who told us how to track when the Greeks were making the change from matriarchy to patriarchy. We were reading the tragedies and the myths, and she would say, "Can you see the changing tracks?" So I always had this idea of a transition that you could track.

Well, I devoted a book to explaining why that is not the case! I mean, it would have been nice if it were. I can see why it would be an appealing story. But really, when you look at the myths that people cite to show this turnover from matriarchy to patriarchy, they are often later myths, not the earliest Greek myths. This makes it clear that there was something going on in the cultural imagination of the Greeks regarding matriarchy rather than this being a mythicized version of their own deep history. So, it doesn't hold up well to archeological or historical scrutiny. But the idea is certainly attractive. It has been widely disseminated. I mean, there are people all the time who tell stories like yours, "I learned this in college."

Rose Mary. In your book, you are far more interested in how the myth has been used and played within the imagination of Western societies. What does it say about Western cultures wrestling with gender?

I think that is what matriarchal myth is all about: wrestling with gender. I think that is why matriarchal myth developed, because it is about women. Interestingly, it has also been advocated by communists, as well as by Nazis. There have been a lot of people who have used this basic storyline in different ways to ratify their vision of the future. The whole issue is about trying to re-conceptualize gender and sexuality, saying there are difficulties with it here and there, that there are things that aren't working. From the Nazi point of view, what was not working was that women were acting too much like men. This story was a way to say, "Women should become more like women"—barefoot, pregnant, and in the kitchen. A lot of different people have used matriarchal myth for various reasons, but essentially it's a way to get outside the culture that we have all absorbed and within which we have lived and really imagine other ways life could be, other ways people could function together, and balance gender relations more productively.

Rose Mary. You mention in your book that we need to reinvent femaleness. What would that look like after all the work you've done?

With apologies to people who do not like the word "thin," I have come to what I think of as a very thin theory of gender. What we can say about femaleness is essentially that it is an identity that is assigned to people at birth. It fits a lot of the people to whom it is assigned; they are able to take on its associations and function within its definition. For other people, this doesn't work out so well. "Femaleness really means having people understand that you are a woman and having them treat you the way they think women are supposed to be treated, nothing more than that. All of the other things that we think of as being part of femaleness, like the Western associations with nurturing, are what people who are born female are usually taught to believe should be a part of their personality. They are rewarded for expressing those kinds of behaviors, so that it's a feedback loop. Those things come to be associated with femaleness, and women experience themselves that way. Men experience them that way, too, even when they aren't being particularly nurturing. People are so invested in believing this that they will look past how people are really acting.

All in all, I would go with a very thin definition of femaleness. It is an ascribed identity. To me, the closest parallel would be race. What is "blackness"? Well, people who are black aren't in a different species than people who are white. We know that now, but people used to say that they were. People used to say that there were all these tendencies. They said, "Black people have *these* characteristics; white people have *these*." They said their brains were formed differently and that they had different gifts. We know now that all that is false. I suspect, although the science is not completely there yet, that the same is essentially true about gender.

It's just that people have a great need to be able to know with whom they are dealing, and it's convenient to have a shorthand— a woman is like this, a man is like this—with which you can anticipate the other's behavior. It's very convenient. People have built up this set of associations, but what is most important about that identity is simply the fact that it is assigned to you. The reason why "blackness" exists as a concept is that people decide you are black, tell you that you are black, and treat you the way they think black people are supposed to be treated. Obviously, the same pattern holds true for people of any other color, nationality, or ethnicity. I think that maleness and femaleness work the same way.

Rose Mary. In your knowledge and understanding, was there any point in history when women had a better social status than they do in Western culture today?

What do you think? Can you think of another time, not imaginary but an actual historical moment that would make you think, "I would have rather lived then as a woman? If I have to be in the category called "woman," I would prefer to live in ancient Greece or Minoan Crete or in Imperial China"? For me, nothing springs to mind. I think it's a very good and very difficult question. As feminists, we are inclined to think, "This is the worst of times." And it is very bad! You look around and you think, why are women admitted to emergency rooms? One of the top reasons is because somebody, usually a husband or a lover, beat them up! So how can you talk about this as being a good time and a place for women? You really can't. There are still so many obstacles between where women are and where women really ought to be, just on the level of fairness and justice, aside from anything else.

So, it's very easy to call this an unusually bad time. But I think honestly it is an unusually good time, not just because there is this ferment and opportunity for change, but also because women have made tremendous gains, just in the last fifty years. When I grew up there were no female newscasters on television; you never saw a female face. Workplaces were filled with men. The fact that this could change so much, and just over the course of my lifetime, makes me really optimistic. I mean, I'm pessimistic, too. There's still a long way to go, and sexism is very entrenched. And while people can see some of the surface issues, they may not see how deeply locked into people's psyches it is.

Therefore, there is still a lot of work that needs to be done. However, I would say we are pretty fortunate to be living now because the only other time that I can think of that would have been better is a mythical, woman-honoring, matriarchal time. It's a beautiful dream. Actually, to answer the question literally, I suspect there are places where it would be better to be a woman than now in Western societies, but I don't know where they are. I assume that there are tribal groups here and there. Maybe it would be better in Sweden than in the United States. I think I would probably move to Sweden, if my main concern was what kind of opportunities I would have as a woman. I don't know where those places are. I have never visited them. All I know is the place I have lived—which is pretty bad for women but has gotten a lot better—and the places I've read about, which mostly seem a lot worse.

Rose Mary. The only thing I can think of is maybe to be a bee or something!
     Certainly another species would give you more. But within primates, I actually think we are doing fairly well! A lot of the primates are worse than we are in terms of male dominance.

Rose Mary. In ancient times, people praised to both gods and goddesses. How did we end up relating God more with masculinity? Why did we accept this?
     Oh, this is a great question. I would say that the default human religion includes worship of both gods and goddesses. If you look worldwide, not just in ancient times, but if you look at most religions today, apart from the three major monotheistic religions—Judaism, Christianity and Islam—everybody worships goddesses. Everywhere you go, people worship goddesses. Even within these three religions there are some very important female figures. For example, in many Roman Catholic areas, Mary is far more important than Jesus. Theologically, the belief is that god, addressed with the male pronoun, is the ultimate deity. In reality, people most often relate to the female, to a saint who is essentially a goddess. Although you are taught to revere Mary and not worship her, that she can intercede and not *do*, and so on, you know those are really fine points. In terms of actual behavior, people's interactions with the Virgin Mary are very much

like Hindus' relationships with somebody like Lakshmi or Durga, or any of the other goddesses. I think that goddess worship really is the norm, not the exception. I don't think it's something that is limited to ancient times; it's a natural human impulse.

I believe that we have ideas about supernatural beings, or more powerful, or more ultimate forces; and because of our own limitations, we try to think of them in terms of things we know. What do we know? Where do we experience love and closeness, protection, and the kinds of things that we may want from a deity? We experience them in our human relationships. Therefore, we start casting god— the ultimate, supposedly genderless god—in gendered terms. When these monotheistic religions developed, why did they decide that this god was a "he and start talking about him as a "father" and "king" and "ruler"? Because that is how things were where they lived. If you want somebody powerful to help you out, you don't ask your mother, because she's not in charge. Your father is in charge, so you ask your father because he's the one who has the legal sway in the household. In many ancient cultures, the father legally owned the children. These were mostly monarchies, so there was one supreme ruler and he was always a man. Thus, the things that you want from god, if you are trying to describe a very powerful, transcendent being, you're naturally going to assume that it is male. You're naturally going to have those associations.

I think this is tremendously problematic. As somebody who was raised Christian and now practices Judaism, I really, really hate this attributing maleness to god, because it seems to me that it makes god a lot smaller, which is exactly what you're not supposed to be doing if you're a monotheist. You're supposed to see god as infinite. If god is walking around with a penis or a vagina, then god is not god. Maybe you can see those as small metaphors, but unless you have a whole lot of metaphors, or none at all, with which to talk about god, then you are making god smaller than god ought to be. In practical terms, it is distressing to me that, if you are told as a child, "God is your father," you will have good associations if you have a good father.

You will think of "father" as somebody who loves you even when you mess up, somebody who always supports you, who's stronger than you and can stand in for you when the going gets rough. He can get out in front of you. This is going to give you a relationship with what I would call your imaginary friend (because I don't believe in god). It gives you a relationship with this spiritual something that is very supportive and good. However, there are many of us who do not have those kinds of fathers. Yet, when you start thinking of god as a father and a king, you're also possibly bringing in all these associations with bad rulers, bad kings, bad fathers, fathers who hit you, fathers who don't want you to be happy, fathers who tell you you're a slut.

As long as we're on the topic, this is also why I have difficulty with the idea of just saying, "Ok we should worship a mother goddess. Let's make a goddess the central deity." Although a lot of people don't want to admit it, mothers are every bit as human and flawed as fathers. If you had a really good mother who loved you, who looked after you and supported you, then thinking of god as a mother might really work for you. But a lot of people don't have those mothers. A lot of people have mothers who were every bit as bad as their fathers.

Maybe this is off-topic, because this isn't really the academic take, but for me, from a religious perspective, we ought to be either using lots and lots and lots of images and metaphors for god, calling god "her" and "she" and "he" and "him," and imagining her as a cow and as the sun or whatever like most polytheistic religions do; or we should move towards a more Daoist idea. In this conception, the one, the infinite, the supreme, however you want to describe it—the potentiality in everything—cannot be gendered because it does not have a body. It's not a person; it's a something. Yes, that is the end of my sermon!

Rose Mary. The unnamable, right?

Yes, yes. I think all religions struggle with this. On the one hand, wanting to believe that god is somehow beyond our words, that we cannot express in language what god is or even what we feel like when we have encountered god; there are no words for it. And yet, we have a profound need to talk to one another about it, so we *have* to use words. Sometimes it gets us into trouble, especially when we grab onto one metaphor and hang on real, real tight, like "Our father in heaven." It leads us astray.

Rose Mary. So, was it really after monotheism that women began to be oppressed?

No, the best evidence we have is that the default culture world-wide, is one in which women are oppressed to one degree or another. Sometimes it is very little, small distinctions of status; sometimes it is absolutely brutal, where girls are married off when they are nine and never have any rights of their own whatsoever. I don't think we can blame monotheism for that. In fact, if we look at non-monotheistic religions, we have so much evidence of polytheistic societies that were extraordinarily male-dominant, including those with a lot of goddess worship like Hinduism and Daoism. In those societies, women really were property. First, you were owned by your father, and then by your husband, and if your husband died you were owned by your son. So, polytheistic religions can be perfectly compatible with male dominance. I think feminists working within a monotheistic context, who are the ones that have been most attracted to the idea of a prehistoric matriarchy or prehistoric goddess worship, have more of a need to flip the gender because they only have that one masculine image and they see that as problematic. I don't have an answer for how you would get the male dominance out of polytheistic religions, though I am optimistic that it can be done.

Rose Mary. I have a question. Is there a feminine principle that perhaps appears in other religions?

Religions that separate a feminine principle and a masculine principle, or a divine couple, are very common. I think they are actually much more common than this idea that there is just one god who is male. The single male god is the exception, really. It's a belief held by the most popular religions today, Christianity and Islam, so we tend to think of it as *the* major human religious idea. However, if you look in depth and over time across cultures, most religions worship both goddesses and gods. Many of them talk in terms of a divine couple that created the universe and it was only the relationship between them that was able to create the world.

You had examples in Chinese religions, in Daoism and Confucianism. Undoubtedly you have seen the yin and yang symbol. The two types, the yin and the yang, intermingle, and each contains a little of the other. One of the main ideas behind this is that yin is feminine and yang is masculine. What you want is a balance between the two. Also, it's not two separate entities, but entities that overlap with each other. There's always a little bit of one in the other. That would be one example of the feminine principle entering into religion. Even in male monotheistic religions a feminine principle works its way in. In Roman Catholicism, the Virgin Mary has become incredibly important. That was a very grass-roots demand from the people as opposed to a mandate from the top. They demanded there be a feminine aspect in the heavenly realm to relate to. In Judaism, you have the Kabbalistic idea of the Shekinah, the feminine presence of god or wisdom. I think it really is the rule rather than the exception that something about the feminine or female deities is part of the overall idea of the divine.

However, problems arise even when you have a religion where the feminine principle is really honored. For example, yin was thought to be incredibly valuable in Daoism. Some Daoist teachers said that men need to cultivate their yin character. It was all about a balance, all about the feminine. Yet, what was really going on in these societies was brutal for actual living women. The sad truth, I think, is that religious ideals don't necessarily correlate that well with what's happening on the ground.

A Marxist notion of religion would say that religion compensates people for what they don't get on earth. This would suggest that if you are looking at a religion in which goddesses are important, in which women play important roles, you are actually looking at a culture in which women are treated much worse. This religious ideal that "the feminine is wonderful; we worship the goddess; we love the feminine principle," is given in compensation for lousy roles on earth. So, it would suggest the opposite. If you have a religion that does not venerate the feminine as much, you might have a culture that actually treats women better. I'm not saying I agree with Marxist theory, but that is what Marxist theory would predict. It would suggest that there could be a real disjuncture between what we do religiously and what we are doing in our lives with real human women. I'm very interested in ideas of the feminine principle and the masculine principle, why people play with those ideas, what attributes they place in each, but I am ultimately more interested in what happens with women during their lives on earth.

Rose Mary. What is so wrong with women that they have to be pushed away? What is wrong with the feminine? Why is there so much energy invested in denying these two from our lives?

Oh, if I knew the answer to that question I would die happy tomorrow. I really do think that this is still the big question for me. Because misogyny, the hatred of women, or just this kind of avoidance reaction to women or to the feminine or to women's bodies; this really does happen all over the world. I don't know where it comes from. I think there are psychodynamic explanations. Take children, to begin with. The first person they really attach strongly to is female, so they have both this great love for the female but also this need to pull away, and so we carry that throughout our lives. Of course, there is an easy fix for that. You just have men raise children the same way women do, and that stops happening. So I see that as something that might explain why misogyny has been so common, but to me, it's not a stumbling block to make a different kind of society. I have encountered that kind of gut level resistance to women, that gut level hatred and pulling away. It certainly surfaces in literature, in films, all over the place. I don't honestly know what the origin of it is. I do see that humans tend to operate in hierarchies because we are a very social species, like a dog pack would. This doesn't mean we can't work against this tendency, but I think we are predisposed to have that reaction.

In really reductive terms, I think that men dominate women mainly because they can, because they are physically bigger. I think if women were physically bigger, men would be subordinate. At bottom, then, men assert dominance over women because they are physically capable of doing it and humans have an untutored urge toward dominance. Then there all sorts of things that get built in, and women learn to believe they are inferior so that it is easier for them to be dominated; and men learn to believe that they are powerful and that they can take up more space, even if they are little guys. Much happens on top of that basic size differential, on top of sexual dimorphism. Yet I think that is the basis for it.

I believe one of the reasons men have been so attracted to ideas of matriarchy or to goddess worship is because they are very conflicted about their supposed superiority. On the one hand they are told that they are dominant, they are bigger and badder, they need to run the show and make the decisions; but they don't always want to. Sometimes, they want their mom, and they want to relate to women in that way. It leaves them in an odd place. The same is true for women; you want to rely on other women but you are also counting on men to give access to certain social things that you can't get without men.

Rose Mary. Do you think that Christianity's whole infrastructure is based on masculine principles?

I think Christianity's core theology is very masculine. I don't believe it necessarily needs to stay that way. There are a lot of people who are able to work within Christianity and within Christian theology in very productive ways to loosen that grasp. They want to demonstrate that early Christianity was open to women's leadership, more inclusive of women's participation and experience and so on. I think that's true. On the other hand, Christianity grew up in a patriarchal culture and it reflected patriarchal values. It was a Jewish religion, and Judaism at the time was a patriarchal religion from a patriarchal culture. As Christianity developed and became part of the whole Greco-Roman world, it became part of yet another patriarchal culture. Therefore, it's almost inevitable that Christian concepts would be expressed in patriarchal and male dominant ways. That doesn't mean they can't be undone. There are a lot of beautiful ideas at the heart of the religion and it is a question of how literally you take things. You can pull apart the fibers and get the icky stuff out, and still keep the fabric intact. Personally, I've given up, but I'm very pleased that there are people who have not. I don't think it's a doomed mission.

Lorís. In a way it's very contradictory because Christ was a more balanced figure.

He's not your big bad male jock kind of guy! As a figure, and in terms of what he taught, he was not about dominance. You could say he was more balanced in terms of the attributes we usually think of as feminine or masculine. I think it would be overstating the case to say that Jesus was a feminist; he didn't talk about male dominance, for or against, though he had plenty opportunities to speak out about it. On the other hand, I think it's very important that this figure at the center of the religion is not a stereotypical male ruler. And a lot of people wanted him to be just that. He was supposed to be the Messiah, the predicted king, the descendant of King David. He was supposed to rise up, take power, and knock out the Romans, but that isn't what he did. There is a lot to be said for the fact that at the center of the religion is the figure of a man who understands humility and talks about personal change and personal behavior. Even so, you can still have a nasty pope and a nasty Christian crusade going out to kill people. It is unfortunate how much can be done with what seemed like a promising beginning. Still, I think it's helpful that Christians have that image to turn to that is not so stereotypically male.

Rose Mary. There are many feminists who connect the decline of the environment with our culture's denial of its femininity. That is, the environment could be portrayed as an expression of the values we carry within. What do you think of this?

I don't find those terms helpful. I think it's an interesting insight, and in some ways you can really show that there has been a model of exploitation towards the environment which is the same model that has been used towards women for centuries. Thus, there is this kind of similarity, this idea that, rather than cooperation and caretaking, you just say, "I need some of that, so hand it over." It's not productive. It's certainly not good for the environment or for women. Insofar as we can address both of those issues at the same time, I think that's wonderful. However, I don't think women mystically embody nature in a way that men do not.

If anything, rather than talking about how women are close to nature, or women are like nature, or that there are similarities in some deep metaphorical way, we should be trying to get men to see how closely *they* are tied to nature. I would say that it's mostly men who engineered our current predicament of climate change and the environment. Given that there is this kind of acquisitive, exploitative attitude on the part of people who are using nature and are using women, it is men who really need to be brought to feel as if they are a part of this whole biosphere. They don't get to stand outside and say, "It has all been given to you, do what you want with it." They need to take a different attitude.

Rose Mary. In your opinion, what changes could we make, both as individuals and as a society, to work towards gender equality in religion?

I think I have spoken to that already in suggesting that either having lots and lots of images to represent the divine, or not having images at all would be helpful. My thinking on this has changed a lot over time, though. When I was younger, I thought a lot about changing theology. I wondered how we should talk about god, and I really thought that was the core issue. I heard the people who were saying, "Oh we just need to ordain more women; they need to be priests and ministers," and I thought they were missing the big issue. For me, the big issue was calling god "him." And I think as I have gotten older I really feel that a lot of what brings gender equality into religion *is* putting women in positions of leadership. It's saying, "This is a communal affair." What we are doing here religiously is a communal effort. Women are on the board of trustees and men are on the board of trustees. There is a prominent priest and there is a prominent priestess, or minister, or whatever you want to call it. Having different gendered people working together and seeing themselves operating at the same level, is a lot more radical than I had first appreciated. That's what is making the biggest difference now. It's not changes in theology, not changes in the way we read scripture; it's just having women standing up in the pulpit and praying and reading before a congregation and people turning to them for an interpretation of religion. That has been a bit of a turn-around for me.

I see a lot of hope in this for the mainstream religions. I think feminist spirituality has been a huge contributor to this change, because this was a group of women who did not just say, "Please, Daddy, can I have a slice of the pie now?" I mean, they commanded, "Get out of the room! We can do this!" That was tremendously empowering. The combination of that and saying, "We do not have to call god "father," we do not have to call god "it"; if god is not a person, it makes just as much sense to call god "she." I think that was a very powerful move. The fact that there were women who were doing that gave a lot of freedom to women who stayed within mainstream religions to move in that direction, to be more self-assertive, to feel more confident about their own leadership. Even though it's not for me, nor is it based on an accurate story about human history, it's ultimately a very effective feminist movement.

Jay. How does one reconcile practicing a religion with being a woman at the same time? It seems like it's a choice you have to make.

I can answer from a personal perspective. How do I practice Judaism and raise Jewish children when the religion is patriarchal? And I don't have to soften that at all: Judaism is a patriarchal religion. Personally, I feel in the first place that the tradition is changing. There is something valuable about deep cultural roots and working with those to create what you want in the future, as opposed to saying, "Hack it all off, we're starting fresh." You never really do that. If you try to hack everything off and start fresh you're still going to be pulling from all sorts of other places and traditions. For me, it's like saying, "Well, if your dad is the head of your family and doesn't treat your mother and your sisters fairly, then you should just leave the family." Well, I don't think that's always the most helpful approach. I think you need to work within it, where people are, to improve their situation there.

Watching my daughters come of age as Jews, it has been a lot about reading the traditional stories and saying, "Wait a minute, he did what? And God told him to do what? And where was his wife?" It's about challenging these stories, which is what is happening in the synagogue we attend. It is happening from the rabbi too, not just among individual congregants. Therefore, it's about struggling from the place you are in, from who you are, who your family is, your extended family, your identity; and moving from there into a less patriarchal future. That's not to say I haven't struggled with this. I was raised Christian, and I left the church mainly because I thought, "This is never going to work. This thing cannot be fixed. This thing is broken and I don't like it. I don't need it, and I don't want it."

To me, what I get out of Jewish practice and what I feel my daughters get out of it is the ritual, the simple honoring of day to day events. You light candles on Friday night and you think about setting down your burdens for a little while and being open to more relaxed ways of being. Once a year, you open up the Torah and everyone looks at the whole thing and you dance around with the scrolls. It's a joyous community event. It's a time when everybody gets together and the rules are tossed aside, just like Mardi Gras or carnival in Christianity. All religions have these kinds of elements. I think so many of them are very community honoring; they are human honoring. They give structure to our lives. Here, we are young, and then we have this event and after that we are supposed to take on new responsibilities and grow into our adulthood. And when we get married, we do it with a sense of being part of generations and generations of people who've done this and engaged in this struggle to try to create a better world and raise their children in the best way they can.

Lorís. I think it makes perfect sense. There's so much truth in that. I mean, you're human! It's not like you're any different from your ancestors. You're still going to do the same things, but to take the time to honor that and feel that sense of belonging to something far greater, I mean, that's what religion is all about!

Jay. When speaking about where the change is going to originate from, a lot of women say, "Well men need to participate as well." In a conversation with Dr. Abigail Disney after her interview, she said, "Until the guys walk out of the bachelor party when the stripper walks in, we're not really going to have true change." At the same time, from my personal experience, I've had discussions with other men —just something stupid about heels, "heels are dumb and painful and no one should wear them, unless it is as a joke or something" —but then, women defend them. So my question is, where does change really come from? Is it a chicken and an egg thing? Is it men who reinforce that dynamic and then women accept it? Or is it women who accept and then men are taught to reinforce that?

The whole gender inequality thing—feminine, masculine, male dominance—it's very much a community project. Men do it and women do it. Women don't teach young girls how to be women in a nice way, and this isn't very helpful or effective for them. Women do this as much as men do, or even more so. I wouldn't see it as either women or men have to take the initiative or be in control; it really needs to be both, ideally through some cooperation. There are different tasks for women than there are for men. If you're a woman and you are trying to get to a place where you don't have to wear heels, or whatever the issue is, you're going to approach it from a different angle than if you are a man.

Again, I come back to the analogy of race. I am white, and I should not be setting the agenda for a liberation movement for nonwhite peoples. On the other hand, I should not be behaving like an asshole. When white people are sitting around and one of them makes an off-hand racist remark, I should protest, "You know, I don't really think that's cool, and here's why." So, I think it's true that men need to walk out of the bachelor party when the stripper arrives. I think men need to start being courageous. Women need to be courageous, too. One of the real tasks feminists need to work on is making men understand that the movement is in their best interests. It's not that power is being taken away from them; it's that a burden is being lifted off their shoulders. They don't have to carry it all. They get to share the burden with people who are strong and capable and who can work as equals with them. They don't have to say, "Oh, alright honey, I know you can't lift that box," or whatnot. Maybe you are stronger and you can help in that situation. However, in another situation in your life, maybe it's easier for her to do the lifting. She can do it for you and not have you feel smaller as a person because of that.

Though I understand many of the reasons, I think a lot of early feminist anger doesn't really give men the opportunity to change. It just says, "You're messed up! You need to stop, stop, stop!" A lot more guys than we imagine would find it a very positive thing to be involved in childrearing. This model where men say, "Oh, I've never changed a diaper," was very, very common a generation ago. I think the changes have been huge in incorporating men into caring for their young children, and men have profited from that enormously. They have closer relationship with their kids. They are more gentle human beings. They know how to love more. So yes, I would suggest selling feminism to men as, "You are going to like this a lot!" as opposed to "Stop doing that!"

Serene Jones

Reverend Dr. Serene Jones, author of *Feminist Theory and Christian Theology, Calvin and the Rhetoric of Piety* and *Trauma and Grace*, is an ordained minister in the United Church of Christ and the Christian Church as well as the sixteenth president of the Union Theological Seminary in New York, the first woman to become president in the seminary's 176-year history. Rev. Dr. Jones holds degrees from the University of Oklahoma, Yale Divinity School, and Yale University, where she served as a Titus Street professor of theology for seventeen years, and chair of the department of Women, Gender and Sexuality Studies. After arriving at the Union Theological Seminary, Rev. Dr. Jones formed the Union's Institute for Women, Religion and Globalization and the Institute for Art, Religion and Social Justice. In 2013, she participated in President Obama's fifty-seventh presidential prayer service at the National Cathedral in Washington DC, and she is currently the Johnston Family chair for religion and democracy and vice president of the American Academy of Religion.

It had been a long time since I had stepped foot in a church other than for a wedding or a family member's first communion. Even though I was raised as a Catholic, my spiritual formation has been focused more on getting to know what I carried within. That is to say, I grew up believing that the more I knew about myself, the more I would know about others and the world. But the task was completely in my hands, and it was up to me to choose what parts of myself I decided to explore. The idea of God having had a carnal body at one point, or God as a separate entity had become foreign to me. So I felt a little shy entering Rev. Dr. Jones's office. I was afraid to say something possibly offensive without meaning it, or maybe completely disagreeing on something she said and not knowing how to deal with it. It's not an easy thing, I thought, to begin suddenly talking about your most profound foundations with someone coming from a completely different background.

What I found was astonishingly different than what I expected. I agreed with everything Rev. Dr. Jones said. We believed in the same things, we just used different words. It didn't matter where we thought God was, or what we thought He/She/It looked like, because in the end we were two human beings speaking about how best to spend the little time we have on this planet. No matter how much we discuss and argue these beliefs, where we go after this life is a journey that will be only for our own soul to see and discover.

Lorís. In ancient times, people praised both gods and goddesses. When monotheism came, feminine representations of human life slowly seemed to disappear under masculine ideals. How did we end up relating God with masculinity and why did we accept this?

Well, that clearly happened in Western culture because we, along with religion, developed stronger and stronger patriarchal modes of government and culture. It all sort of consolidated into one big patriarchal vision of the male-head. Now, why did we accept it? That's what's baffling to me. You know, you look into any organization, you look into any culture around the world and you ask the question, who's doing the work that matters the most? You can't go anywhere in the world and not find that the women are growing the food. They're harvesting the food. They're cooking the food. They're having the children. They're educating the children. They're taking care of the sick people. They're taking care of the old people. They're selling and exchanging all the goods that make a village work. So, why are they not in control?

Lorís. It seems that under Western values, if you don't bring money to the house, your work is not worth anything. Taking care of the children of the house doesn't bring money.

Well, we've set up an economy in which we don't value child care. It doesn't bring money to the house because we don't pay for it. But, that's a social decision, to think that raising children is not as valuable as other forms of labor, and in cultures where women are, in fact, making the money, men take it from them and control it. That happens over and over again, too. So simply giving women more money doesn't solve the problem.

Rose Mary. From the times of Aristotle to the present there have been innumerable philosophers and theologians who have spoken loud and clear about the inferiority of women. St. Thomas Aquinas spends a fair amount of time proving the inferiority of women. Previously, St. Augustine did the same. Many of us still carry those beliefs. How can men and women overcome and achieve equality when that subtle oppression has been culturally engrained in the collective unconscious for centuries?

It's deep. It is so deep. And you can go into the most feminist communities today and the thing still rears its ugly head because it's so deep in our psyches. We breathe this stuff in when we don't even know it. You can't find a bigger feminist than me in terms of the world of Christianity and theology, and yet even I find myself sometimes standing up in Church and saying, "God, may He be with us." And I'm like, "'He'! 'He'? Why do I even say it? It just came out of the depths of me!" Because it's been so ingrained! And we need to have a world in which that ingrained dynamic is interrupted. I want my daughter to grow up and think that if she ever heard of God referred to as a He, it would shock her. "Oh, mom, God's a 'He'? I thought God was a She!"

Lorís. And you first have to be able to recognize something before you can fight it.

And it feels like it's natural. It's so ingrained. You think, "Well, this is the way the world is." And that's the hard part. I tell the story of my daughter. The moment she was born—literally, she had not been thirty seconds in the world—before the hospital put a little pink hat on her head. Everyone in the hospital began to interact with her like she was a little girl. Immediately, a set of assumptions was ingrained into her about who she is.

Rose Mary. You mention in your book, Feminist Theory and Christian Theology, *that oppression affects the very way one thinks about oneself. Sometimes it is difficult to recognize oppression. Sometimes, it originates from oneself when we interject social rules. For example, "Women need to remain virgins, serve God and men, and forever live being careful not to tempt men." Adam and Eve are a perfect example of how women were launched to the world of religion as the sinners, evil itself embodied. If men and women are supposed to complement each other, this means that oppression in women must inevitably oppress men as well in a certain way. What are your thoughts on this?*

Well part of what I'm describing there is that if we have a set way that women should be, and we have a set way that men should be, it ends up constraining both; because men no more fit the role of what men should be than women fit the role of what women should be. In that sense, both parts of the equation are disadvantaged. If we could get rid of this weird calculus of men and women, people could be what they are. They could grow and blossom into the fullness of what they're meant to be.

Rose Mary. You mention in your book that liberating women is the sole key to liberating the world. This interconnection between women and their environment does not exclude the inner connection between women and their own femininity. Would you say that the first step to acquire this liberation needs to be through the inner work?

Absolutely. Changing society helps the inner work happen because you have to be in a supportive environment to do the inner work, but until we get those deep stories changed inside of us, it doesn't matter how much we change a structure here and there. These outer changes don't matter if, three years down the storyboard, the story is going to recreate itself because we haven't changed what we tell ourselves about reality. If we believe somewhere that men and women are different because the feminine is inferior to the masculine, then it's going to happen again and again and again. That's how we'll create our lives.

Lorís. There are many feminists who connect the decline of the environment with our culture's denial of its femininity. That is, the environment could be portrayed as an expression of the values we carry within. What do you think of this? Where does the environment fall in Christian belief?

When I think of the environment I think of our creative world, the world of materiality around us, and I'm not sure that the feminine is more connected to the environment. But what I think happens with this dynamic around femininity and masculinity is that we get so good at denial, massive denial, about the things that it takes to make life work. So, just like we don't want to deal with the fact that women's bodies are the source of life; so, too, with the environment. We think, "Oh, we can just keep raping the earth. We can just keep attacking this nature." And because we don't want to deal with the consequences, we just shove it aside and we pretend like it's not happening. It's happening, and it's devastating.

Rose Mary. Do you think that our Christianity's whole infrastructure is based on masculine principles? How, or how not so?

I think that if you read back through Christianity, you always find another story, and that's the story of the strong women who have been very devout and committed leaders, who have been taking care of the poor and the children, who have been doing the hard work of social justice, and time and again their stories get slammed down. We don't want to acknowledge that they exist, but there's now 2,000 years of really tough, brilliant women who have been inspired by Christianity at its best. I also think Christianity is going through a massive change right now, and the masculine Christianity is in its death rows.

Rose Mary. Could you explain to our audience what feminist theory and theology is and its importance?

Feminist theory is a body of research and thinking that looks at the way in which, for thousands of years, human beings have constructed this notion that there are feminine characteristics and there are masculine characteristics. It examines how we've taken those and imposed them on the bodies of women and men. It thinks about that whole dynamic of how we came up with that and how weird it is that we're stuck with it.

Rose Mary. Women have historically lived various forms of oppression, one of them being religion. Since the Church was born, women were relegated to a place that, for centuries, was not accessible to priesthood. Can you elaborate on this subject?

Yes, there are two big factors in Christianity in particular. One is that Christianity was born into a culture that was totally patriarchal. The Romans were patriarchal. The cultures of the Middle East were patriarchal. So, Christianity was born in the midst of patriarchy. And then, you have Jesus, the Messiah, the big figure there, and he's a man! Well, an early group of Christians came along and said, "Oh, because Jesus was a man, that means only men can be at the top."

Rose Mary. Jose was telling me about the gospel of St. Thomas, and I read Pagels (1979)[23] *and she spoke about that. It seems that that discovery of the Gnostic gospels in 1945 changed all the dynamics of how we conceived Christianity, and women had a better place* (Robinson, 1990). *Did it really affect the way the Church was developing? Because I really haven't seen a change.*

A lot of conservative Christian communities just deny the fact that in early Christianity women had dramatically different roles. In early, early Christianity, there would be no Christianity if it weren't for wealthy women who were hosting emerging Christian communities in their homes. In those communities there was an insistence that men and women were equal. It was like a baseline starting point. Then we get another form of Christianity growing up alongside it that actually wins the day, and that view decides that women are inferior. It's very tragic when you look and see what happened.

Lorís. From your experience and from what you have learned throughout your lifetime, if you were asked to define what the feminine is, how would you characterize it?

When I think of the feminine, I think of things like intuition, emotion, connection, embodiment, nature, love; as opposed to masculinity, which is reason, logic, individualism over the collective, not emotion but clear-headed thinking, order. I think of the feminine as

---

[23] Elaine Pagels is an American author focused in the history of religion best known for her book *The Gnostic Gospels* (1979).

the space of sort of chaotic, intuitive connection; and the masculine as the space of order and law and the correct configuration of things.

Lorís. Our documentary plays with the idea that our society devalues feminine characteristics in both men and women, and this is a contributing factor to women always falling one step behind. For example, some unspoken assumptions remain flowing in our psyche such as "intuition is not as strong as reason," "emotions are a sign of weakness," or "receptiveness and un-certainty go in opposition to profitable results." How do you view this argument? Does it follow with your experience or with your observations throughout your life? Would you share some examples?

Those distinctions are in fact the way we view the masculine and the feminine, and in large part they get mapped onto the bodies of men and women. So you look around and you say, "Well, there's more women doing this kind of thing and more men doing that." But in both men and women, there are many examples of "the other being a part of who they are." Secondly, and this is a part that really perplexes me, all the qualities that we associate with the feminine that are usually degraded, counted as less, are in fact—when you look at how societies function—more important. They are the things that actually make the world go round, and they're the things that connect us deeply to what make us who we are. So why is it that things that are more important at the end of the day have less power? It doesn't make any sense.

Lorís. Is there anything else you would like to add?

As a professor of theology, Christianity, and religion, my work early on was on a reformation theologian named John Calvin, who worked at the time of the reformation, five-hundred years ago. He was around during a time when Christianity turned inside out and became a new thing. I think we're at one of those moments right now. I think Christianity is being remade from its toenails up to the top of its head; it's acquiring a new body. Fifty years from now, what counts as Christianity is going to be something we don't recognize right now. Now, my worry is that it could become a more patriarchal Christianity.

Rose Mary. Do you think that Catholicism or Protestantism is headed that way?

I think that there's a large group in Catholicism and Protestantism that is so afraid of change that they're becoming more entrenched, and they're becoming more patriarchal and more anti-woman. But sometimes when it comes to change, right before it changes, it gets the worst. What people also don't talk about is that there are all these people who have left Protestantism and Christianity, massive numbers, who have left because it's a problem, and those are the people in whose hands the future rests. Those are the people we work with at the Union here. Those are the people that I think carry our future. That's where my daughter is.

Greg Gondron and Tom Hopwood

Greg Gondron is a musician, singer, and ASL interpreter in Houston, Texas, and the director of training
and operations at the men's nonprofit organization, the
ManKind Project (MKP), which is a sponsor of the
New Warrior Training Adventure (NWTA). He received his BS in speech and hearing sciences and his
MS in deaf education from Lamar University. Previously, Greg specialized in deaf education as a teacher
and interpreter in a regional day school for the deaf.
In 1998, after a fifteen-year career in the field of
education, Greg attended one of the ManKind Project's trainings and was profoundly transformed. He
began staffing and engaging in MKP leadership
trainings. To this day, Greg has staffed and led over
110 MKP trainings internationally, and he continues
to lead trainings and facilitate healing and transformation work for men and women.

Tom Hopwood is a leader emeritus with the Mankind Project and sits on the board of directors for Houston Achievement Place. He received his BA in history from Monmouth University. After twenty-five years running major companies he left the corporate environment to work with men in the US and the UK. In 1994, he founded Executive Advice, a business that allows him to work with men and women to find the courage to develop a sense of purpose and fulfillment for themselves and for their community.

A loving and active father to his two daughters and four grandchildren, Tom lives in Houston, Texas, where he indulges in his love of photography and nature, often losing himself in the woods with his camera.

Initially motivated by the desire to send my father and brother off on an adventure, I had never heard of the ManKind Project before I contacted Tom. I remember telling him, "I have been looking for an organization like this for years." I had always wondered if women might not be the only ones presently involved in these sorts of endeavors. To my surprise, Tom and Greg opened a new mysterious world of men welcoming the feminine back into their lives. Coming from a family with very old-fashioned gender roles, this new community seemed like the Promised Land, the missing link of feminism and the ultimate key to whatever good was to come in the future. I was thrilled and desperate to know everything: who these men were, how they thought, what they sounded like. I wanted to know about their wives, their children, their favorite movies and conversation topics? To this day, the men's section in the film has been the most intriguing to me. I only have Tom and Greg to thank for welcoming me to the Other's side.

Lorís. Can you speak to us about the Mankind Project's mission and its importance in our society? Why would it appeal to a regular guy?

Greg. I want to preface this answer and all of them by saying that this is my opinion. I believe that if you ask any man who has been through the New Warrior Training, which is the flagship program that we run, you'll get diverse answers.

Mankind Project's New Warrior Training Adventure has been around since 1985. It grew out of the men's movement prior to that time. It was founded by three men, and it was meant to be, well, what it was meant to be. That sounds a little loose, but it was an opportunity for younger men, older men, men in our society to go through a rite of passage, the opportunity for a new way of being. It was a chance to wake up, to become conscious, and also to do battle within. For those reasons, the Mankind Project and the New Warrior Training Adventure is a portal for men who are willing to take risks and to transform.

Tom. To echo Greg, my experience is probably more important than my knowledge as well. I remember watching a lot of Joseph Campbell[24] and being moved by the power of myth, seeing all these images and stories. I was so interested, but I wasn't doing anything. I was running a large company, and I thought, "Who is this? What is this all about?" Then the men's movement started, and Robert Bly[25] was a big influence. I remember going to a workshop up in Minnesota,

---

[24] Joseph Campbell is an American mythologist and author. He is best known for his concept of the "hero's journey."
[25] Robert Bly is an American poet and activist. He was the leader of the mythopoetic men's movement, and he is best known for his book essays, *Iron John: A Book About Men* (2004).

and then one day somebody said something about the New Warrior training.

There, I saw so many different aspects of men, men who would hold other men in their fears, nurture them in a way I had never, ever experienced before. Something shifted inside of me. I think what shifted on some level was this idea of, "Who am I? Why am I, and when am I?" I knew what I was not because I was always left with this question—running a company, let's say—but knowing that was not me. I was shut down emotionally. I couldn't have a dialogue; probably couldn't even name a feeling I was having other than anger. The New Warrior experience isn't just the experience of the weekend; it's the only work I know of that gives some transcendent purpose to what a mission is. I still have the same mission that I had twenty-two years ago when I did the work. It hasn't changed one word. It is "to co-create world community by empowering men and women to the ecstatic joy of service." It hasn't changed one word because it was natural. It gave me something that I had never experienced before, but I had to see that it was real in other men. That's why I think the warrior is much more of an archetypal energy, rather than something repressed and denied just within men.

Lorís. Why has the men's movement died?

Tom. That's a really great question. Why does any work die? Does it, really? Or does it just have a different form that manifests on a larger collective basis. You go and have an experience, and in time it runs its course. I believe New Warriors have been around close to— what, thirty years now?

Greg. Thirty.

Tom. Thirty years. That's the longest-sustained work I know of that deals with the deep sensitivities of men. Much of the work of New Warrior is about men getting in touch with the psychological wounds that block them from having a transcendent purpose. Men's work doesn't stick around if there's no feminine energy that gives it purpose. I come from the Vietnam era. Back in the seventies free love and all the things that went along with it were huge. Women introduced us to something bigger than just fighting wars that were needlessly fought. What did we do? We traded it off. When we said, "Make love, we would rather make love," we forgot that we had work to do in the world. It becomes seductive at some point.

Greg. I might add that, just as we have transformed, the work itself is transforming. Its purpose or its audience may not be what it was. The essence of it is powerful enough and impactful enough that it has sustained itself for some reason all these years. We have adapted in some ways, in terms of where we reach out into our audiences, and the type of men who we are attracting to come and do the work. Like Tom said, attraction is what draws men out of curiosity into exploration. "What is it about you, or what do you have that I want to have? Where did you get that?" That is really a doorway to expose what the work is about.

Lorís. How would you define a healthy masculinity? Does this differ from how society sees it?

Greg. One of the tenets of the work around healthy masculinity is the significance of moving from boyhood to manhood. There is a blueprint already in place that we may not already be aware of. As we age, a lot of things block our truths. In those blueprints are templates, what Jung refers to as archetypes. Each of these archetypes, or energies, within men can be tapped through this work and can lead or guide men, if they choose. That is key; they must choose to move from this boy-centered energy or belief, this sort of egotistic, "Me, me, me, what's in it for *me*?" kind of competition. The work can lead us into and through a transformational experience, which is what the weekend is about. It's about coming into a healthy masculinity, the discovery of what is possible as a man.

Tom. Even the word "healthy" is a construct. What one person might call "healthy," another person might say is "sick." We live in a culture that says it's weak to have your feelings. It takes a strong man to want to be able to identify a deeper connection to his emotional body and hopefully work his way through some of the wounds that he has so they can serve him out in the world. A man who doesn't know his own wounds will act them out somewhere in the world, mostly in his relationships, and especially in his close relationships. It's not that he intends to do it, but it's going to slip out because he has not taken responsibility for himself.

Most men are just as subjected to patriarchy as women are. They're bullied, shut down. They're told, "Do not create, and just slide by," and left wondering whether they'll ever do something of value in the world. As a result of that, when you're around what I call "male nurturing"—which has a pretty strong edge to it—it evokes a fear. And it's a healthy fear, maybe even a healthy terror. It says, "You know, I may be able to do this, because I see it in someone else; they make a stand for something that I would be silent about."

We learn that these forces are there, and we want to tap into them because of the state of the world we find ourselves in today. Patriarchy is the highest form of male cowardice, the highest form, because it hides in it its arrogance. The reason I can say that is because I was a part of it; and to some degree, when I am unconscious, I continue to be a part of it. If I know it inside me, maybe I can feel safer to say what needs to be said around those who project it out and squash the creative forces in both men and women.

Lorís. To you, what is the feminine? People understand feminine as the pink and the cute, whereas the real feminine is not being recognized for its true meaning. I have not been able to find a word that grasps the idea of the feminine without saying "feminine." The closest I've gotten to is "soul." So, I want to ask you about that.

Greg. Well, again, if you'd asked me fifteen years ago, prior to doing any internal work, I would have given you a completely different answer. However, for me today, the feminine is a construct, and I resist trying to define it. But I do see the feminine as the nurturing, the creative, the birthing, the supporting, the holding. That can apply to men or to women or to any being. It's the part that is intuitive, the part that is in touch with feeling, the part that gives itself permission, the part of me that is unbridled in freedom, the feminine. It's the braver part, in some ways. It doesn't fear, but pushes through, metaphorically and literally. It's the part of each of us, that *allows*.

Tom. The word "feminine" works for me because it is beyond; it's what expands me to have an experience or a thought. It's a possibility, a hologram of something that might be. I love the word "feminine." I think it was Campbell who used the term "the Tao." For men, our own repressed feminine is a connection to the source. I love the term, "the source." It's where there is an explosion, an expansion; the feminine actually has to push the solid walls of what we men have built in this world.

I think the feminine has a certain ferociousness when it speaks its truth; it really cannot be denied. Patriarchy doesn't let up, and the feminine says, "We are screwing up the planet. Stop it!" So what do we do? We still screw up the planet. But it doesn't stop the truth. Where does that insight come from? Where does a thought come from? I believe it comes when we allow ourselves to be tapped into these collective intelligences at the source. "Feminine'" really does work for me.

Lorís. When you do your retreats and your weekends of the New Warrior, how do you address the feminine? Do you address it with the term, "feminine" or with a different word? I mean, how does it appeal better to men? What resonates better with men?

Greg. I would say that it depends on the work. There are a lot of metaphors for the feminine. I don't know that we use "feminine," but we use metaphor a lot in our work, and the archetypes, and the analogy of the earth being the feminine. We borrow that from cultures throughout history, the idea of the earth being the part of the feminine that births and nurtures and sustains and endures. I don't know that the word per se is scripted in the training itself, but for those who continue to do the work, then it becomes consciously about what feminine is for that man.

Tom. Rather than the language, it's about the experience that can't be put into words. Where do you get a deeper sense of what love means to you? You don't have words for it; you have an experience. When love is that intense, it can be strong but compassionate. It brings in the polarities of the energies of the real world. Maybe in some ways it expands the possibility that the new mind, or the expanded mind, might have new neural pathways to experience something that doesn't need a definition. It just means "go and do something of value to you in the world." That is the feminine spirit to me.

We shut down so many things. I believe Aristotle had it right. He used the word "flourish." What a beautiful word that is! Now, flourishing doesn't mean I'm just going to live happily, joyous and free. It means I don't waste any experience that helps me move closer to who I am in the world. Actually, I like that, "the flourishing feminine." It works for me. Does it work for you?

Greg. Yes.

Jay. I have a bunch of ideas. It's fascinating to hear you guys talk about this, especially in contrast to all the other interviews we've done, because they've mostly been women. I've had a moment of revelation that the "male" side of men goes through a lot more fear than women do. I don't feel like a woman is ever afraid of being a woman, whereas a man does have that sense of the risk they would take in society if they tried to live a fuller life.

The second thing that has been really different for me right now is listening to these ideas talked about in the context of the world in general, and—like you said, Tom—the context of doing something valuable for the world. It's like a different type of struggle. It seems like it's taking the face of a genderless struggle, more than something specific to a particular gender. Maybe that's why it seems like the movement died, because it's just so open to everyone. It's not necessarily about a man's movement.

Loris. We've talked a lot about the word "feminine," leading you to think only of women, and keeping men away. Men are shying away from things that pertain to them, and the problem mainly originates in the language.

Tom. We get caught up in the semantics rather than in the experience. I constantly have men in a place where words can't really express what's taking place inside them. When I have an experience I say, "Come join me and have your own experience. Don't copy my experience, okay? You have to have your own to find out what it is that moves you, so you can find your purpose in life." If I tell you how to do it, I just formed a religion, and that's the last thing I want to do.

These experiences are an archetypal part of the collective, and they're genderless. You have great poets like Rumi who say, "There is a field out there, beyond what is right and what is wrong. Meet me there." For me, he's saying that you must work beyond the duality of constructs like man or woman, right or wrong. Beyond that, what you might find is that we are all part of the same world, the same cosmos, and all trying to do the very best we can to find out how we belong in that larger context.

Lorís. Our culture has a sort of obsession of the female body, whether it be to sexualize it or to heal it. However, there has been very little talk about men's relationships with their bodies. From what you have seen and experienced, what kind of relationship do men have with their body? Has the media had an effect on it?

Greg. Men have the opportunity to become conscious of their bodies, not just their physical body or their appearance, but of the truth being held in their bodies, that answer lying within, the battle occurring within. The whole process, from the simplicity of identifying a feeling, to distinguishing it from a thought, to making a conscious choice, is part of the wake-up call that takes place in the training. Men are challenged on these weekends to recognize that the answers are not going to be with the leader, and they're not going to be out there. We constantly bounce back and mirror back to within, to make our journey, to find our mission, to identify what we're feeling, and ultimately, to see the interconnectedness between all of us.

Tom. My experience is that men are, for the most part, disconnected from their body, disconnected from the intelligence that our body can draw from. If I'm not connected to my body, I will project that out. I will project it out to men, to women; I will project it out into the world. Why do images seen in pornography try to own something of beauty that really doesn't serve any purposes? It's not just a magazine; it's about ownership. It's so seductive. Part of it is because of man's own disconnection with the joy that the body can create in many different ways other than just sexually. That is participating with life in its fullest. When you start to open up and work through the emotional body, the spiritual body opens up to all the senses—touch, taste, feel, sound, everything. It vibrates.

The body is the instrument; it's the temple that allows us to be connected to everything around. What we often have done, especially in the business world—we can speak from experience on that—is teach women how to shut down. It's very simple. You want to be successful in business? You just look like this patriarchal dick that is running a business. If you look like us, you, too, can have what we have! Which is not much, but we have it. Then we put all these ads on TV, and we flood you with what beauty ought to be. There's a collusion that takes place. We don't put ads out for, "Who are you, really?"

But there is an awareness that is taking place that is shifting those views. I am hopeful that will expand.

Greg. In my fourteen years in this work, I've seen time and time again the men who come on our training weekends shackled with how they have defined themselves, what they have been told a man is. I've seen them search time and time again, initially on the training, just to *identify* what a feeling is, much less to express it. The immediate narrative prevails: "Well, if I feel or I express, then somehow I am deemed feminine, or a woman, or a little boy." They have been inundated with all these messages about what it is to be a man as opposed to a woman.

When men find the key to unlock their own shackles, and the freedom and the brilliance and the gold that they discover in themselves—we use the term "gold" a lot in the work—and the relinquishing of definitions and constructs of who I am or was; they discover themselves, and it's beautiful.

Lorís. If our human nature dictates that we be social beings, where is the cultural value of shutting down men's emotional communication? And how does this hampered emotional communication affect the relationship between father and son?

Greg. One of the basic teachings on the weekend is to identify emotion—energy in motion. I like the separation of "e" into "energy," so that "emotion" means "energy in motion." In the work that we do, we circle up and we check in with what we're feeling. We check where each other is. We check in, and it enhances relationship. If I am aware of what his body is feeling, and he is aware of what my body is feeling, what I am holding, what I am containing, imagining and hallucinating; it creates relationship. It creates trust, bonding. That's some of the emotional intelligence that our work renders, men being able to identify and have permission to identify who they are, who you are as a man.

Tom. Shame is so pervasive in our world. Brené Brown[26] here in Houston has done some incredible research around shame factors for men and also women. Her work began primarily around women until she realized she was excluding something: Men get shamed too. She observed that the number-one thing that puts men in shame is criticism from women. Much of it has to do with our own complex, dealing with women, dealing with the mother, not being enough or being too much, or whatever that case may be. Often we look to fit in certain places. Often we try to fit in where we know we don't belong, but we work hard to fit in, never feeling like we belong.

---

[26] Brené Brown is an American psychologist and author best known for her bestselling books *The Gifts of Imperfection* and *Daring Greatly*.

She also found that the number-one piece that puts women into shame is their body, and the images that they are constantly bombarded with. Unless we can identify and have a language to get beyond our own shame, how can we really support and learn to love others, stand by their side and not continue to do harm in the world? The basic tenet, not just of this work, but of life, is to do no harm. I have to know about shame, what puts me into shame, and what keeps me out of shame. Then, I am empowered not to respond in the way I used to before.

Men shame one another, and it's not pretty. It's flat-out bullying, and the subtleties of locker room shame almost become a ritual abuse, almost become acceptable, and everybody sits around and smiles. You don't have to go far to find other examples, a cocktail party of guys sitting around minimizing others for their own egotistic power.

There is a lot that suggests that there is a switch of energies from the masculine to the feminine, from patriarchy to a much deeper sense of consciousness. The movement is actually underway, though it may be measured in teaspoons. You would not be here having this conversation twenty years ago. You are part of this movement to wake ourselves up again, to recommit ourselves to try to be the best we can, especially with younger men. Now, we middle-aged neurotics can do all our work about our childhood wounds, but the real work is with the young men who need more mature men to validate their fears about life and say, "Let's do it together. I'll be by your side." What we have said over the years is, "I'll be there for you," but we find addictions, afflictions, sex and other things, toys. We have an over-abundance of so many things. Never has a world, especially in our culture, had so much and had such a scarcity of soul.

Lorís. Let's talk about success. How does the average man come to define success? When and why does the idea of success become so seductive for many men and how are they affected? Is this view of success equivalent to power?

Tom. The word "success" is again one of those elusive words. What are the metrics of one's success? It has sure shifted for me over the years. In many cases, what looks like a success today is a solid

401K, knowing that things are going to be safe, that you are a good citizen, or at least have the persona of being a good citizen in the world. A lot of that is true. It comes back to what we were talking about before, what Aristotle said. Responsibility—financial and otherwise—is an important piece, but are you flourishing? I may have two cars and a house, my two children attending the best schools in the world, and on the outside I look like I'm a success, but what's really going on in my inner life? Do I really feel like I'm a success, or do I feel like something is missing? What if I were living the life that I intended? Only the individual can self-diagnose that based on of the level of his or her own despair. If I'm really honest with myself, where is the feminine in all of that?

I think Greg said it very well: The feminine says, "Wake up! Wake up! I'll support you out there finding your way." It says to the young man, "Don't take care of me. Go off and find your way. You must leave this house." The feminine is willing to cut that cord and not mother him into his twenties or thirties or forties. He ought to be scared, so much so that he has to make the choice in his fear to step out in the world. Often it takes a life or death situation for many to realize that the greatest tragedy, as Jung said, is the unlived life of the parent. The child sees that, and at a very early age. We need models of healthy parenting from both men and women, so that the feminine stays alive.

I'm actually very hopeful. I get to work with a lot of very young people and I have to say, we're in good hands. It may feel like the negative side of life is expanding, but the positive is getting larger, too. We might not see it because this negative here is very, very present. The shadow just may be golden.

Greg. We have collectively come to realize that there is an opportunity for death, and in dying, an opportunity to rise. I think that the feminine plays a vital role in that death, that "dying to self" that many religions teach. It's in line with what happens in our trainings: dying to what I thought I was, to who I thought I knew, to all those stories and definitions and constructs, in order to wake again and then return and be welcomed back.

There is also a sense of the sacred in a ritual space that is created and held by elders. On our training weekends, men actually go through a separation from the mother, if you will, a separation from what is comfortable and familiar, from the boy. There is an opportunity to go through this separation. We use the term "descent"—I think Jung uses this, as well—descent into the darkness inside. They descend and have this experience, and then are welcomed back into a community of men and women to celebrate that death and return, that awareness and realization of potential, of purpose and mission.

Tom. The piece that I would like to add here is that in order to be true to self, one becomes a part of a group. The idea is not just to absorb and take in some of what they experience in the group, but to individuate in breaking out of the group. You always have to break out of a group. We need the group as a launching point. We need that foundation, and we never know who is going to be our teacher in that group. I pick up a little pearl from this one, another from that one. I pick up a pearl from an empowered woman. I pick it up from a Jungian or from a Freudian, or from wherever. Pretty soon, I have a necklace.

What kills the male is the static masculine that stays rigid in belief systems or structures. It's like my old brain. It's so rooted in the past, so rigid, but when somebody says, "Is it absolutely true what you believe?" the feminine makes me go down a different path. I ask myself, "What if I didn't believe this? What if, like Marion Woodman, I was the other side of the belief?" If I get stuck on one side of a paradox, I become a stereotype. If I do have the experience of the other side, the other experience of life—male or female, life or death, this or that—then I have a different choice to make, and I get to break through some constructs.

Lorís. In the documentary we have been playing with the idea that, for a society to change, it must come from the individuals, which means change comes from within. For us to create a space for the feminine in our culture, we must first create a space within us. Do you believe we have done this? Can you elaborate on the subject?

Greg. I cannot speak for others but I have moved in that direction because of this work. I am gay, and at one time I saw it as a curse and a detriment. However, I have been blessed because now I see this as a perk and a bonus to give myself permission to unfold, to risk, and to have compassion and empathy, all those things that society has coined as "feminine." My albatross has turned out to be my saving grace, if you will. In this community of men and women who are becoming conscious and embracing difference and authenticity, I have been able to shed my negativity and be unconditionally loved and accepted and embraced. We get to see difference. Tom and I were talking earlier about how the old belief that "we are all the same, we are all men" has shifted in our consciousness. In our likenesses we are the same, but in our differences we grow.

I was hesitant to bring this subject out because of the old taboo and the shame I carried for a while and that I was able to discard through being in relationship. This work in particular, and the relationships I have co-created in this kind of work, have validated who I am and vice versa. It has given me authentic relationships, and that's something I could not wake up and just feel. I'm at a place of authenticity and awareness of who I am as a man.

Tom. Love is an intelligence, not a construct. You participate based on the depth of your own willingness to open up. Within me, I start to open up to the possibility, just the possibility, of no separation between what is internal and what is external. However, on a larger scale, what is external to me also resides within me; there is a relationship that has formed. Many times it's easier to form that type of relationship with nature or art. When it comes down to other people who don't look at the world the same way I do, and my ego wants to separate me from them, how can I realize that they are an extension of who I am?

Part of the piece is to do no harm. Harm to myself or harm to others. I have to stay conscious, and I don't always do that. If I'm going to be in some type of transcendent service, what I'm really here to do is to absorb some of the suffering of those who don't even know they're suffering. Some of my deepest wounds have turned out to be some of my greatest gifts, because I know my deepest pain. I know what my deepest fears are, and I can sit across from people and absorb some of that. If in some way I'm reducing the pain and the suffering of another in that moment, I am making a difference. I use the phrase "I am" in a collective way. I didn't do anything except show up and be aware and be conscious of having a certain level of intimacy, not just with myself but also with what or who is around me.

I always wondered why they used the word "recovery" when they ought to use the word "discovery." If I can find out who I am, then I'm going to have fun. I use "fun" to describe the part that gets repressed the most in a culture that's so bent on duty and on creating or winning something it may not even want or need to begin with. What gets repressed most is joy, flourishing, having that absolute connection through laughter. You know who keeps that alive in me? My grandchildren. When I look at younger people, there is a symbiotic flow of purpose and legacy, and of hope that they, too, will have the space to create. In terms of the masculine, the feminine, all these energies, in the end, I'm not exactly sure how any of this works, but I'm glad I'm a part of this process that has moved me to feel deeply, to sense strongly, and to enjoy life in a way that I didn't realize was possible.

Lorís. Is there anything else you would like to add?

Tom. What is the most profound question you have about your own self?

Lorís. I guess it would be finding meaning in life. Why am I meaningful or how am I going to find meaning? I think at this point in my life, that's the biggest question I've been asking myself. Also, as you said before, it's a process. Even if I did find an answer right now, I don't think it's going to be the same next year, or when I'm thirty. For now, that's what I've been questioning myself.

Tom. I will pass that back to someone like Marion Woodman who said, "The soul is going to ask that question, every single day."

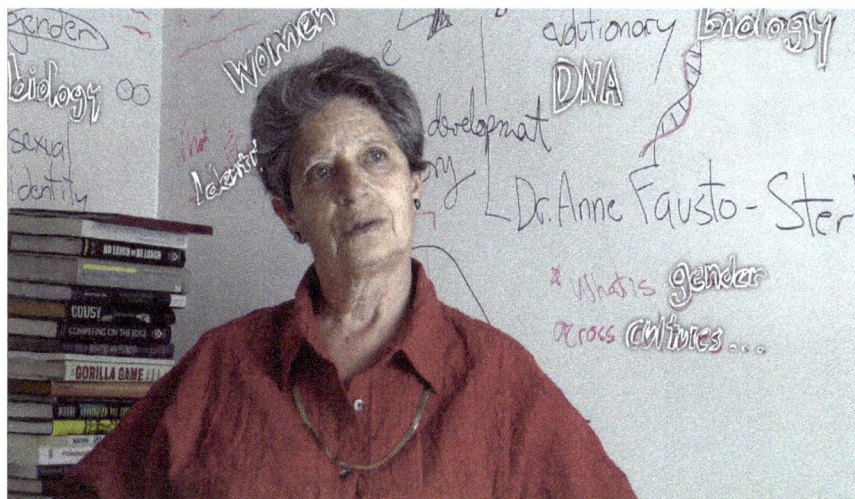

Anne Fausto-Sterling

Dr. Anne Fausto-Sterling is a leading authority in biology and gender development and the author of *Myths of Gender: Biological Theories about Women and Men*, and *Sexing the Body: Gender Politics and the Construction of Sexuality*, among others. She is the Nancy Duke Lewis Professor Emerita of biology and gender studies in the department of molecular and cell biology and biochemistry at Brown University and a former director of the Science and Technology Studies Program. Dr. Fausto-Sterling's work has achieved international recognition as it defies deep-seated scientific beliefs in an approachable and appealing manner. Her research covers the areas of women in science, gender in science, intersexuality, homo-sexuality, the construction of heterosexuality, and rethinking the nature/nurture divide. In addition, Dr.

Fausto-Sterling is a Fellow of the American Association for the Advancement of Science.

Dr. Fausto-Sterling brought me back to the practical perspective I had when I began the film: women are oppressed for their gender. Despite the time and conversations spent differentiating "the feminine" from "woman," the truth remains that western ideals of gender associate women with the feminine. Talking to Dr. Fausto-Sterling brought me back to a reality outside of inner life and psychological principles. There is a truth that coexists with the feminine and the masculine, and the yin and the yang, the animus and the anima, and that truth points to the fact that no matter what qualities characterize us men and women, women are still devalued in Western culture with respect to men. A feminine man still enjoys a higher social status than a masculine woman. Dr. Fausto-Sterling reminded me of this, she did not let me forget that there were traditions that stood firm despite my youthful idealism.

Lorís. In your experience, what is femininity?

Even within the United States, people from different parts of the world living in communities here have different definitions of femininity. Honestly, I never try to give it an exact definition. I know it when I see it, but the minute I try to pin it down, it's elusive. What we are really talking about is a spectrum of human behavior, and humans as a group are enormously variable in their behaviors. So something that I may call "feminine" might not necessarily come from a female. There is huge variability in behaviors among men and women, and the behaviors overlap. If we talk about the feminine, we have to talk about it as a theoretical construct and not as something that is related to a male or a female body.

Lorís. You mention in your book, Myths of Gender, *that scientists, journalists, students, etc., have begun to search out the real truths about sexual differences. What are these differences? Do they really exist?*

The problem with figuring out what sexual differences are, again, is that we have huge variability within groups between different men and between different women. You don't have an absolute difference unless we're talking about the actual reproductive organs. What you have are averages, what scientists call a "normal curve" or a "bell curve." You have a distribution of behaviors from one end to another for males and for females, and they overlap enormously. When someone says, "We found a sex difference," they usually mean that they have found an average difference with a great degree of overlap or a smaller degree of overlap.

Statistically, you can make them look very real. For example, a tiny difference can be statistically significant if you use a very large population. If you're just using a small population, say if you were studying fifteen boys and fifteen girls; to get a statistically significant difference, it would have to be a very large difference. So, there aren't many differences. There aren't any that I would say are absolute other than the ones having to do with reproduction. Then, there are some that are larger than others. Again, it's culturally bound. It's also historically bound. So, in the nineteen twenties, the first clerical typists were all male. The modern version of this, a computer operator doing secretarial work, is most likely a woman. So, there are these changes in cultural trends that have occurred historically as well.

Lorís. We like to describe the feminine as a kind of diffuse energy within everyone. It's a source of creativity, of receptiveness, of intuition, un-certainty, emotions, and at times, chaos. These are terms that have been closely related to females. At the same time, there appears to be a devaluation of feminine characteristics in our culture. What are your thoughts about this?

I think it's devalued when it occurs in a woman, and it's valued when it occurs in a man. I mean let's take an example from modern politics. If Hillary Clinton cried as often as John Boehner cries, she would be laughed off the stage. Just in the last election when she was competing against Barack Obama for the nomination, the one time she got teary-eyed, everybody got all excited. But John Boehner gets up on the podium and cries all the time, and everybody says, "Oh how cute. He gets teary-eyed." Our expectations of masculinity and femininity are different. Our expectation of women in politics is that they should throw away the emotional side and try to be ideally masculine. Although, as I said, the actual carrying out of masculinity in men is much more variant than most people imagine.

Lorís. For many years, philosophers, priests, scholars, and others have used Darwin's theory of evolution to argue that women were behind men, evolutionarily speaking. Can you elaborate on this phenomenon?

The use of the theory of evolution to account for the different roles of men and women has really gone on for a very long time. It's had funny ups and downs. In the early part of the nineteenth century, people argued—Darwin included, I think—that women were the more variable sex and men were the more stable sex. They had a whole story to tell about why that was true. It explained why women were not reliable enough to be given the vote and why biology dictated that they needed to be out of the public sphere.

That viewpoint actually shifted, however, partly in response to data that psychologists collected in the late nineteenth and early twentieth century suggesting that men were way more variable and women were the more stable state. But then the conclusions drawn also shifted. Variability came to be seen as a good thing, in that it would spawn a certain number of socially unfit people but would also spawn the geniuses and the people who were off the scale on the positive end. The stability would mean women were perfect to stay at home and raise children, because they provided the stable setting.

So if you look historically at these theories, you see that when they switch, the social conclusions also switch in a way that makes one very suspicious. I would say that, at best, using evolution to explain the current state of affairs has to be done extremely cautiously. It's one thing to gather empirical data on animals and look at how they interact; it's another thing to take those data and use them to draw conclusions about social roles for men and women in a contemporary setting.

Lorís. What is your personal opinion with respect to sociobiologists' ideas about how we are determined by our genetics and gender, and how gender is a strong agent in social roles? Can you give us some examples?

I would divide sociobiologists into two groups. One is a group of scientists who do very careful and quite interesting studies on animal populations. The positive thing about these studies is that the ones that are well done are long-term and very detailed. So, you may have someone studying a population of deer on an island continually for ten or fifteen years. They'll observe the matings with detailed observations. They will identify individual animals; they'll know who is doing what. They'll weigh the offspring knowing what the mating pattern was. They'll take DNA samples, so they'll be able to see whether the mating they see is actually the one that fostered the animal that was born. Then, they can take this huge mass of data which has lots of very specific information about individual animals and their behavior and analyze it and draw conclusions about the mating patterns or the birth patterns of a whole population of animals in which they also know what each individual is doing, and which they studied over several life cycles. When they do that, they often find a great deal of variability in behaviors from year to year. That's why the long-term generational study is important.

I have a colleague who studied territoriality in bluebirds. She found that the male bluebirds were very aggressive and defended the territory. That way they could do mate guarding and make sure they were the only one that impregnated the female. She also found that the aggressive behavior was only true when there were very few nesting sites. If she provided lots of other nesting sites, the males adopted other strategies to attract females, including caring for the hatchlings. The conclusion was that different environments produced different behaviors. She also found through DNA testing that the males who guarded the nests were not always the fathers of the hatchlings who were in the nest. That careful study, then, actually produced data that was surprising and moved beyond the kind of gender assumptions we bring in from our human world.

I have no problem with those kinds of studies. I think they're great examples of science. Now, the studies that are done on humans can't be done that well for obvious reasons. Our generation time is too long, and the observations would include a kind of intrusion in the family life that is not acceptable. So people turn to another type of data set. The people who do this work these days usually call themselves "evolutionary psychologists" rather than "sociobiologists." They tend to take big samples or email samples, data samples from college sophomores, for example. These samples are problematic from my point of view in a number of ways. They're not developmental so you can't get a good history through several generations and you can't watch behaviors during upbringing and beyond. They're not random, and they especially are not culturally random. So even though people say, "We've studied eighteen different countries"; if you look, ten of the countries are from Western Europe or the United States and Canada, and maybe two of them will be from South America and one from Africa. So they're not necessarily countries where you would expect huge gender differentiation. I tend to look at that work with a very skeptical eye.

Lorís. Can you talk to us about the historical beliefs about how men were superior to women and why they needed to stay at home?

The evolutionary history of gender or sex differentiation is much debated; there are lots of good theories written about it from different points of view. I would say that there is no single acceptance theory. You'll hear theories about how men hunted and women gathered, how women gathered because they had the babies and so they stayed closer to home. It's all speculation because we don't have behavioral fossil records. There's a whole subfield of scholars who produce these theories. In the nineteenth century everyone from Darwin to Frederick Engels had theories about the origin of the modern family. As you might imagine, Darwin's theory was more biologically based, and Engels's was more social and economically based. I think a lot of the theory-making depends on the intellectual background that you bring to the approach, so a sociologist is going to look at things differently than a biologist.

Lorís. We have consulted many books that talked about matriarchal societies, groups who saw a mother give birth and started idolizing—

Engels had a whole theory about the matriarchal society, that it was more communal and went back to an idea of primitive communism. They're great theories, but I don't think we have much way of knowing, either way. I just have to raise an eyebrow at some point. I think they're interesting to explore, and I'm totally in favor of thinking theoretically about these things; but I was trained back in the days of empiricists, so I don't know how we could get evidence in favor or against.

Lorís. In our culture, we have an unspoken assumption that science and technology are more important than old traditions or myths, yet many people have not changed behavior that stems from gender ideas in those old traditions and myths; this, despite the fact that science and technology have shown us the huge overlap of similarities between the sexes. Do you agree or disagree with this idea? Can you give us some examples from your experience?

I both agree and disagree. I do think that cultural change is very difficult and I think we are in a time right now in which people are very skeptical of science. We see this in other arenas, the skepticism of global warming, for example, as we sit here in one of the hottest summers we have had in a long time. I wish I understood better why people reject empirical information in favor of other beliefs. I do think that with regard to sex and gender, we have had a lot of change, but we have also had people holding on to certain kinds of ideas. One of the common myths about culture versus nature is the idea that somehow culture can just change. In fact, I think culture is enormously stabilizing. It can take several generations to change ideas.

I do think we're facing a reality in which science isn't enough for people. They often reject it altogether. It's a sociological phenomenon I don't entirely understand. On the other hand, we have seen enormous change. If someone had said to me even twenty years ago that gay marriage would become an accepted platform in the Democratic national party, I would be asking, "What planet do you come from?" And now, it's true. I think twenty years is a quick switch. When will we have a time when 80 percent of the population accepts it? Probably not even in another twenty years, but maybe in another sixty, or eighty.

Loris. I had a conversation with my mom about that recently. I said that right now the gay community is much more accepted than before. She was saying, "not so much, maybe in your environment, but not overall." I disagreed, and we got into a debate. I realized it's a cultural difference; I'm seeing more into the future, that it's changing, the direction in which it's headed.

It definitely is, and in states like Massachusetts, where gay marriage is legal, it has changed even more quickly because it's no longer strange to refer to your married relationship. For example, I spoke today with a salesperson working out of Boston, and she said, "I presume you will get this message to Paula; she's your friend." I said, "No, she's my wife." She was like, "great," because that's the law of the state now. It will be the law of the land. People will get used to it, but it will be a very uneven change. That has been true with the other major civil rights changes, too. They didn't all happen at once.

Loris. In Houston, we were presented with the term effemiphobia *by Brandon Mack. It pointed to the male gay community's hierarchies where the most masculine, rough, aggressive men are at the top, and the most effeminate men are at the lowest level in the hierarchy. There were even identified names for the categories, like "fairies," "bears," and "leathermen." I wonder if you see some sort of hierarchy like that among women.*

Well, there are different names or categories, at least among the women I know. I certainly can't speak for the younger ones, because it's a whole different world for them. There are the terms "butch" and "femme," and there's a lot of joking around and playing with those terms and the ideas of being masculine or feminine. Among my friends we do a lot of traditionally "masculine" activities, like wilderness camping or white water canoeing, and among our group there's a lot of play with those words and ideas. Many of us have partners who don't do the same activities, so it's "the husbands' weekend out." I don't think it's hierarchical. We all recognize that each of us in our relationships takes on different roles at different times, depending on what is necessary.

Jay. Do you think that's a reflection of a cultural gender association? Maybe males tend to categorize more?

I do. I do think that the gay male community is structured socially and sexually in a somewhat different way than the lesbian women's community, and I do think that it's reflective of overall gender diffe-rentiation in our culture.

Lorís. Many intellectuals continue insisting that we have an undeniable biology that affects our behavior as a sex. Is this true? Could you elaborate on this idea?

Again, it's really hard to say what is meant by an undeniable biology. There are many ways in which cultural feedback produces different neural development. For example, interesting things have been written about this in terms of how boys and girls throw a baseball. There's that old insult that many of you have heard and certainly has been directed at me, "You throw like a girl." As it happens, you have to learn how to throw "like a guy"; and when you do it's because you have been coached and had repeated practice from the time you were a little child, even if it's only throwing pebbles into the water. Your whole neuro-muscular system learns a certain pattern of growing. It's actually in your nerves and your muscles and the neuro-muscular connections to your brain where you learn to do that.

I have a colleague who is an anthropologist. He studies this very macho dance in Brazil, *capoeira*. As an anthropologist, he lives with *capoeiristas*. He studies them and talks to them. He is interested not only in how they have learned *capoeira*, which is a very physically demanding sport; but primarily in how they imagine themselves as men. When he started tossing a ball with one of these *capoeiristas*, he noticed that they throw like girls. Throwing a ball in Brazil is not as common as soccer, and these guys had never learned to throw the way men throw in a country where baseball is the big sport. So, you see that differences can be biological but also cultural.

Lorís. When you said that biology goes along with culture, I thought, "Of course, it does." Sometimes when something is said differently, it clicks. My brother and I grew up in a really traditional background; we're Lebanese, but we were born in Mexico. In that tradition the gender roles are very set. Coming to the United States changed everything. Our younger cousins always ask us things about gender roles, and to them, you can't touch the biology. It stands on its own.

It's in the ways in which we learn to walk, to dance, to present ourselves. I have another friend who is a lesbian who, in her younger years, was absolutely spectacular looking and obviously had the potential to be a traditional model, but she walked like a man. Someone trained her to adopt a feminine walk so that she could compete as a model. She learned how to do it, and she could snap her body into it. The body learns and it remains in the muscles and the neuro-muscular abilities. That is biology. I think at the very heart of things, the dichotomy between culture and biology is a false dichotomy because they work together.

I always tell people, you have to think developmentally. You can't just look at an adult behavior and understand where it came from; you have to ask how that behavior developed. Was there a point in time when a behavior you think of as different in men and women was not different? When did the boy's and girl's behavior diverge? What were the things that led them to diverge? Biology is certainly part of it, but you can't separate it easily from cultural influences.

Lorís. How can we change this pattern of ideas? What would a more balanced view of sex and gender look like?

My big crusade is to get people to think developmentally. We need to ask where difference comes from, how it arises, what is the process by which it appears, and also, what are the processes which maintain it. You may have something that is stable, a stable behavior or belief or point of view, but it's being produced by a set of processes that stabilize it. If it is important to change, then you have to ask what the props are, the support systems that keep it stable, and what happens if you start destabilizing the supports. The dynamics theory says you produce chaos when you do that, but then a new form of stability appears.

If you buy the analogy, think of something like being able to walk. That's a very stable trait, unless you have an accident. You could have an accident in which you damage your leg so badly that it takes you a year to learn to walk again. You have completely destabilized your walking system. You have to produce new ways of walking, new neuro-muscular and brain connections. You can again produce walking as a stable state, but it would not be the same walking as what you had before. It will be a different set of things going into producing that walking behavior. So you have a stable trait, something that disrupts it and produces chaos for a while, and then something new and also stable that emerges from it.

Lorís. It's like chaos is an important factor.

It can be, yes. I think whenever anyone is going through a big change, especially of an emotional sort, but also a physical or a physiological sort, there is a period in which things seem chaotic and out of control and really difficult. That is part of the re-stabilization process.

Lorís. In your book, Myths of Gender, *you pose the question of why scientists who claim to search only for the truth have failed to solve the problem of gender and sex differences. Do you have an answer to this question?*

I do. After I wrote *Myths of Gender*, I spent a number of years thinking about that question and writing about it separately, which led me to a different field of scholarship called Science and Technology Studies. Scholars in this field are interested in how scientists produce scientific knowledge. They're interested in the actual production of knowledge.

Every scientist has a cultural location and they have a set of beliefs and values about how the world works that they bring into their experimentation. They may bring it into how they choose to design an experiment, what kinds of data they choose to gather, what theoretical framework they apply. Each of those things will carve a window to look out onto a bigger picture, but the window may be faced one way or maybe faced another way. Depending on how you face it, you miss something. This is true of all scientists, and it doesn't mean they're bad scientists, or that they're trying to distort data; it just means that they are who they are, and no matter how hard any of us tries to get a 360-degree view of the world, we can't. The world that we come from inevitably shapes the window we're looking through. There are a lot of studies published on gender and on other areas of science that clarify this point of view about how scientists create knowledge. I think it goes a long way toward explaining why I think that scientific findings about gender will begin to change as the cultural expression of gender changes.

Lorís. In your work you have many times referred to the idea that many of the positive changes women have achieved in the social sphere have faded due to our culture's apparent recalcitrant ways. Do you think there is a projection of our own beliefs onto reality? Have we focused too much attention on changing the outside world, and not enough on our inner lives?

I don't think we focus too much attention on changing the outside world as opposed to our inner lives, because I think big social structures really affect our inner lives. The energy that feminism released in the nineteen seventies was extraordinary, but it's also not surprising in retrospect that the expectations released by that energy could not be met in the time frame people hoped for. On the other hand, there has been a push back that has been stronger than anything any of us expected. That push back is very strong right now.

It goes back to something I said earlier in this interview, which is that cultural and economic change is a very slow process. Both economic systems and cultural systems are usually very stabilizing; so when you push against them, you do change them but slowly. If we look only at the employment arena, women have moved into many more different kinds of jobs than they had open to them in the nineteen seventies. If you look at my own profession in the university, certain kinds of hires were simply closed to women when I started out, and now that's against the law and there are a lot of women entering the field. Is there 100 percent equality? No. There have been huge changes, and there are still things to be done. It means that changing the social is a much slower process than we understood in the early enthusiasm of the feminist movement.

meggan watterson, m.t.s.
Author and Founder of REVEAL

Meggan Watterson

Meggan Watterson, author of *REVEAL: A Sacred Manual for Getting Spiritually Naked,* is an international speaker and spiritual leader. She holds a master's degree in theological studies from Harvard Divinity School and a master's of divinity degree from Union Theological Seminary at Columbia University. She is the founder of REVEAL, an annual event in New York City that celebrates ritual, dance and voice; and she facilitates the REDLADIES, a spiritual community that emboldens women to delve into their bodies and integrate them into their spiritual lives. Her dedication is focused on inspiring seekers to live a fearless life of authenticity and audacity by giving them tools to listen to their soul voice. Meggan currently lives in Brooklyn with her little boy and his imaginary goose, Goldie.

Meggan was one of the youngest experts we interviewed for the film. Her youth took me back in the midst of so many encounters with people much older than me. I hadn't experienced this work through the voice and dreams of someone closer to my generation. When I met Meggan, I understood that to her, inner work was equivalent to the color red. It was the color of her lipstick, the color of her book, of her website and probably her aura. It was such a fresh feeling to listen to the words she chose to speak about these topics, words that came closer to the life I led than what I had heard from others. I felt an immediate affection for her, even though I had only met her once. I've always had to pay special attention to people capable of seducing my soul so quickly. I'll understand later.

Lorís. Based on your lived experience, what is the feminine to you?

The feminine is an attribute that both men and women possess. It is that attribute that allows me to be receptive and to go within. Meditating, taking a moment, no matter where I am or what I am doing, just to stop and go within, that to me is a feminine principle, a feminine attribute. We all contain the feminine. I don't know how or when women had to drop anchor with the feminine and men had to drop anchor with the masculine. We have really missed out with that equation. For me, the feminine is an attribute that we all possess.

Lorís. In the documentary when we touched on the media, many of the young people we interviewed spoke about feeling pressured to reach unattainable standards of perfection. This happened not only with self-image, but with other areas such as professions and relationships. We have all been burdened with an external standard of who or what we ought to be in certain situations of life. What is your opinion on the media and its relationship to the individual's inner life?

Whether it is the media or our friends, there is a need for us to disengage from the voices and the ideas that come from outside of us telling us who we need to be and what we need to do. We need to dare to go within to figure out whom we are and what it is that we've come here to do. We can literally spend our entire lives figuring out what other people want or expect from us, some crazy unattainable perfection. It's just chasing an illusion, chasing other people's ideas of who we need to be. What is true tends to be the most simple and the most terrifying. We can only find our own truth by going within. That's the only place we are ever going to find it, *within*.

Lorís. There's a big risk to that, isn't there?

There's a huge risk! But there's a greater risk in following somebody else's truth for your life and getting to the end and saying, "Oh my god, I never lived." That's a much, much greater risk to take.

Loris. Could you talk to us about the feminine in relation to the body? People in Western society grow with the Cartesian understanding that our mind, our soul, and our bodies are entirely different things. Could you elaborate on this idea?

I always go back to my personal experience. I've had a lot of scholarship, but the only thing that matters is what I experience in my body. Whenever I feel I can speak from a place of authority, it's because I have experienced it. I always had this idea that finding the divine as I was growing up would mean transcending the body, somehow denying or ignoring the body. This seemed especially true of the female body since so many images and ideas of the divine are male and masculine. However, what I found when I began to go on my own pilgrimage was that it was only by becoming fully embodied and daring to be really present in my body that I began to hear and understand what the divine was for me. I found that from within there was no separation. I can't hear my soul voice without being fully in my body. Rather than transcending the body, the trajectory of finding the divine is the exact opposite; it's coming home to the body. That's when you can begin to connect to what is eternal inside. It takes daring to be fully present.

Lorís. Why do you think we're raised that way? We're told that to reach individuation you have to do it all up here, in your head. You have to pressure the body to keep up with your ambitions.

We've had this idea for so long that the body is somehow less than the soul, but it's not. A lot of these ideas go all the way back to the beginning of religion. We could talk about the separation between the human and the angel, the male and the female, the light and the dark— everything was split and put in a hierarchy. Everything was placed above or below the other. None of those ideas ever really worked for us, and I believe that everything is beginning to level out. We're beginning to see that our object here is to be a soul-embodied. We are here to see each other eye to eye, no matter who or what we are. This idea that the flesh is somehow sinful and lowly is not serving us at all. The body is inherently sacred.

Lorís. In our section on relationships in the film, there's much discussion of the ideals and expectations we come up with about the other person with whom we are relating. Many mention Jung's theory of projections, saying that we always look in the other for what our own soul needs to develop for itself. Is there really a "perfect" way to have a relationship? What are your thoughts on this?

There is so much around about finding the right person—what you need to look like, how you need to sound, who you need to be, what shoes you need to be wearing. I'm so much more concerned with a person's relationship with his or her own soul. I feel like when you're doing what you love, if you figure out who you are and what it is that you're here to do, that you want to share, in what way you want to lead this unique love that you have inside of you; you're going to find who you love. So many want to find a kind of wholeness in another person, that feeling of, "You complete me." The problem is that, often, what we need to find and provide is something that can only come from inside of us, something we can only provide for ourselves. These bits of ourselves that get lost and fragmented throughout our lives, we sometimes put those on someone else, as if to say, "Here is a shovel and a hammer and a huge box of nails. Go find all my lost bits of self and put them all together again!" But that is our work! Not someone else's. In the process of healing ourselves, of doing the hard, gritty work that is also filled with grace, we become whole to ourselves, and learn to provide for ourselves and love ourselves deeply. This healing process cultivates our capacity to love ourselves in the way we are hoping that somebody else is going to love us. When two people who have done the work of becoming whole come together, it's two worlds coming together. It's an interdependence, rather than a codependence. So much more is possible then.

Lorís. I think that takes a lot of responsibility. To say, "You know, I am not going to ask this of you. Just give me two minutes, let me go figure it out myself…" Many people do not want to take that responsibility because of all the work it involves. It also involves pain to realize that you are missing something, and you owe it to yourself, nobody owes that to you, nobody owes you anything. I think it takes too much work that we are not raised to cope with.

It goes with you no matter what. No matter what happens, wherever you go, you always have access to it. It's unconditional, and nothing is ever going to sever you from it. That is a gold watch right there at the end of a struggle! Once you have attained that, you look back on it and you say, "That work was nothing. It was nothing for this unlimited access to a limitless love I have within me always, no matter what."

Lorís. It becomes desirable, less of a task.

Exactly, that's the shift that happens. It is not a sacrifice. The work that you have to go through is the pressure that creates the diamond.

Lorís. From what you have experienced, is Western society based mainly on masculine principles? Now that women are gaining more positions of power, are they acquiring these masculine principles?

Again, I think the goal is for there to be a balance. Everyone has to figure out what their own relation to masculinity is. I went to an all-women's college, and there were some women there who were more masculine than any men I had ever met. Likewise, I have met men that are more feminine than I am. I think that it's about opening up our ideas and our expectations of men and women and how much they embody either attribute, masculine or feminine. Ultimately, the ideal is that we are all able to express our own balance. No two people are going to have the exact same expression of masculinity and femininity, but there is tremendous healing when we are all able simply to express whatever sacred combination of the two we embody, whether we're male or female. Our sex does not have to determine whether we can express masculinity or femininity. We can express them both as we come into who we really are and express who we really are with authenticity.

I go back to religion and spirituality because that's really all I know. I had an "Aha!" moment, a rude awakening, or just one of those moments when my jaw dropped, when I was really young and realized that all of the sacred scripture that pretty much comprises most of the world religions in the West have been exclusively created by men. That floored me, terrified me, but also excited me later. I realized, we hadn't heard from a whole half of the population throughout the majority of all time about what the divine was for them. What are the rituals? What are the prayers? What is the path of finding the divine? What does that look like? Carol Lee Flinders, in her book about feminism and spirituality, mentions that for a monk, the classic expectations are silence, submission, and solitude—all of which are part of a woman's everyday life! That's not anything new.

On a global scale, there are so many women who are silent and secluded, forced to be submissive. How is that spiritual for us? That's our everyday life. So, what does it mean for us? What does it look like? Maybe it's turning that on its head and maybe it means for us to eat meat, drink wine, run around, and speak all over the place. We haven't heard yet from women who have been expected to be feminine, who have been seen as an expression of the feminine. We haven't heard yet what their experience of the divine is. We are beginning to. That's going to create some tremendous shifts in what we have seen and understood in terms of the masculine and the feminine and the balance of between the two.

Rose Mary. When women have wanted to express their divinity, they've been perceived as crazy, don't you think? They've been dismissed in history as if there were something wrong with them.

Burned or silenced. Yes, absolutely. One of my favorite mystics, Marguerite Porete, was asked by the church fathers to write about her experience of being connected to the divine love inside of her, of reaching union with the divine from within. She called the book *The Mirror of Simple Souls.* In it, she reveals that you do not need anyone outside of you; the spiritual is between you and the divine! There's no middleman, literally. That is the holy relationship. The church found that to be way too heretical. They burned her book first, and then they burned her at the stake. Luckily, her book survived, but at the time it was too dangerous in suggesting that the divine is accessed from within. This was true whether you were a man or a woman; sex did not affect the capacity to connect with the divine.

Lorís. Wow, that was a very brave thing to do, to speak up like that.

Yes, she was the abbess. She was the head of the nunnery. She was told to write it, but the writing condemned her because she admitted that her experience of the divine was the ultimate freedom. No one can tell us who and when the divine is. It's something found within. It was happening, as Rose Mary said, not just among well-known figures but all the time. I would definitely say that witchcraft was prosecuted for the same reasons. It was the expression of being able to commune with spirits, of healing with herbs and other remedies, powers that really terrified people. All of that was shut down. I think that was a feminine way of expressing the divine, but it was too frightening.

Lorís. To think that today that would simply be called "organic."

Well, to think that *Harry Potter* is such a hit. This is where the story comes from! We have suppressed all of it. We are Hermione and Harry; we all have an inner Hermione.

Lorís. Is there a space for the feminine in today's organized religions? Is it present at all?

I can't really say because I walked out of my church at age 10 and I haven't been back! I can't really say if the feminine is present, but I love the ritual. I'm a ritual junkie and fanatic. I tend to go to a lot of temples and synagogues and masses. At a young age, when I heard "the Father, the Son and the Holy Spirit," I perked up, and thought, "Well, where is the mother?" I asked the question very simply, very innocently. "That does not make any sense!" I thought. That equation does not make sense. Why would we not honor what we see in life? If we are made in the divine image, then where is the mother? I guess my life is a reflection of that question. I was in the Unitarian Church and I still felt there was not enough mention of the idea of the divine feminine. There were not enough women present and teaching and enjoying a spiritual authority equal to that of men. I would say now that it has changed. There are so many women who are part of the practice and the ministry of organized religion.

However, I would definitely say there is still a glass ceiling. It's reflected in the naming and inauguration of the new pope. I have deep respect for all of those who have profound belief and faith, who really feel that religion is the right path for them and can accept the privileges of all these men in cardinal red as they are sequestered to decide the vote. But I keep thinking, "Don't the nuns get *one* vote? Don't they not even get *one* say about who is going to be at the head of it all when they're sacrificing and serving Jesus as much as any of the male priests?" Because of the way I have been raised and my personal experience, I can't understand that. I look at it, and I can't wrap my head around it. I can't understand how such a process could reflect spiritual leadership of a people. It doesn't include women's voices and women's concerns at those top levels; there are no women cardinals. I would love for Sister Joan Chittister to have been considered for the position of pope! I can honestly say that if that were even a possibility, I would be a Catholic. I would be a Catholic gratefully, because I would love it all—from eating the little wafer to drinking the wine, all the rituals, and the meaning that they give life. For me, though, all of those services and rituals are leaving me out—my body, my experience, my truth, my sex, my sexuality! It denies those parts of me that I can't deny. I have had to leave the church and create those rituals and ways of reaching the divine on my own, create my own community. It would have been so much easier if I could have felt that women are seen, heard, acknowledged in religion, and revered for their wisdom just as much as men. I still hope for that day! I don't know if I'll be alive when it happens. Jung said at one point that the church is going to die unless the church finds the mother. I believe that. The women in my generation have thrown the baby out with the bath water for the most part because their religious traditions are not acknowledging their experiences as women nor the wisdom that they accrue and have access to *because* they are women. Instead, they're leaving the churches and finding other creative ways to express their spiritual selves.

Lorís. I never thought about it that way. If there were women popes and cardinals, would I still be a Catholic? I probably would.
Jay. For the booze and the crackers?
Lorís. Well, no! It's just that there would be someone to model what I as a woman am going through as well. Ultimately, they're spiritual leaders and they are supposed to guide you to reach your own sense of spirituality.

Right. It goes back to our earlier conversation about the balance of the masculine and the feminine. All you're seeing is men representing the ultimate spiritual authority of the divine. How are we going to trust that voice of the feminine inside of us if all that we see outside of us are these masculine role models in places of highest spiritual authority? What would it mean for example to have a popess, a she-pope? I don't even know what you would call it! What would it do for the small voice inside of us that tells us who we are and reminds us of the love that is our birthright? For me, the closer and closer we get to being able to see men and women, the masculine and the feminine, balanced outside of us, that the closer we are to achieving that balance inside of us.

Lorís. Exactly! That's a question we've been exploring in our film, the idea that this outward imbalance is only a reflection of our inner balance. It has been hard to express that to people without them understanding through a previous lens for these concepts.

One of your questions asked, "Where does it start?" It starts inside of us. If we want to see balance in the masculine and in the feminine, and more of a balance in relationships between men and women, it starts inside of us. It starts with us really being able to claim and embrace the masculine and the feminine inside of us. It begins with those inner shifts, those inner revolutions that happen. That inner healing is ultimately at some point going to be translated outside of us.

Gary Bobroff

Gary S. Bobroff is the author of *Crop Circles, Jung & the Reemergence of the Archetypal Feminine*, and the facilitator and developer of *Archetypal Nature*. He has degrees from Pacifica Graduate Institute of Santa Barbara, CA and the University of British Columbia, Canada. He writes and speaks internationally about archetypal themes and life's deep mysteries.

When I announced my Kickstarter campaign for my film on one of LinkedIn's Jungian groups, I became a little obsessed with my post's ratings. It wasn't my intention, but my passion sort of got out of control for this post, and I ended up checking its status several times a day. There was one other post I never "beat," and it bugged me in a ridiculously silly manner. I finally clicked on this superior other post to see what it was about, and to my surprise, it was about the feminine. And it was amazing. Who was this G.S. Bobroff? I immediately googled him and found another article of his, and his website, and his book… I don't recall finding his email, so I had to leave an overly zealous comment in his article asking him, begging him, to please look at my Kickstarter campaign and learn about what I was doing. I don't know why I thought it was so important for him to know. A few days later he did comment, but because I had no more space for further interviews, we agreed on his participation in the next film—which he dubbed *Ensoulment II - Return of the Soul*. In the meantime, he graciously conceded a written interview for version I.

Lorís. From your experience, how would you define the feminine and how did you come to relate crop circles to the feminine?

"Feminine" and "masculine" are words we use to describe characteristics of nature. Speaking of them psychologically, they are not equivalent with "female" and "male" or "patriarchy" and "matriarchy." To use the terms in a Jungian sense is to address universal characteristics that are a part of human nature.

Jung's understanding of the feminine is complex, dynamic and coherent but far from simple. In addition, to my own experience of this quality, and after writing a Master's thesis about a Jungian interpretation of crop circles with Dr. Lionel Corbett as my advisor, I spent years looking at everything that Jung, von Franz[27], Ulanov[28], Woodman[29] and other Jungians wrote about the feminine in order to

---

[27] Marie-Louise von Franz was a Swiss psychologist and disciple of Carl G. Jung.
[28] Ann B. Ulanov is an American author and Jungian psychoanalyst best known for her book *The Feminine in Christian Theology and in Jungian Psychology*.
[29] Marion Woodman is a Canadian author and Jungian analyst best known for her books *Addition to Perfection: The Still Unravished Bride* and *Dancing in the Flames*.

address this mystery properly from a Jungian point of view and turn the thesis into a book for general readership.

"Feminine" and "masculine" were understood in earlier eras through metaphorical associations like "solar" and "lunar," "yin" and "yang" or "eros" and "logos"—where "eros" refers to a feeling of joined-ness and "logos" to truth and clarity. While the "masculine" can be associated with truth and the objective distance that is required for seeing clearly, the "feminine" is associated with emotional connection, feeling, and the lunar knowing of the unconscious and the body. The masculine is associated with spirit, upwardness and the solar daytime of a clear view of what is near; the feminine is associated with the body, downwardness and the lunar night time in which we dream and see the distant stars.

One of the most significant psychological characteristics of our modern time is the absence of the feminine. We have lost our connection to nature, to the inner life and to the miracle of life in the outer world. It is only through such an illness that we are capable of destroying the world in which we live.

Crop circles occur in living grain, the ancient symbol of the goddess. In our psyche, this symbol lives on. Jung said plant symbols point us in the downward way, the yin way. We live in an era which is high on an inflation of ego-masculine character. We believe in rationality, linearity and tidy oversimplifications. Into this illness comes the healing dream of crop circles, a mystery which defies easy answers and invites us to participate with a genuinely unknown other. Crop circles deflate the ego and evoke feeling. Both in its media— grain, living wheat—and also in its mystery, the crop circle expresses an archetypally feminine nature.

Lorís. In your book, you relate crop circles to Rorschach images: "As Fielder has noted, they are kind of Rorschach tests reflecting the psyche of the day and telling us more about the nature of the observer than the observed." Can you talk more about this concept?

The history of our reactions to crop circles shows us that our responses document more of a truth about ourselves than about the phenomenon itself. A woodcut from 1678 shows a "mowing devil,"[30] and the story describes the same crop circles that we see today. Enlightenment-era responses to it try to establish a natural weather phenomenon, which shows the masculine desire to imagine that it knows everything and that there is no real mystery out there. We confuse measurement for mastery all too often in our quest for scientific understanding.

Today the modern response for the most part is to see it as a hoax. And the government-sponsored, human-made formations in the UK, along with their accompanying media blitzes, make it easier for us to do so. Our era likes to think that there is no Other out there—no God, no alien beings, no intelligence in the universe other than us. That's a fairly profound level of grandiosity! We go along with this by not doing our homework, not looking at the research, not going to see them for ourselves. We do the same, when we brush off synchronistic experiences as "merely coincidence." In doing so, we reinforce our own disconnection from the living mystery inside of us.

Lorís: You speak about how our society experiences the unknown. Would you say that the feminine stands in this category of the unknown? Does language take part in how we interact with this phenomenon?

Yes, the feminine is the miracle of life. The seed is placed into the "dead" ground and emerges alive. Culturally today we have lost all connection to this mystery, the mystery through which we are born. You know you've lost conscious connection with something when you express it compulsively, and we express our non-relation with the feminine through materialism. The word "materialism" comes from

---

[30] A pamphlet printed in Hertfordshire, England in 1678 shows an image of the Devil with what looks like a crop circle. Research on it has been done by author Andy Thomas.

the Latin *mater* or "mother." Having lost the inner mother, we compulsively grasp for things. For example, our Thanksgiving is not
characterized by any pious gratitude for nature's gifts but rather by
ferocious shopping and competing with others for material possessions.

The ego-masculine desperately wants certainty. That's part of
what's going on in American politics today with the Tea Party; they
want to go back in time to the comforts of a simpler era. The new
unknown factors challenge what we think we know, and if we really
participate with that, we must let go of our certainties and begin the
process of growth. Part of what we are figuring out in our era is that
we live in a world that is meaning-rich, but that meaning is not
singular, not one dimensional; it's multivalent. One of the qualities
of the feminine is seeing that the meaning we're discovering in the
world is true in a variety of forms all at once. The masculine wants
one single answer, one right way and that's just not how our world
is. Marcuse wrote about this as our preference for "one-dimensional
reality over all contradiction" (1991), and Jungian analyst Marion
Woodman observes that "negative masculinity cannot think in
metaphor." Jung saw in us that "it is still the case today that discrimination and differentiation means more to the rationalistic
intellect than wholeness through the union of opposites. That is why
the unconscious produces the symbols of wholeness (1967, page 456).

*Lorís. If crop circles embrace the Self archetype, what roles do the masculine
and feminine principles play in such a paradigm?*

The Self archetype is the "part of us that knows there is a center"
as Ann Ulanov summarized beautifully (1988-2000, pg. 126-128).
There is a part of us that knows what we need even when our conscious mind does not. The Self archetype contains our best interests
from the point of view of both consciousness and unconsciousness.
The images that we use to express this force in us are centered: the
circle, mandalas, stain-glass windows, labyrinths, pyramids, and
temples like Stonehenge. There is a magic in form, and these centered
forms are one way of expressing something powerfully transfor-

mative in nature. In some traditions, the sick person is placed right into a sand painting mandala for healing.

The masculine and the feminine are only related to the self today in the way that they play a role in the nature of our illness, our imbalance. The old masculine gods haven't been animating us for a long time, and we're in a period of massive transition, but that transition has a particular character. We're on the other side of a long historic journey. Primitive psychological unity with the feminine from our prehistory is long gone. We gave up the Mother, the Earth and the feminine in pursuit of masculine truth, clarity, morality, rationality and objectivity. Now we have too much masculine, too much distance, too much disconnection from context. We are living under a massive psychological inflation that is masculine and grandiose, and the illness that allows us to destroy our planet.

The Self archetype is the force in us that leads us toward balance. But we also must go forward. We're not getting back to the garden, so to speak. It's not a question of going *back* to the Goddess. As Tarnas and others like to say, we're like a suitor choosing to consciously engage with the feminine again (2007, pg. 1-5); the metaphor of our moment is one of a conscious wedding. We can choose to see, to connect, to embrace the world and our struggles and loves in it; or we can resist transformation and invite Kali and perhaps the end of all life on this planet. As Jung said, "the world hangs on a thin thread and that thread is the psyche of humanity" (1986).

Lorís. After all your investigations on crop circles and the feminine, did you encounter anything that challenged your original beliefs, those you had before beginning your book?

Crop circles are an invitation to a mystery without a solution. To consider it with the whole of our being means being in dialogue with a host of inner responses. Denial comes up, as the ego-masculine part of us wants to get off the hook and simply reject the phenomenon altogether. Fear arises in us as we consider the numinous other that is on the other side of this creation. But most of all, I find that crop circles bring me to want to be more fully engaged with the world in its mystery and crises.

The dark side of our time is our destruction of the Earth, something we accomplish through our inner loss of connection to the feminine, through our rejection of a part of ourselves, a part of nature, a part of God. Yet we live in a time in which a new, healthier understanding is arriving through us too.

For me, crop circles are emblematic of our new era. Simple answers no longer suffice today and no authority stands with all the solutions for us. We are each on our own to try to struggle with the new wonders. Our conscious recognition of the fact of synchronicity and quantum physics does the same. These new mysteries are the positive side of our uncovering of the feminine nature of reality, a world in which psyche and matter are not divorced from each other as our imbalanced ego-masculine grandiosity has wanted to believe. We are discovering that we live in a world in which the psyche and the heart extend out past ourselves into the world around us. We are discovering that we live in a heart-shaped world. If we are lucky, coming to embrace this revelation will help to keep us from destroying it.

Mary Hamilton

Mary Hamilton is a dancer, educator, Jungian therapist and author. A graduate of the Canadian National Ballet School, Hamilton implemented the first secondary school dance course in Canada in 1973, when she began teaching theater with Marion Woodman. She later became professor at the University of Western Ontario where she taught modern dance, improvisation, and choreography, and earned a reputation as a pioneer in dance and theater education. In 1980, she co-created and began teaching the BodySoul Rhythms Intensives internationally, which she continues to do today. Mary is a member of the Canadian Group Psychotherapy Association and author of several books, including *Under the Horse's Ass: A Love Story Human and Divine*, *The Dragonfly Principle: An Exploration of the Body's Function in Unfolding Spi-*

rituality, and *Leaving my Father's House: Journey to Conscious Femininity* with Marion Woodman.

I met Mary when I was nineteen years old, at the same time that I met Paula Reeves. Her name, Mary, is one of the most soothing sounds in the world to me, like a breeze dancing in the leaves. She gives me a sense of spiritual freedom, as if she can fly anywhere on Earth at any moment her heart desires, like a dragonfly, perhaps. I admire her deeply and I have welcomed so many of her words into my permanent consciousness. I live by what she taught me, and her wisdom will forever be the second pillar of truth in my con-sciousness.

Rose Mary. In your opinion, what is the feminine?

For me, the feminine is the great round. It is the encircling embrace. It takes into itself, like a great womb. Where it takes in, the mystery of transformation happens. From that transformation something new emerges and is given out. You have this movement, this pulse of coming into itself, transforming and giving out. You will notice that my movement is cyclical so that feminine is nature. The body, the trees, the flowers, the birds, anything that is of substance is of the feminine. The masculine is the catalyst that ignites it from within. Therefore, the feminine embraces, encircles, takes into itself, transforms and gives out. You have this repetition, always new, never the same—taking in, transforming, giving out. Thus, we have the seasons. Every season is different, yet it is the same. Every sunrise, different, yet the same. For me, that is the feminine. Within the differences, it sees and experiences what it gives off as beauty, beloved. The feminine is of love. Nature in its most spacious place is of love. You realize, this matter is of love. If you watch nature bloom, you see such beauty. Who could ever turn against that kind of beauty when you have the eyes of the feminine to see? The feminine is also the valuing. What it brings forth in its life is a value because it exists, not because it has to do anything or be anything. It already is in its pure, raw existence. Beautiful.

Rose Mary. Many people have expressed their feeling that the word "feminine" is not a good fit for its meaning. What do you think?

Language is interesting because it is abstraction from direct experience. So much depends on who you are. If you work a lot with dreams, the feminine comes in the form of woman, the round, nature; and the masculine, a man, logos. The feminine has got such a bad rep in culture and in nature. It's something we can just rape. It's something that is simply there for our convenience, to be used and abused. In some cases, I find "the feminine" hard to use. I prefer to use "the substantial field," because of all the baggage associated with "masculine" and "feminine." Not everyone can discern the meaning, because they haven't had the experience. That is not a judgment. They just haven't had the experience of being both feminine and masculine.

One has matter, mattering, and that mattering is ignited by some catalyst—spirit, god, whatever you want to call it. The visceral experience of that igniting is its reality. When you choose how to put that into language, you have to be very careful. You have to be very careful when you are speaking to others. If you say "feminine," many will think of a *Vogue* magazine style of a woman's image. They don't realize that it is huge, that everything that manifests has both a feminine and a masculine principle; otherwise, it is nothing. This union is the absolute. Out of nothingness comes the something. Now, you can call that "mother earth," or simply, "mattering is happening and it is ignited by something within." So you see that language, how you choose your words, is important.

Rose Mary. How have the media's images of perfection affected the feminine?

I know from experience and from teaching so many women and young girls that the images presented in the media are unattainable.

They are perfection. As soon as you have an ideal out there that you're supposed to match up to, you turn against yourself because you are always a failure. You cannot be what the images represent. Therefore, there is this terrible turning against yourself, the body object. Then, the criticism comes in. After that, the hatred. When you get to, "I hate this body," all you want is to carve pieces off. The medical profession is doing that, it carves pieces out, puffs others out. It's like a banana thinking it has to be an orange. No matter how much it is cut and carved, hated and despised, it will never be what it is trying to be.

Therefore, the life effort is spent on appearances, on trying to be something you cannot be, rather than the living experience and the gift of your own life. And when you have an ideal out there that you're striving for, it generates a terrible war with self and other. You never live your own life, nor do you see the beauty out there because you are always judging by an ideal that is not real. You lose your sense of value and self-worth. Additionally, you split off parts of yourself. In the body, you split here at the neck. The head is okay; the body is not. The problem with the split from here at the head to there at the body is that you can't control it. You can't make it something that it is not. It will always be what it is.

Rose Mary. In a way, it's as if the body is causing that anxiety because of how it is perceived, especially the female body.

When we hate something, it's because we are afraid of it, we feel a sense of powerlessness. Our natural being is vulnerable, sensitive. We hate our bodies, and so we split out what we hate, and we put it out there or put it down here. Then, to feel powerful, we attack it. It's called splitting. You split off that which you hate in yourself so that you have an enemy. You can spend the rest of your life fighting it out there, without ever having to face that it is the hatred you have for your own flesh in your own body that you inherited, when you took on the human flesh. It was not necessarily your parents, or the culture. It's so deep, this belief that man's role is to dominate nature, that the goal is mind over body. No, no. The body supports.

Rose Mary. What role does the body play in the unfolding spirituality that is emerging in Western culture?

The spirit, spirituality, is carried as a quality in the space between the notes. As a dancer, you can have two people dance exactly the same technique, yet one will be so soul-infused, and the other will be just a technician. When you go into the body, you experience yourself as far more than a physical concrete form, but as a field. When you start to read the field material and begin to experience viscerally what is going on in you, you realize you are these waves. When we go deeply into the quality of the wave that comes through us, it is a wave of love. A deep, deep current of love weaves through our breathing, weaving through the pulsations of the blood, the heartbeat, even the synapses in the brain.

Since I am a body person, my background is in the psychology of the body; when you go deeply, deeply into the body, into the experience of your thinking function, your feeling function, and your physical function, your actual sensation; when you work through that and you untangle that which is yours, that which you inherited, that which is the culture; you often find a black void. That void can be very terrifying. We think it is nothing. When you go into that nothingness, that deep, deep sense of not being a body image, you realize there is a spaciousness. The spaciousness is so intelligent; it is so beyond the narrow limits of our narrow mind that thinks we are a something; that the egocentric *I* becomes a *we*.

We become the boundaries, soft and mutable. You expand out and realize that we are one humanity. We are one human system, one planetary system. We are one solar system. When you live and become and know from a visceral point of view—very different from a mental concept—then you live that oneness. "I am of love. You are of love. We are all of love. We are all made of the particles and the space and the breath and the wave of something so much vaster." No matter what your language is, no matter what your upbringing is, you will give it a name: God, field, Allah, Buddha, Christ. However, there is a common denominator. When we go deeply, deeply into our visceral experience you know you are a unified field. And this, I believe, is where the future of humanity is heading with quantum physics in the sciences, toward the understanding that we are a unified field.

Rose Mary. Projections play an important role in our lives. We include a section on projections in the context of relationships. How can an individual realize that he or she is projecting, and how do we learn from those projections?

Projections are how we were designed to learn. When we project out we do not realize that it came from inside. We project out and we see it out there. Once you understand the principle of projection, rather than say, "Oh, what a beautiful being that is!" you can think, "I can pull it in and determine if this, this body of mine, is a beautiful being." You go in, and then you can start to experience it. At that point, projections are real. I do know that when I am in a field in which everyone is projecting something onto me, it really affects my behavior. It can either make me feel up and out, or very diminished and wrong. Children are very, very sensitive to projections. They internalize what their parents project. Even a gaze. If you have been with someone who has a very introverted feeling function and is very judgmental, all they have to do is look at you and you crumble. You don't know why, but under their gaze, you're like that. If you are with someone who truly loves you, you feel, "Oh! I'm okay." Those projections are very real.

How do we pull our own projections back in? As soon as we know we have envy, or jealousy, or desire, we can be sure there is a projection going on there. So, we pull it in and you realize that the projection itself is unlived potential in us. It might very young. If I project onto a professor, "Oh my goodness, I wish I could speak like that," the possibility is there within me, but I have to get the training. I have to work on that projection and pull it in. Nevertheless, the capacity is there. So for me, projections are ways that the little being inside of me, who knows that she is all things, casts the lines and catches the fish, calls it in and asks, "How do I develop this? How do I nourish it?" That brings us back to the feminine, how do I nourish those parts of me that have not been nourished?

When we start looking at the negative projections it's much harder. Especially when you realize there is a killer energy in you. It's so much easier to have someone on the outside—governments and politicians are very good at creating an enemy overseas. As long as that enemy is out there, you're motivated. You get your strength and you can fight. Yet, when the enemy is inside, you realize that you are capable of murder if put in the right situation. Part of the human condition is that our animal nature will kill to survive and to protect itself. Once you know that in yourself, you feel enormous compassion toward others who have to live with these kinds of projections. There is enormous strength in this.

There is real discernment here in recognizing that the strength of hatred puts me into my essential being. If I project it out, I become a killer. But when you really pull in those projections, you find that you have a capacity you were born with that you never dreamed of. These capacities are latent seeds ready to be developed. How you develop them and how you express them is a personal responsibility. I personally know I would not kill, but I would come pretty close if one of my children were in danger, and I remember feeling that strength! But I wouldn't do it, and there is the consciousness. If you are not conscious of it, it comes out.

That's why workshops are so valuable. You can experience that kind of huge energy and work with it. Every archetype has two sides. Every projection will have something that is self-enhancing and something that kills, always. Thus, you discern, find the mid-point, take hold of the strings you want, and weave together the new. Then you realize you are being woven, but you have to be aware of the extremes. So, projections are the way that humanity learns. I don't know if animals project, but I think it's something in the human mind that is a great teaching tool!

Rose Mary. When most of the world's population is made up of women, why does the phenomenon of the glass ceiling exist?

I think we still have a long way to go in terms of the unfolding of humanity and our understanding of men and women. I think in the Western world we are very lucky that girls have been taught that they can be whatever they want to be. Now the concern is the men. These young boys who are being depotentiated, they don't know what they are to do. Still, the house-husband is not valued, though there are many who would much rather be at home cooking and taking care of the kids than out trying to make it in the world. So you see that glass ceiling has been very much ingrained into the physical being, and at the same time it is also an outer reality.

Rose Mary. Do you find it detrimental to the development of a human being to deny feminine attributes?

Absolutely. The feminine is the feeling, the valuing, the "of love." If these aspects of us are not developed, we become cruel machines. So that by developing the feminine side of you, it is like accessing the gold that can be shaped into any form. If you are only the form and you are identified exclusively with the form, you will live a very limited life. However, when you realize the feminine in you, you're always transforming, shifting, changing, moving through like nature. The variety and diversity are incredible. You mature in ways that you would never believe possible if you didn't have these attributes. And rather than lugging the body around, if you are in touch with your own true nature, there is no lugging around. Wherever you are, you are home. Wherever you are, there is this exquisite feeling of being-ness.

Lorís. Lastly, Mary, we're asking everyone for their advice as to how to live a more balanced life between masculine and feminine energies. Could you give us some examples that one could practice on a daily basis?

I would say, go back to your own self. In many cases, we have been educated not to trust ourselves, and we believe we have to go to an outside authority who will tell us what to do. Thus, my advice would be to take some time, preferably before you start your day, maybe even when you are brushing your teeth, to look in the mirror and ask, "Who am I? What is my gift? What do I cherish about my life and myself? What must I be mindful of? What are the projections? What is the function of my being today and how can I live it fully?" In this way, you bring awareness to your day. If not, once that alarm goes off you're just a mindless robot, run, run, running. In stopping and reflecting on these questions, there is a pause; and in that pause, the quality comes through. Yes, you have your list, you have your plans of things you have to do; but what is the quality that is so deep within you that you want because it is who you are? There is a desire to permeate your life with that. What is that?

If you forget that, you go to bed at night and you think, "Oh, I was a robot again." However, if you remembered it, you think, "Oh, what gratitude! I had an opportunity to be with people whom I love and who love me and we could be together. In that being together, we each brought forth our gift." In the balancing, the feminine loves and embraces and digests and transforms and absorbs, and the masculine animates it and allows it to be brought out. You have to have both. If you only have the one, the feminine, nothing happens. If you only have the other, the masculine, there is no connection. When the two are woven together in that deep current of love, then whatever you do will be permeated with who you are. This is the gift you give to life; the gift you are because you are! You can't be anything other, even though you may try!

Conclusion, After Thoughts

Almost three years have passed since I began the *Ensoulment* project, film and book. My view on the feminine has changed drastically in this time, so much so that I can no longer identify it on its own. It is almost impossible to encounter isolated examples of its existence. The masculine is always there, present, interwoven and knit in with the feminine. On the rare occasion that I am able to look the feminine in the eye, it quickly vanishes and resumes its fluctuating nature. Yet in those moments, I smile. I feel as if an old friend has briefly waved at me from a distance, reminding me of our journey together.

Thinking back on the areas we covered—the media, the body, men, relationships, the workforce and religion—I am struck by the ideas that formed my mindset before I began the film. My understanding developed in so many ways, particularly with respect to the areas of men, relationships, and religion. I chose these areas because I thought they were the parts of our everyday that consumed or influenced us most. My only point of reference was to look at my own life and determine what shaped my thoughts, dreams, and desires. The only section I could not reference to my personal life is the one dealing with men, but this theme was part of my initial desire to explore feminism in the film. The project's exploration of men changed me profoundly. Not only did I begin to get a sense of what genders other than my own have to deal with, but I came to a clearer understanding that we are all in this mess together. We are all guilty of both hurting and helping others depending on when and where destiny brings them into our lives. Thus, I have grown a bit wary of any discourse that leaves the other gender out, because it is not enough to switch the spotlight onto the underdog anymore. Now, we must turn all the lights on and begin to understand our place in relation to the other and in relation to the world.

The section dedicated to relationships became a personal passage for me, unveiling the biases and preconceptions about romantic relationships that I didn't know I had. I used to be transfixed by the beautiful tales of romance told by my elders, enamored by the stories in the movies about love at first sight. Everything I saw or heard about dating or marriage drastically clashed with my lived experience. As I listened to my interviews over and over again, I created a solid understanding of the concept of projections. I began to understand the damage caused when people in my generation indulged in violent swings of rejection or admiration without the least awareness of how these projections might act upon the receiver. I listened to the pain in my friends' broken hearts after the sudden disappearance of a lover. I heard something in their pain other than projections, something I couldn't wrap my head around. I began to fear the despair I saw in my friends, worrying that if I moved an inch here or there, I might be hurt or could hurt another. No matter how cautious I was, this unintended pain inevitably found its way into my relationships.

I became aware that the need to pull your projections back was a two-way street. To be free from projections we would all have to pull back, but I rarely encountered a motivation to do so from others. This hurt me deeply, and on many occasions I tried exploring the subject with friends or love interests, but for the most part I was quickly dismissed out of disinterest or confusion. Though I'm extremely grateful to have found a man I'd like to share my life with—and who has provided endless support during this project from beginning to end—I still can't shake the sense that I've lost a bit of hope in others. Maybe it's just a phase. Maybe it's only part of growing older.

Even more than men and relationships, the project's exploration of religion shook the foundation of all my beliefs. Though we never found the answer to our biggest question—When did organized religion shift to purely masculine principles? —I was surprised to find an explanation of my own forming in the reflections that followed our conversations. It is a story of possible beginnings that I'd like to share with you.

In primitive times, when volcanoes and storms had spirits of their own, human belief systems attributed food scarcity and sickness to the gods and goddesses. They knew very little of science, and the stars were the only gift nighttime had to offer them. However, as years passed and eras changed, they began to understand the world through medicine, sophisticated shelters for their families, structured wars to frighten off invaders and ordered systems of work and civilization. Life stabilized, the weather was predicted, diseases were cured and families grew exponentially. The faster populations grew, the more they craved organized institutions to manage their societies. The quicker these institutions replicated, the more efficient their systems of survival became. Consequently, our psyches began to shift, unnoticed, into the masculine realm: realms that brought food to the table and guaranteed stability for our children's future. While I no longer believe religion was the determining factor, as it was sometimes suggested in the film, I do believe that religions today need to undergo a vital transformation in order to embrace the new energy that we are calling to flood our world.

People often ask me what my final thoughts were after finishing the documentary, "What is the feminine to you?" they probe. My answer to that depends on the day. I've had three long years to reflect on the feminine in my life, where I am excluding it, where I embrace it. What is the feminine to me? Because of its nature, I can't seem to describe it. It is clothed in dissimilar shapes and colors each time we meet, and it very rarely arrives through my brain. I recognize and welcome it when I sense it, but to communicate that relationship with words never appears to convey the phenomenon fully.

In my daily life, I feel as if I am mostly in a masculine state, thinking about work, about maintaining a healthy routine for my body and making sure I spend enough time with family and friends. But once in a while I receive a sort of message from myself in the form of images or bodily sensations within. That's when I feel I meet the feminine again. It's quick and clear. It says what it has to say and then vanishes. For a split second, I can feel the feminine in its essence, naked and wordless. The feminine is who I am when words do not exist. It's the breath I take in to give me life, the undeniable mystery that perplexes my scientific reasoning, the speechless voice that I should never turn away from because it is what binds me to the universe's rhythm of life.

Over these years, I have developed my personal narrative away from an exclusive focus on the feminine and its place in the outer world, and toward the ideal of balancing the feminine and masculine energies in the inner world. There are so many initiatives out there that highlight the need to change government policies, so many petitions that advocate new laws and documentaries that propose alterations in media production. How are we to transform the way we live if we are always pointing to someone out there to do all the work? Who are these people that are making the laws? Are they not driven by an inner world as well? And who are the people who are conforming to these laws and consuming what is given to them? Do they have no say in how they decide to live their lives? All these efforts to change our external reality will be futile if we continue to look away from the change that needs to be made within. This is everyone's individual responsibility. We owe it to ourselves and to those we love to be, as Gandhi said, the change we'd like to see in the world. Perhaps, if each one of us took more time to look deep inside ourselves, we would be a more respectful people as a whole. Maybe we would pay more attention to the harm we have done to the Earth or allow compassion to influence the allocation of our company's profits. Such attention to creating a balance inside would surely develop organically into an outer balance as well. If this documentary and book has the power to transform anyone's life, it has definitely begun with my own. I have come to understand that before I convince anyone of what I believe, I must first believe it and embody it myself. I've learned that it's not enough to know something cognitively, or even experience it. Something deeper drives our decisions, and if we can't find it in ourselves to *want* to change, society will continue as it is.

Interviewing so many astounding individuals has left me permanently engraved. These encounters have forged a new lens within me through which I see the world. I could write twenty-four essays to try to describe the way I experienced each of the conversations in this book, but the one message that permeates them all is the importance of maintaining an equilibrium in each and every single aspect of my life. To do this, I have had to remind myself constantly to stop, sit still, and listen. It's too easy to get absorbed by work, to forget my dreams and ignore my body, but I made the decision to live by the words I collected throughout this passage. I have treasured these words and tattooed them onto my core, where they radiate and call me to attention whenever I find myself losing balance.

There are days when I feel a sudden panic, a fear that this awareness might wear off once the project has found its way farther from the present and deeper into my memory, leaving me lost in the stress of daily routines. I'm afraid of losing the intention that drove me to embark on this work in the first place. But then I remember that I already have my anchor, in the evidence of what once was. The only reminder I'll ever need of how far I've come is wrapped up in the film and in these pages, where the beginning and the end are always one and the same. As this book comes to a close, after everything I saw, after everyone I heard and everything I read, the greatest revelation of my journey is accepting that the end does not exist, only a new path waiting to be discovered.

Lorís (left) with her mother, Rose Mary, and brother, José Antonio.

Bibliography

Bly, R. (2008). *Leaping Poetry: An Idea with Poems and Translations.* University of Pittsburg Press

Bly, R. (2004). *Iron John: A Book About Men.* Philadelphia: Da Capo Press

Bobroff, G. (2014). *Crop Circles, Jung & the Reemergence of the Archetypal Feminine.* Berkeley, CA: North Atlantic Books

Brown, B. (2012). *Daring Greatly: How the Courage to Be Vulnerable Transforms the Way We Live, Love, Parent, and Lead.* New York: Gotham Books

Brown, B. (2010). *The Gifts of Imperfection: Let Go of Who You Think You're Supposed to Be and Embrace Who You Are.* Center City, MN: Hazelden

Campbell, J. (2014). *The Hero's Journey: Joseph Campbell on His Life and Work.* Novato, CA: New World Library

Da Vinci, Leonardo. (1508). *The Virgin and Child with St Anne and St John the Baptist.* Charcoal, black and white chalk on tinted paper mounted on canvas. London: The National Gallery

de Castillejo, I. (1997). *Knowing Woman. A Feminine Psychology.* Boston: Shambhala Publications, Inc.

Disney A. (2009). *Pray the Devil Back to Hell.* Warren, NJ: Passion River Films

Eller, C. (2000). *The Myth of Matriarchal Prehistory: Why an Invented Past Will Not Give Women a Future.* Boston: Beacon Press

Eller, C. (2011). *Gentlemen and Amazons: The Myth of Matriarchal Prehistory, 1861-1900.* Berkeley and Los Angeles, CA: University of California Press

Ensler, E. (2008). *The Vagina Monologues.* New York: Villard Books

Fausto-Sterling, A. (2000). *Sexing the Body: Gender Politics and the Construction of Sexuality.* New York: BasicBooks

Fausto-Sterling, A. (1992). *Myths of Gender: Biological Theories about Women and Men.* New York: BasicBooks

Hennen, P. (2005). *Faeries, Bears, and Leathermen: Men Community Queering the Masculine.* Chicago: The University of Chicago Press

Hollis, J. (1994). *Under Saturn's Shadow: The Wounding and Healing of Men.* Toronto: Inner City Books

Hollis, J. (1998). *The Eden Project: In Search of the Magical Other.* Toronto: Inner City Books

Hollis, J. (2006). *Finding Meaning in the Second Half of Life: How to Finally, Really Grow Up.* New York: Gotham Books

Hollis, J. (2009). *What Matters Most: Living a More Considered Life,* New York: Gotham Books

Jarrett, J.L. (1997). *Jung's Seminar on Nietzsche's Zarathustra.* Princeton, NJ: Princeton University Press

Johnson, R. and Ruhl, J. (2007). *Living Your Unlived Life: Coping with Unrealized Dreams and Fulfilling Your Purpose in the Second Half of Life.* London: Penguin Books, Ltd.

Johnson, R. and Ruhl, J. (2000). *Contentment: A Way to True Happiness, Balancing Heaven and Earth.* New York: HarperCollins

Jones, S. (2000). *Feminist Theory and Christian Theology: Cartographies of Grace.* Minneapolis, MN: Augsburg Fortress

Jones, S. (1994). *Calvin and the Rhetoric of Piety.* Louisville, KY: Westminster John Knox Press

Jones, S. (2009). *Trauma and Grace: Theology in a Ruptured World.* Louisville, KY: Westminster John Knox Press

Jung C.G. (1967). *Alchemical Studies.* Princeton University Press, NJ: Princeton University Press

Jung, C.G. (1970-1979). *The Collected Works of C.G. Jung.* Princeton, NJ: Princeton University Press

Jung, C.G. (1989). *Memories, Dreams, Reflections.* New York: Vintage

Jung, C.G. (1982). *Aspects of the Feminine.* Princeton: Princeton University Press

Kilbourne, J. (1999). *Deadly Persuasion.* New York: The Free Press

King, J.L and Hunter, K. (2004). *On the Down Low: A Journey into the Lives of 'Straight' Black Men Who Sleep with Men.* New York: Broadway Books

Lopez-Pedraza, R. (1996). *Anslem Kiefer: The Psychology of "After the Catastrophe."* New York: George Braziller

Lopez-Pedraza, R. (2000). *Dionysus in Exile: On the Repression of the Body and Emotion.* Asheville, NC: Chiron Publications

Marcuse, H. (1991). *One Dimensional Man: Studies in the Ideology of Advanced Industrial Society.* Boston: Beacon Press

Pagels, E. (1979). *The Gnostic Gospels.* New York: Random House

Paris, G. (2011). *Heartbreak: New Approaches to Healing – Recovering from Lost Love and Mourning.* Minneapolis, MN: Mill City Press, Inc.

Paris, G. (2007). *Wisdom of the Psyche: Depth Psychology after Neuroscience.* New York: Routledge

Reeves, P. (2003). *Heart Sense: Unlocking Your Highest Purpose and Deepest Desires.* York Beach, ME: Red Wheel/Weiser, LLC

Reeves, P. (1999). *Women's Intuition: Unlocking the Wisdom of the Body.* Berkeley, CA: Conari Press

Robinson, J. (1990). General Editor. *The Nag Hammadi Library in English.* San Francisco: Harper San Francisco

Gómez del Campo, G., Porter E., and Salum R.M. (1994) *Vitrales.* Mexico City: Edomex

Stone, M. (1976). *When God Was a Woman.* Orlando, FL: Harvest/ Harcourt Brace

Tarnas, R. (2007). *Cosmos & Psyche: Imitations of a New World View.* New York: Plume

Tacey, D. (2004). *The Spirituality Revolution: The Emergence of Contemporary Spirituality* and *Edge of the Sacred: Jung, Psyche, Earth.* New York: Brunner-Routledge

Whitney, M. and Whitney. M. (1983). *Matter of Heart.* a Michael Whitney-Mark Whitney Productions film. Sponsored by the C.G. Jung Institute of Los Angeles.

Wolf, N. (2002). *The Beauty Myth: How Images of Beauty Are Used Against Women.* New York: HarperCollins Publishers, Inc.

Wolf, N. (2007). *The End of America: Letter of Warning to a Young Patriot.* White River Junction, VT: Chelsea Green Publishing Company

Woodman, M. (1982). *Addiction to Perfection: The Still Unravished Bride: A Psychological Study.* Toronto: Inner City Books

www.ingramcontent.com/pod-product-compliance
Lightning Source LLC
Chambersburg PA
CBHW040138270326
41928CB00022B/3255